APPLEWORKS THE PROGRAM FOR THE REST OF US

SECOND EDITION

Michael L. Sloan

Scott, Foresman and Company
Glenview, Illinois London

ISBN 0-673-18937-6

Printed in the United States of America.

Library of Congress Cataloging-in-Publication Data

Sloan, Michael L., 1944-
AppleWorks: the program for the rest of us.

Includes index.
1. AppleWorks (Computer program) 2. Business—Data processing. I. Title.
HF5548.4.A68S58 1988 650'.028'55369 87-9775

1 2 3 4 5 6 RRC 92 91 90 89 88 87

Trademark notices appear on the page following the Acknowledgments.

Notice of Liability

The information in this book is distributed on an "As Is" basis, without warranty. Neither the author nor Scott, Foresman and Company shall have any liability to customer or any other person or entity with respect to any liability, loss, or damage caused or alleged to be caused directly or indirectly by the programs contained herein. This includes, but is not limited to, interruption of service, loss of data, loss of business or anticipatory profits, or consequential damages from the use of the programs.

Scott, Foresman Professional Publishing Group books are available for bulk sales at quantity discounts. For information, please contact the Marketing Manager, Professional Books, Professional Publishing Group, Scott, Foresman and Company, 1900 East Lake Avenue, Glenview, IL 60025.

ACKNOWLEDGMENTS

I would like to thank the following individuals and organizations for their assistance in the writing and editing of this book:

Ray Morin of Apple Computer, Inc., Rolling Meadows, IL

Jack Taylor of Rundell and Sloan Ltd.

Jennifer Corbin, for her assistance with the preparation of the manuscript

Mark Hoffman of Egghead Software, Lombard, IL

Tom Oliva and Terry Berndt of the Glen Ellyn Computer Center, Glen Ellyn, IL

Vince Aderente of Farnsworth Computer Center, Villa Park, IL

Jack Finnegan of Farnsworth Computer Center, Aurora, IL

Daniel Lauer of American Computer Equipment, Wheaton, IL

Cat Skintik of Custom Editorial Productions, Inc., Cincinnati, OH

and my wife, Claudia, to whom this book is dedicated.

Spellworks™ is a trademark of Advanced Logic Systems, Inc.

AppleWorks™, Apple Writer™, Access//™, Business Graphics™, MousePaint™, Quick File™, ImageWriter™, Profile™, DOS 3.2™, DOS 3.3™, and ProDOS™ are trademarks of Apple Computer, Inc.

Apple® and the Apple logo are registered trademarks of Apple Computer, Inc.

RamWorks® III is a registered trademark, and Z-Ram Ultra™, TimeMaster H.O.™, RamFactor™, TransWarp™, Viewmaster 80™, and Applied Engineering™ are trademarks of Applied Engineering.

Dazzle Draw™ is a trademark of Broederbund Software, Inc.

MultiRam //e Card™ and MultiRam™ CX are trademarks of Checkmate Technology, Inc.

CP/M® is a registered trademark of Digital Research, Inc.

Discwasher® is a registered trademark of Discwasher division, International Jensen, Inc.

Epson™ is a trademark of Epson America, Inc.

HabaMerge™ is a trademark of Haba Systems, Inc.

MegaWorks™ is a trademark, and ReportWorks® and Megahaus® are registered trademarks of Megahaus Corporation.

Wordstar™ is a trademark of Micro Pro International.

Okidata™ is a division of Oki Electric, Inc.

RamPak 4GS™ is a trademark, and Orange Micro® is a registered trademark of Orange Micro, Inc.

GraphWorks™ is a trademark of PBI Software, Inc.

Pinpoint™, QuickLabel™, GraphMerge™, InfoMerge™, Pinpoint Spelling Checker™, and Point-to-Point™ are trademarks of Pinpoint Publishing and Virtual Combinatics, Inc.

Catalyst™ is a trademark of Quark, Inc.

Qume® is a registered trademark of Qume Corporation.

Graphics Department™ and Sensible Speller™ are trademarks, and Sensible Software® is a registered trademark of Sensible Software, Inc.

DIF™ is a trademark of Software Arts, Inc.

VisiCalc® is a registered trademark of VisiCorp.

FlashCalc™ is a trademark of VisiCorp/Paladin.

CONTENTS

CHAPTER 1

STARTING OUT IN APPLEWORKS

This chapter consists of four sections. The first was written for those of you who are just starting to use your computer. The remaining three sections are for everyone using *AppleWorks* for the first time. If you are already familiar with the startup and printer configuration of *AppleWorks* and have already made copies of your *AppleWorks* Startup and Program disks, please feel free to skip this chapter and go on to Chapter 2.

I. YOUR APPLE COMPUTER

Your computer system consists of a number of components connected together (similar to a component stereo system). The main component is the Apple II itself. It processes all of the computer information (words, numbers, etc.) and plays the same kind of role as an amplifier does in a stereo system.

Just as your stereo system gets its musical information from a record turntable, for example, your Apple gets information from its keyboard. And, just as your stereo can record and play music from its cassette tape recorder, your Apple can store and retrieve information with its disk drive(s). Finally, as your stereo outputs music to speakers, so your computer outputs data to its monitor screen and printer.

Connecting the individual pieces of your computer system is fairly straightforward. But if you are not sure about how to connect your system together, *have your Apple dealer show you how.*

The Apple Keyboard

Apple currently sells three models of Apple II computers: the Apple IIc, a new version of the Apple IIe with a new keyboard, and the all new Apple IIGS. Older model Apple IIe's and IIc's have virtually identical keyboards, and keyboards for the IIGS and the new model IIe are the same. (*Note:* The Apple II+ keyboard is discussed in Appendix C.) While the layout of a computer's keyboard is similar to a typewriter's, there are some differences and added features you should know about.

First, your computer distinguishes between the letter "O" and the number "0" and between the letter "l" and the number "1."

As with a typewriter, you will use the SHIFT key to get capital letters as well as the *upper* symbol on any key. For example, look at the second key from the left on the top row of keys. If you type this key by itself, you'll produce a "1" character. If, however, you hold down the SHIFT key while you press the "1" key, you'll get a "!".

Now look at the key marked CAPS LOCK. It's at the lower left corner of the keyboard. This key is actually a two-position switch. Press it once and it locks in the "down" position; press it again and it returns to the "up" position. With the CAPS LOCK key in the "down" position, all alphabetic keys (A, B, etc.) will print in upper case (i.e. capital letters). CAPS LOCK does *not* affect any other keys. (You still have to use the SHIFT key to get an exclamation point, !)

Over on the left side of the keyboard is a key marked CONTROL. This key is used the same way that the SHIFT key is used. That is, you hold the CONTROL key down while you type another key. The effect of using the CONTROL key is not as obvious as when you use the SHIFT key. First, the CONTROL key only modifies 32 of the keys on the keyboard—all 26 alphabetic keys (A–Z) and the following 6 symbol keys: @, ^, _, [,], and \. The combination of using the CONTROL key with one of these 32 keys produces what is called a *control character*. Control characters do not show up directly on the screen or on the printer, but they are used to produce special effects such as underlining or bold printing, which will be discussed later.

At the bottom of the keyboard, to the left of the wide Space Bar, is the OPEN-APPLE key. This key has an outlined apple pictured on it ( ) and is used the same way that the SHIFT and CONTROL keys are used. You hold the OPEN-APPLE key down while you type some other key. Almost all commands in *AppleWorks* are produced with this combination.

The key marked ESC (called the ESCAPE key) is at the upper left corner of the keyboard. *AppleWorks* uses this key to move from one part of the program to another.

At the upper right corner of the keyboard is the DELETE key. *AppleWorks* uses this key to delete or erase characters.

Finally, there are the four cursor control keys in the lower right corner of the keyboard. The cursor is an indicator (either a blinking underline symbol or a blinking box) on the monitor screen showing where the next character typed will appear. The cursor keys allow you to move the cursor—up, down, left, or right—so that the next character typed can be anywhere on the screen.

One caution: All keys on the keyboard are repeating keys. This means that if, for example, you hold the "A" key down for more than half a second, you'll get several A's. This is particularly important when you press special keys such as the ESC or RETURN keys, because generating several ESC or RETURN characters instead of one may produce unexpected results. You are encouraged to develop a light touch at the keyboard.

II. COMPUTER COMPONENTS FOR *APPLEWORKS*

In order to use *AppleWorks*, your Apple computer system will have to contain certain required components. This is true for all computer programs, but the components vary from one program to another and from one model of computer to another.

The Apple IIGS and IIe Systems

DISK DRIVES

AppleWorks requires at least one disk drive, although two drives make some operations, such as copying diskettes and saving files, easier.

Apple sells two types of disk drives, 5.25″ and 3.5″. The two sizes refer to the size of the disk each uses. Disk drives are used to store computer data—your *AppleWorks* files, for example. And the main difference between the two drives is the amount of data that the drive can store on its respective disk. Odd as it may seem, the 3.5″ disk can store almost six times as much data as the 5.25″ disk can.

Apple IIe's and IIGS's can use one or two drives of either or both types. That's right, if you wanted to, you could connect two 5.25″ *and* two 3.5″ drives to your computer.

AN 80-COLUMN TEXT CARD

AppleWorks requires an 80-column display from your computer. New Apple IIe's and Apple IIGS's come set up for 80-column display. Older model IIe's require a separate 80-column text card.

There are two types of 80-column text cards available from Apple for the Apple IIe. The Extended 80-Column Text Card provides an older Apple IIe with an 80-column display and doubles its internal memory from 64 thousand (64K) bytes to 128 thousand (128K) bytes. (*Note:* See the discussion on memory below.)

The second type of 80-column card adds the ability to operate an RGB color monitor to the Extended 80-Column Text Card. It's called the

Extended 80-Column/AppleColor Card (see the discussion on monitors below).

MEMORY

The internal memory of your Apple (called Random Access Memory or RAM) is where both the *AppleWorks* program instructions and the *AppleWorks* documents you're currently working on are kept. *Apple-Works* has been released in several versions. The current version, 2.0, requires your Apple to have a minimum of 128K (that's 128 thousand) bytes of memory. (*Note:* One byte of memory can hold or store one character of information. The letter "A," the number "5," and the symbol "=" are each characters.) Current Apple IIe's and IIGS's have 128K of RAM. Older IIe's were shipped with 64K of RAM. If you're unsure how much RAM your computer has, ask your local Apple dealer.

MONITORS

Monitors come in either monochrome (one color, usually green) or color. If you decide that you want a color monitor, don't try to connect your Apple to your TV set or to a standard composite video color monitor. If you do, you'll find that the 80-column display is almost unreadable. If you own an Apple IIe and you feel you must have a color monitor, then you have two options. First, you can use two monitors, one monochrome, the other composite color (or your own TV set). Second, you can purchase what is called an RGB color monitor. This type of monitor has much better resolution than an ordinary color monitor and can clearly display 80-column text. And, in order to use an RGB color monitor with your Apple IIe, you'll need a special RGB interface card such as the Extended 80-Column/RGB AppleColor Card mentioned above.

If you own an Apple IIGS, you can plug an RGB monitor directly into your computer. The RGB interface is built in.

PRINTER INTERFACE CARD

The printer interface card allows your computer to communicate with your printer. Printer interface cards are of two types, serial and parallel, and the only thing you have to be careful of is that your printer and printer interface card are the same type—either both serial or both parallel.

There is one other caution. If you purchase a non-Apple brand printer interface card (e.g., Grappler, Tymac, etc.), you will have to perform one extra step in the process of setting up *AppleWorks* to work with your printer. This process is discussed later in this chapter.

PRINTER

Here the choices are many and varied. The only suggestion I have is that you see the printer of your choice in operation and look at its output (quality of printing, speed, special features, etc.) before you buy it. Remember that your printer interface card and printer must be of the same *type*, either both parallel or both serial. If you buy all of your computer equipment, including the *AppleWorks* program, from the same computer dealer, you can be fairly sure that everything will work together.

AppleWorks itself directly supports *all* Apple printers as well as Epson printers in the MX, RX, and FX series and certain models of Qume printers. Any other brand of printer will have to be specially installed as a "custom" printer, which we will discuss later.

HARD DISK DRIVE

The purpose of using a hard disk drive, such as Apple's 5 megabyte (that's 5 million bytes) Profile, 10 megabyte Profile, or 20 Meg SC20, is to avoid using diskettes for program and document storage and, instead, store everything on the hard drive. Adding a hard disk drive to your computer system is definitely optional and can be done at any time.

The Apple IIc System

If you have an Apple IIc, you have fewer options. Your IIc already contains one 5.25" disk drive, 128K bytes of RAM memory, built-in 80-column display, and two serial interface ports. The only choices you need to make are whether to add a second disk drive (recommended) and which monitor and printer to buy.

MONITORS

In addition to the information on monitors in the above discussion on Apple IIGS and IIe components, there is one other fact you should know if you intend to use an RGB color monitor with your Apple IIc. The IIc will *not* operate an RGB color monitor directly. It requires an "RGB adapter" currently available from a company called Video 7 (see Appendix A).

PRINTERS

Again, look at the discussion on printers in the section above. While the Apple IIc has its own serial printer ports built in, you *can* use a parallel printer with your IIc, if you desire. At least one company, Discwasher (see Appendix A), sells a serial-to-parallel converter box that plugs into the IIc's serial port and allows the use of a parallel printer.

III. THE *APPLEWORKS* PROGRAM

Before your Apple computer can perform the various functions of *AppleWorks*, it must first receive instructions. The *AppleWorks* disk contains these computer instructions. Every time you want to use the *AppleWorks* program, you have to load in these instructions, because every time you turn off your Apple, it forgets them.

Making Copies of *AppleWorks*

When you buy *AppleWorks* 2.0, you get two copies of the program. One copy is on both sides of a 5.25″ disk, and the other comes on a 3.5″ disk. (*Note:* See the discussion of disk drives above.) Before you use *AppleWorks*, you should make your own working copy of the program, and then store the original *AppleWorks* disks in a safe place. That way, if your working copy of the program becomes damaged, you can easily make another copy.

If your computer system uses 5.25″ disks, you *must* copy the original *AppleWorks* disk before you can run the program. If your system uses 3.5″ disks, you can run the program from the original disk, but I strongly recommend copying it and using the copy in your day-to-day work.

You'll use the Apple System Utilities disk to copy the *AppleWorks* disk. I'm using version 2.1 of the System Utilities. If you have an earlier version, you can get the latest one from your local Apple dealer.

The first step in the copying process is to "boot" or start up the System Utilities program. Insert the utilities disk into your Apple's disk drive, and turn on the computer. (Don't forget to turn on the monitor, too.) After a few seconds you'll see the program's title screen.

If your computer is an Apple IIe or IIGS, you'll be asked which display you prefer, 40 or 80 columns. Press the "Y" key on your keyboard to indicate that you prefer an 80-column display.

Remove the System Utilities disk from your disk drive and set it aside. Your screen should look like Figure 1-1. This is the System Utilities' Main Menu. It lets you select the operation you want to perform. You want to copy, or duplicate, a disk, so press the "5" key on your keyboard, and then press the RETURN key.

I'll give you two sets of step-by-step instructions for the copying procedure—one for the Apple IIe or IIGS, the other for the Apple IIc. So find the set of instructions appropriate for your computer system.

FIGURE 1-1 System Utilities Main Menu

```
System Utilities                                                 Main Menu
Version 2.1           Copyright Apple Computer, Inc. 1984, 1985
__________________________________________________________________________

                      Work on Individual Files

                      1.  Copy Files
                      2.  Delete Files
                      3.  Rename Files
                      4.  Lock/Unlock Files

                      Work on Entire Disks

                      5.  Duplicate a Disk
                      6.  Format a Disk
                      7.  Identify and Catalog a Disk
                      8.  Advanced Operations

                      9.  Exit System Utilities

Type a number or press ↓ or ↑ to select
an option.  Then press RETURN.
__________________________________________________________________________
For Help: Press -? or -?
__________________________________________________________________________
```

Copying *AppleWorks* with an Apple IIe or IIGS

If your computer's disk drives use 5.25"disks, you need to copy both sides of the original *AppleWorks* disk onto two separate disks, so you'll need two blank disks. If your disk drives use 3.5" disks, you'll copy the entire program onto one 3.5" blank disk.

Before you actually start the duplication process, label your blank disks with a soft-tipped marker. (*Do not use a pencil or a ball-point pen or you may damage the disk.*) If you're using 5.25″ disks, label one of them "AppleWorks Startup" and the other "AppleWorks Program." The single 3.5″ blank disk can be labeled just "AppleWorks."

1. The Utilities program wants to know how you intend to specify the location of your source and destination disks (more about them in a moment). For copying disks, you only have one choice. You'll specify the location by **SLOT AND DRIVE**. Press the RETURN key to accept this choice.
2. Disk drives on the IIe and IIGS attach to the computer through interface cards that plug into slots on the computer's main circuit board. These slots are numbered, and the System Utilities program needs to know which slot your disk drive is plugged into. It's guessing slot 6, and unless your drive is plugged into some other slot, just press the RETURN key to accept slot 6.
3. Each slot can accommodate one or two drives, so now the program wants to know which drive will contain the source disk. (*Note:* The source disk for this exercise is the original *AppleWorks* disk.) The default choice (that's the one the program makes for you) is drive 1. Accept this choice by pressing the RETURN key again.
4. Next, the program wants to know where the destination disk is going to be. The destination disk is the blank disk you just labeled. Press the Return key to accept the choice of **SLOT AND DRIVE**.
5. Again, the Utilities assumes the destination drive is plugged into slot 6, so press the Return key to accept slot 6.
6. But when the program asks for the drive number of the destination disk, the choice depends on the number of drives in your computer system. If your system has two disk drives, press the "2" key to indicate drive 2. But if your computer has only one disk drive, press the "1" key.
7. Now the program wants you to insert the source disk in drive 1. If you're copying the 5.25″ disk, hold the disk so that the label that reads "AppleWorks Startup" faces up, and insert this disk in drive 1. If you're copying the 3.5″ *AppleWorks* disk, just insert it, label side up, into the drive. Press the RETURN key to tell the program you've done this.
8. Next, the program says to insert the destination disk. If you have a single-drive system, remove the source disk and replace it with the destination disk. If you have a two-drive system, place the destination disk in drive 2. Press the RETURN key after you've inserted

the destination disk. If you're copying the 5.25″ *AppleWorks* disk, use the blank disk you labeled "AppleWorks Startup" for the destination disk.

9. The program wants to know what to name the destination disk. (Every disk has a name, called the *volume name.*) The program chooses the volume name "/APPLEWORKS." Accept this name by pressing the RETURN key. (*Note:* Do not change the volume name. Your copies of the *AppleWorks* disk *must* be named /APPLE-WORKS.)
10. If your destination disk has been used before, you'll be asked if it's OK to "destroy" the contents of the disk. Assuming that it is OK, press the RETURN key. (*Note:* If your destination disk is brand new, you won't see this warning message.)
11. If your computer system has two drives, sit back and let the System Utilities do its work. It will first format (or initialize) the destination disk, then it will copy the contents of the source disk onto the destination disk. But if yours is a one-drive system, the program will prompt you to exchange the source disk with the destination disk several times. Just follow the instructions on your screen and be sure to insert the correct disk.
12. When the copying process is complete, you'll see a message on your screen saying **Duplicating ... Done!** (See Figure 1-2 for a typical screen display. Depending on the number and kind of drives you have, your source and destination may be different.) After you see this message, remove the source and/or destination disk from your drives.

If you're copying the 3.5″ *AppleWorks* disk, press the ESC key and stop here. You are through copying. But if you're copying the 5.25″ disk, press the RETURN key, go back to step 1, and repeat the entire process. This time use the other side of the original *AppleWorks* disk, the side labeled "AppleWorks Program Disk," as the source disk and the other blank disk as the destination disk.

When you've finished copying *AppleWorks*, remove the disks from your drives, turn off your computer, and store the original *AppleWorks* disks in a safe place.

Copying *AppleWorks* with an Apple IIc

If your computer's disk drives use 5.25″ disks, you need to copy both sides of the original *AppleWorks* disk onto two separate disks, so

FIGURE 1-2 Copying *AppleWorks* with a IIe or IIGS

```
System Utilities                                          Duplicate a Disk
Version 2.1                                                  ESC: Main Menu
----------------------------------------------------------------------------
                    Source Disk : Slot: 6, Drive: 1

                    Destination Disk : Slot: 6, Drive: 2

                    Operating System : ProDOS

                    New Volume Name : /APPLEWORKS

                    Formatting ... Done!

                    Duplicating ... Done!

----------------------------------------------------------------------------
Disk Copy complete. Press RETURN to continue; ESC to return to the Main Menu.
----------------------------------------------------------------------------
```

you'll need two blank disks. If your disk drives use 3.5″ disks, you'll copy the entire program onto one 3.5″ blank disk.

Before you actually start the duplication process, label your blank disks with a soft-tipped marker. (*Do not use a pencil or a ball-point pen or you may damage the disk.*) If you're using 5.25″ disks, label one of them "AppleWorks Startup" and the other "AppleWorks Program." The single 3.5″ blank disk can be labeled just "AppleWorks."

After you choose option 5 from the System Utilities Main Menu, your screen will display a list of all the drives you have connected to your Apple IIc. Figure 1-3 shows the list for an Apple IIc system with an external disk drive. If you have attached a 3.5″ drive, you'll see it listed as "External DISK 3.5 #1." A second 3.5″ drive would be listed as "External DISK 3.5 #2."

1. The Utilities program wants to know where to find your source disk, the disk you're copying from. Your source disk for this exercise is the original *AppleWorks* disk. The default choice (that's the one the program makes for you) is the Apple IIc's built-in drive. If you're copying the 5.25″ *AppleWorks* disk, accept this choice by pressing the RETURN key. If you're copying the 3.5″ disk, you'll see the choice, "External DISK 3.5 #1" as the second choice. Press the "2" key, then press RETURN.
2. Next, the program wants to know where the "destination" disk is going to be. The destination disk is the blank disk you just labeled. If you're copying the 5.25″ *AppleWorks* disk and you have an

FIGURE 1-3 Selecting the IIc source drive

```
System Utilities
Version 2.1                                          Duplicate a Disk
                                                     ESC: Main Menu
------------------------------------------------------------------------
                   Where is your source disk?

                   1.  Built-in Drive

                   2.  External Disk  //c




Type a number or press ↓ or ↑ to select
an option.  Then press RETURN.
------------------------------------------------------------------------
For Help: Press ⌘-? or ●-?
```

external 5.25″ disk drive, choose the option, **External Disk //c**. If you don't have an external drive, choose option 1, **Built-in Drive.**

If you're copying the 3.5″ disk and your computer system has two 3.5″ drives, choose as the destination, **External DISK 3.5 #2** by pressing the number corresponding to the choice. Otherwise, choose **External DISK 3.5 #1.**

3. Now the program wants you to insert the source disk in the drive you specified as the source drive. If you're copying the 5.25″ disk, hold the disk so the label that reads "AppleWorks Startup" faces up, and insert this disk into the drive. If you're copying the 3.5″ *AppleWorks* disk, just insert it, label side up. Press the RETURN key to tell the program you've done this.
4. Next, the program says to insert the destination disk. If your source and destination disk drives are the same, remove the source disk and replace it with the destination disk. Otherwise, place the destination disk in the other drive. Press the RETURN key after you've inserted the destination disk. If you're copying the 5.25″ *AppleWorks* disk, use the blank disk you labeled "AppleWorks Startup" for the destination disk.
5. The program wants to know what to name the destination disk. (Every disk has a name, called the *volume name.*) The program chooses the volume name "/APPLEWORKS." Accept this name by pressing the RETURN key. (*Note:* Do not change the volume name. Your copies of the *AppleWorks* disk must be named /APPLE-WORKS.)

6. If your destination disk has been used before, you'll be asked if it's OK to "destroy" the contents of the disk. Assuming that it is OK, press the RETURN key. (*Note:* If your destination disk is brand new, you won't see this warning message.)
7. If your computer system has two drives, sit back and let the System Utilities do its work. It will first format (or initialize) the destination disk, then it will copy the contents of the source disk onto the destination disk. But if yours is a one-drive system, the program will prompt you to exchange the source disk with the destination disk several times. Just follow the instructions on your screen and be sure to insert the correct disk.
8. When the copying process is complete, you'll see a message on your screen saying **Duplicating ... Done!** (See Figure 1-4 for a typical screen display. Depending on the number and kind of drives you have, your source and destination may be different.) After you see this message, remove the source and/or destination disk from your drive(s).

FIGURE 1-4 Copying *AppleWorks* with a IIc

```
System Utilities                                              Duplicate a Disk
Version 2.1                                                     ESC: Main Menu
------------------------------------------------------------------------------
                    Source Disk : Built-in Drive

                    Destination Disk : External Disk //c

                    Operating System : ProDOS

                    New Volume Name : /APPLEWORKS

                    Formatting ... Done!

                    Duplicating ... Done!



------------------------------------------------------------------------------
Disk Copy complete. Press RETURN to continue; ESC to return to the Main Menu.
```

If you're copying the 3.5″ *AppleWorks* disk, press the ESC key and stop here. You are through copying. But if you're copying the 5.25″ disk, press the RETURN key, go back to step 1, and repeat the entire process. This time use the other side of the original *AppleWorks* disk, the side labeled "AppleWorks Program Disk," as the source disk and the other blank disk as the destination disk.

When you've finished copying *AppleWorks*, remove the disks from your drives, turn off your computer, and store the original *AppleWorks* disks in a safe place.

Using *AppleWorks* for the First Time

Now that you have made copies of *AppleWorks*, you can begin to make the program work for you.

First, as you have no doubt discovered if you have read any computer books or manuals, computer people speak a language all their own. Many of these "computerese" terms are so esoteric that you could be a computer user for 20 years and never hear them. Other terms can be useful to know.

Throughout this book, you will see the term "default" or "default value." Each section of *AppleWorks* has many different features and options. Most of these features and options can take different values. For example, in the word processor section there is an option to print out your document either single, double, or triple spaced. The default value, the choice that *AppleWorks* makes for all new word processing documents, is single spaced. So, anytime you see the term default, think of it as a choice that *AppleWorks* has made for you—one you can change if you want.

Another term you'll come across is "boot." Simply put, to boot a system or program means to start it up.

STARTING UP *APPLEWORKS*

To boot *AppleWorks*, place your copy of the *AppleWorks* Startup disk in disk drive 1 (the internal drive, if you have an Apple IIc). If you're running *AppleWorks* from a 3.5" disk, insert this disk into your 3.5" drive. Turn on your Apple computer or, if it is already turned on, hold down the CONTROL and OPEN-APPLE keys and press the RESET key. (*Note:* The above procedure is call a CONTROL-OPEN-APPLE-RESET and is used to restart the computer. You should always use this method to restart, rather than turning your Apple off and on again with the power switch. However, you should *only* restart your computer when you begin a new program and *never* do it while you are in the midst of using a program.)

APPLEWORKS' VERSION

After about 10 seconds, your screen should look like Figure 1-5. There are two interesting pieces of information on this screen. The first is the version number that appears on the line beginning **Copyright . . . .** The version I have used in this book is version 2.0. If you have an earlier release of *AppleWorks*, you can get version 2.0 from your local Apple dealer. There is a charge for "upgrading" an older version of *AppleWorks* to version 2.0. Currently, that charge is $50, but it may be different by the time you read this.

FIGURE 1-5 Starting *AppleWorks*

```
                              TM
                    AppleWorks
                Integrated Software


          By R.J. Lissner and Apple Computer, Inc.
     Copyright Apple Computer 1983-86   V2.0     USA

--------------------------------------------------------------------------------
Place the AppleWorks PROGRAM disk in Drive 1 and press Return      56K Avail.
```

AVAILABLE MEMORY

The second useful piece of information from this first *AppleWorks* screen is the amount of memory *AppleWorks* says it has available for your documents. This value is found in the lower right corner of the screen, and should be **56K Avail.** or greater. Remember, this is the amount of memory *inside your Apple* that is available for word processor documents, spreadsheets, etc. It has nothing to do with storing those files on a disk.

I said 56K *or greater* because *AppleWorks* version 2.0 will take advantage of any extra memory your computer might have. Apple sells memory upgrades (additional memory) for all three types of Apples (IIe, IIc, and IIGS), as do other hardware manufacturers. These add-on memory cards can increase the size of your *AppleWorks* Desktop to several hundred K. In Chapter 6, you'll find a discussion of add-on memory cards, but for the rest of this book, I'll assume that your *AppleWorks* Desktop is the standard, 56K, size.

To understand what this value means, suppose you were typing a long word processing document. With 56K of memory, *AppleWorks* would have enough room for about 17 single-spaced typewritten pages of text—figuring 60 characters (letters, numbers, spaces, etc.) per line and 54 lines per page. And, yes, *AppleWorks will* warn you when you're getting close to running out of memory.

ENTERING THE DATE

Let's continue with the start-up process. If you're running *AppleWorks* from 5.25" disks, remove the *AppleWorks* Startup disk and insert the *AppleWorks* Program disk into drive 1. Press the RETURN key and your screen should look like Figure 1-6. If you're running *AppleWorks* from a 3.5" disk, just press RETURN. *AppleWorks* is asking you to type in today's date in the format: mm/dd/yy. You can accept whatever date *AppleWorks* has chosen as a default value by pressing the RETURN key, but I suggest that you actually type in the current date. The reason is that *AppleWorks* uses this date to "date stamp" every file that you save onto a disk. When you look at a list of files on a disk, you'll also see the date each was last saved. (*Note:* See the discussion on clock/calendar cards in Chapter 6.)

Do you see that small box that's blinking about once a second? This is one of the two types of cursors *AppleWorks* uses and is called the *overstrike cursor*. The cursor shows you where the next character you type will be placed. As you type in the date, notice that each character you type replaces a character on the screen. If your date has fewer characters in it than does the default date, press the space bar once or twice so that only your date shows. Now press the RETURN key. This completes the start-up process and your screen should display what *AppleWorks* calls the Main Menu.

FIGURE 1-6 Setting the date

```
File: None                  GETTING STARTED       Escape: Restore former entry
==============================================================================




                    The date must be 1983 or later,
                    and in this form:  3/20/86




------------------------------------------------------------------------------
Type today's date or press Return:  9/16/87                         56K Avail.
```

IV. CONFIGURING *APPLEWORKS* FOR YOUR SYSTEM

The Main Menu provides access to all the parts of the *AppleWorks* program. In later chapters of this book, we will discuss all of the Main Menu options, but, right now, we are concerned with configuring, or customizing, *AppleWorks* for your particular Apple computer system.

Figure 1-7 shows the Main Menu, which should now be on your screen. The purpose of a "menu" is to present you with a selection of choices. To make a selection, you can either type the number of your choice or use the up- and down-arrow keys to "highlight" your choice. Then you press the RETURN key and the selection you have chosen is made. The selection I would like you to make is the fifth one listed: **Other Activities**. So, press 5, then press the RETURN key, and your screen should look like Figure 1-8. (*Note:* If you press the wrong number, you can delete it by pressing the DELETE key on your keyboard.)

Choosing the Default Drive for Your Data Disk

Before we go any further, look at the top line on your monitor screen. On the left is the "Data-Disk drive Indicator." Right now, it shows that it expects your data disk (that's the disk you'll be saving

FIGURE 1-7 ***AppleWorks'* Main Menu**

```
Disk: Disk 1 (Slot 6)          Main Menu                 Escape: Erase entry

      Main Menu

      1.  Add files to the Desktop

      2.  Work with one of the files on the Desktop

      3.  Save Desktop files to disk

      4.  Remove files from the Desktop

      5.  Other Activities

      6.  Quit

Type number, or use arrows, then press Return  5                 56K Avail.
```

FIGURE 1-8 The Other Activities Menu

```
Disk: Disk 1 (Slot 6)            OTHER ACTIVITIES            Escape: Main Menu

  Main Menu
     Other Activities

        1.  Change current disk drive or ProDOS prefix

        2.  List all files on the current disk drive

        3.  Create a subdirectory

        4.  Delete files from disk

        5.  Format a blank disk

        6.  Select standard location of data disk

        7.  Specify information about your printer(s)

Type number, or use arrows, then press Return                       56K Avail.
```

your *AppleWorks* documents on) to be in "Disk 1 (Slot 6)" or the "Built-in disk" on a IIc. If your computer system has just *one* disk drive, *skip* the next paragraph.

If your computer system has *two* (or more) disk drives, you'll want to tell *AppleWorks* to look for your data disk in another drive. To do this, select option 6, **Select standard location of data disk**, from the Other Activities Menu. Figure 1-9a shows a typical list of disk drive options for the Apple IIc. Apple IIe and IIGS owners will see a list similar to that in Figure 1-9b. If you have two disk drives, your choice for the location of your data disk will probably be the second one on the list—**Ext. Disk //c** for IIc owners, **Disk 2 (Slot 6)** for IIe and IIGS owners. Select this drive by pressing the "2" key, then press the RETURN key. You should now be back at the Other Activities Menu and the Data-Disk drive Indicator should say **Disk: Ext. disk //c** or **Disk: Disk 2 (Slot 6)**.

The Standard *AppleWorks* Screen

The top line of a typical menu screen contains other information besides the current data disk drive number. At the center of the top line is the name of the menu or activity you are currently using. At the right of the top line is a special indicator that tells you what will happen if you press the ESC key on your Apple's keyboard. On your screen it says

FIGURE 1-9a Disk drives for Apple IIc

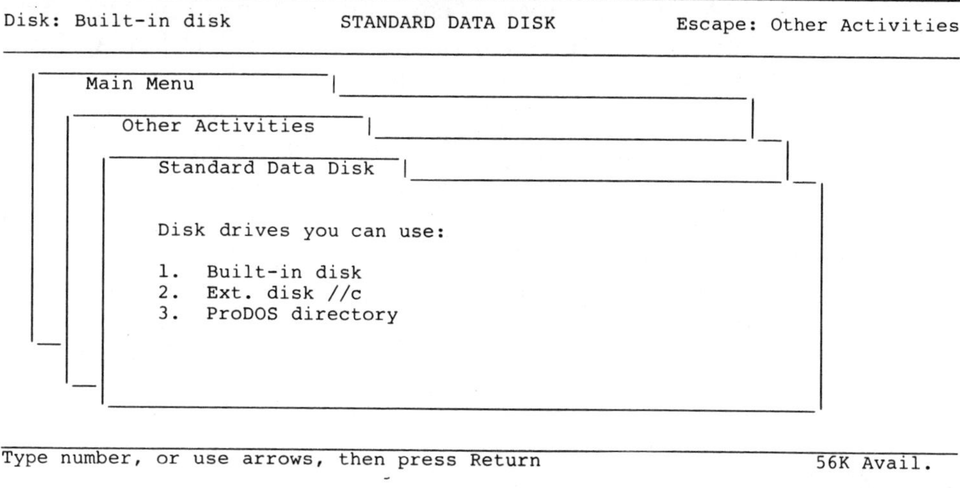

```
Disk: Built-in disk          STANDARD DATA DISK          Escape: Other Activities

     Main Menu
        Other Activities
           Standard Data Disk

           Disk drives you can use:

           1.  Built-in disk
           2.  Ext. disk //c
           3.  ProDOS directory

Type number, or use arrows, then press Return                         56K Avail.
```

FIGURE 1-9b Disk drives for Apple IIe and IIGS

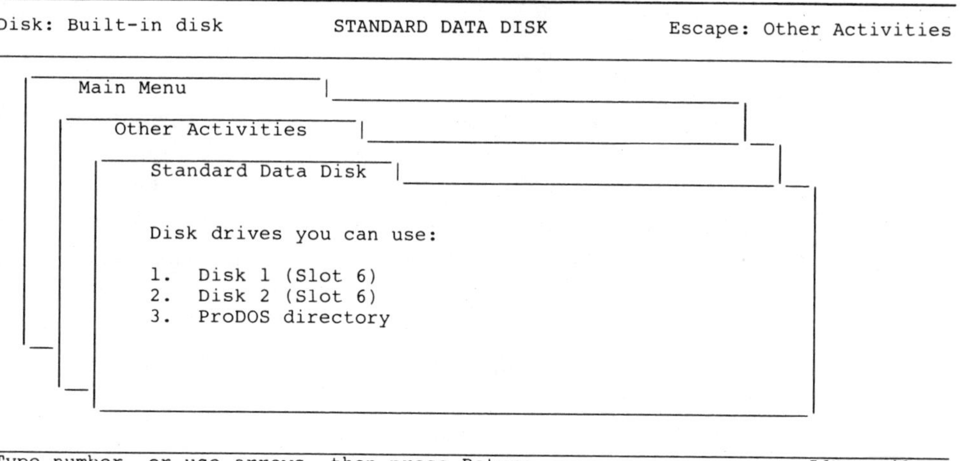

```
Disk: Built-in disk          STANDARD DATA DISK          Escape: Other Activities

     Main Menu
        Other Activities
           Standard Data Disk

           Disk drives you can use:

           1.  Disk 1 (Slot 6)
           2.  Disk 2 (Slot 6)
           3.  ProDOS directory

Type number, or use arrows, then press Return                         56K Avail.
```

that pressing ESC will return you to the Main Menu. Pressing the ESC key is the way to exit any menu except the Main Menu. Try it out. Press the ESC key and see that you have returned to the Main Menu. Now select option 5 and go to the Other Activities Menu again.

Most of the screen is used to display the Other Activities Menu. Notice that the menu appears outlined with the shape of a file folder. This is part of the desktop metaphor used by *AppleWorks* throughout the entire program. You can see the outline of the Main Menu file folder "behind" the Other Activities file folder. The implication is that the Other Activities folder is "contained" in the Main Menu folder, and this is reinforced by the fact that when you're in Other Activities, pressing the ESC key returns you to the Main Menu.

At the bottom of the screen is an instruction line, **Type number, or use arrows, then press RETURN**, and at the far right of the bottom line is the Available Memory indicator, which we talked about earlier. This indicator tells you how much internal computer memory is currently available for you to use. As you type in word processor, data base, or spreadsheet documents, the Available Memory indicator will gradually decrease. When it reaches 0, you won't be able to type in any more words or data. Later in the book, we'll discuss what to do when this happens.

Formatting a Data Disk

The next thing you want to do is to format a disk to use for your *AppleWorks* data. The formatting process prepares the disk to store your *AppleWorks* documents.

Blank disks can be used on any brand or type of computer that accepts 5.25" (or 3.5") disks. But every computer uses its own method to "record" and "playback" data on its disks. The formatting process allows your particular brand of computer to set up its own unique record and playback scheme on the disk. Formatting a disk also erases any and all information that may have been previously recorded on it.

Some computers, and your computer is one of them, have more than one method of formatting disks. The method chosen depends on the *operating system* being used at the time the disk is formatted. Since *AppleWorks* runs under the *ProDOS* operating system, your data disks will be formatted using the ProDOS scheme. Other operating systems available to your Apple computer (but not to *AppleWorks*) include *DOS 3.3* and *Pascal.*

To format your data disk, select option 5, **Format a blank disk**, from the Other Activities Menu. A new "file folder" should appear on top of the Other Activities folder, as in Figure 1-10. Take a blank disk and label it "AppleWorks Data." If your computer system has *two* disk drives, insert this labeled data disk into the second drive and *skip* the next paragraph.

If your computer system has only *one* disk drive, remove the *AppleWorks* Program disk from the disk drive and insert the labeled data disk into the drive.

FIGURE 1-10 Formatting a data disk

```
Disk: Disk 2 (Slot 6)          DISK FORMATTER          Escape: Other Activities

   Main Menu
     Other Activities
       Disk Formatter

       The formatter will use the disk drive
       shown on the top line of the screen.

       A disk name consists of up to 15 letters,
       numbers, and periods.  The first character
       must be a letter.

Type a disk name:                                                  56K Avail.
```

The instruction line at the bottom of the screen says **Type a disk name:**. Under ProDOS, the operating system used by *AppleWorks*, all disks are given names when they are formatted. You can give your data disk almost any name, up to 15 letters or numbers long. You can even use periods, along with your letters and numbers, and the letters can be either upper or lower case. (*AppleWorks* converts all letters in disk names to upper case.) There are three restrictions when you name a disk: You must type a letter as the first character of the disk name, you cannot use spaces, and you must not name the data disk "AppleWorks." In fact, to make some of the later exercises less confusing, let's name the data disk "DATA." Type the four letters, **D,A,T,A,** and press RETURN. The instruction line should now read: **Press Space Bar to continue**. Press the Space Bar.

(*Note:* If your data disk has been previously formatted, you will see a warning message telling you that your disk is not blank and asking you if you *really* want to format it. Type **YES** and press RETURN.)

Your data disk should now be formatting. After about 30 seconds, you should see the message in the center of the screen: **Successfully formatted**. If your computer system has two disk drives, *skip* the next step.

If your computer system has one disk drive, remove the formatted data disk from the drive and insert the *AppleWorks* Program disk.

Press the Space Bar once, then press the ESC key to exit formatting and return to the Other Activities Menu.

Configuring *AppleWorks* for Your Printer

The last part of our configuration process tells *AppleWorks* what kind of printer you are using. To do this, select option 7, **Specify information about your printer(s)**. Your screen should now look like Figure 1-11.

FIGURE 1-11 Adding a printer

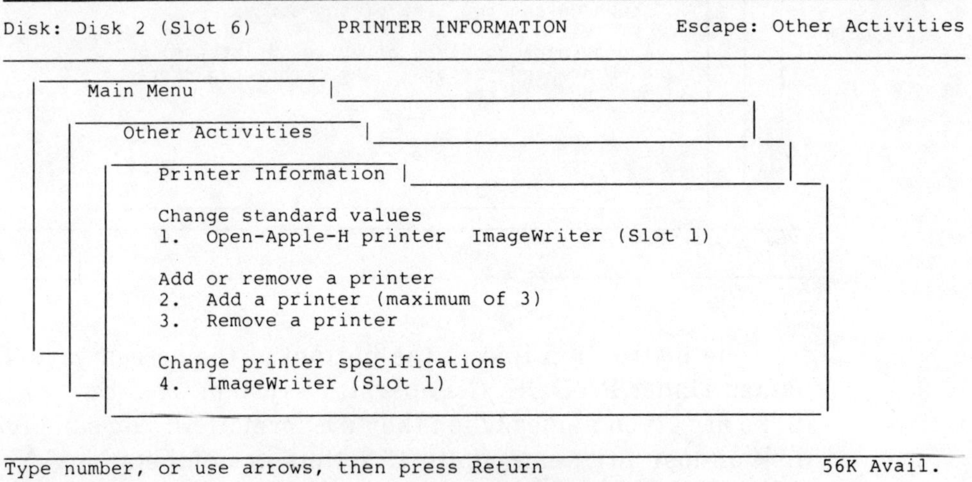

```
Disk: Disk 2 (Slot 6)       PRINTER INFORMATION       Escape: Other Activities

   Main Menu
      Other Activities
         Printer Information

         Change standard values
         1.  Open-Apple-H printer  ImageWriter (Slot 1)

         Add or remove a printer
         2.  Add a printer (maximum of 3)
         3.  Remove a printer

         Change printer specifications
         4.  ImageWriter (Slot 1)

Type number, or use arrows, then press Return                      56K Avail.
```

THE PRINTER INFORMATION MENU

The first thing you'll do is remove any printers that may be present. (*Note:* If your screen only shows options 1, 2, and 3, you can skip the next paragraph.)

Select option 3, **Remove a printer**. In the Remove a Printer folder, you will see that printer #1 is highlighted. Press the RETURN key and that printer will be removed. You should now be back at the Printer Information menu. Repeat this step until your screen shows only options 1, 2, and 3.

You will now tell *AppleWorks* which printer you will be using and where it is connected to your Apple computer. Select option 2, **Add a printer**, and your screen should look like Figure 1-12. (*Note:* If your version of *AppleWorks* is earlier than version 1.2, you won't see an entry for the Apple Scribe printer and the Custom printer selection will be number 11.)

FIGURE 1-12 Selecting a printer

```
Disk: Disk 2 (Slot 6)          ADD A PRINTER      Escape: Printer Information

   Main Menu
      Other Activities
         Printer Information
            Add a Printer
            Identify your printer, or a compatible series

            1.  Apple Dot Matrix          9.  Qume Sprint 5
            2.  Apple Imagewriter        10.  Qume Sprint 11
            3.  Apple Daisy Wheel        11.  Apple Scribe
            4.  Apple Silentype          12.  Custom printer

            5.  Epson MX series
            6.  Epson MX/Graftrax+
            7.  Epson RX series
            8.  Epson FX series

Type number, or use arrows, then press Return                     56K Avail.
```

ADDING A PRINTER

If you are using any Apple printer (ImageWriter, Daisy Wheel, etc.), any Epson printer (MX, RX, or FX series), or a Qume Sprint 5 or Sprint 11 printer, you will find your printer listed in the Add a Printer folder. Type the number that corresponds to your printer and press RETURN. (As with all typed responses, if you type the wrong number, press the DELETE key to erase your mistake.)

But what if your printer isn't listed? In that case, you must select Custom printer, choice 12.

After you make your choice, you'll be asked to **Type a name:** for your printer. The name can be anything you want. Again, for convenience, suppose we call it "My Printer." Type **My Printer**, and press RETURN.

You now have to tell *AppleWorks where* your printer is connected to your Apple. If you have an Apple IIGS or IIe, your choices will be those in Figure 1-13a. If you have an Apple IIc, your choices are shown in Figure 1-13b. In most computer systems, your printer will be in **Slot 1** if you have an Apple IIGS or IIe, or **Port 1** if you have an Apple IIc. Type the number next to the location of your printer (probably "1") and press RETURN.

FIGURE 1-13a Assigning a slot to the printer

```
Disk: Disk 2 (Slot 6)          ADD A PRINTER          Escape: Printer Information

   Main Menu
     Other Activities
       Printer Information
         Add a Printer

         How is the printer accessed?

         1.  Slot 1
         2.  Slot 2
         3.  Slot 4
         4.  Slot 5
         5.  Slot 6
         6.  Slot 7
         7.  Print onto disk or on another Apple

Type number, or use arrows, then press Return                        56K Avail.
```

FIGURE 1-13b Assigning a port to the printer

```
Disk: Ext. disk //c            ADD A PRINTER          Escape: Printer Information

   Main Menu
     Other Activities
       Printer Information
         Add a Printer

         How is the printer accessed?

         1.  Port 1
         2.  Port 2
         3.  Print onto disk or on another Apple

Type number, or use arrows, then press Return                        56K Avail.
```

PRINTER OPTIONS

Depending on whether you chose Custom printer, and which model computer you are using, you will have 4, 5, or 6 customizing options displayed (see Figure 1-14). If you have an Apple IIGS or IIe, *Apple-Works* will show you the option, **Interface cards**. If you have selected

FIGURE 1-14 Setting printer options

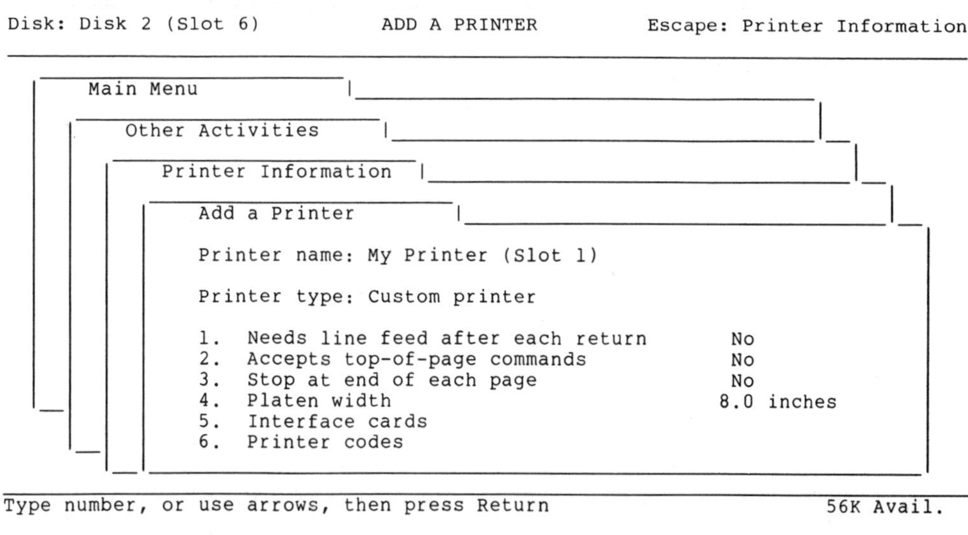

Custom printer as your printer type, *AppleWorks* will show the option, **Printer codes**.

Let's discuss options 1 through 4 first, because they're always present. Option 1, **Needs line feed after each return**, asks you whether your printer requires *AppleWorks* to send a *line feed* command after every *carriage return* command. Most printers generate their own line feed commands every time they receive a carriage return command from the computer. Some printers require both carriage return and line feed commands to be sent by the computer. If you look in your printer's manual, it should tell you whether your printer requires line feeds. In order to change any of the first three options, from "Yes" to "No" or vice versa, type the number of the option, press RETURN, and type the letter "Y" (in upper or lower case, without pressing the RETURN key).

Option 2, **Accepts top-of-page commands**, should *always* be "No," regardless of what type of printer you have. The reason for this choice has to do with printing mailing labels and is a bit too involved to go into here, so trust me and select "No" to option 2.

Option 3, **Stop at end of each page**, controls whether *AppleWorks* will pause after each page in a multipage document and wait for you to press a key on the keyboard before continuing. If you are using single sheets of paper, the response to option 3 should be "Yes." If you are using continuous-feed paper, the answer to option 3 should be "No."

Option 4, **Platen width**, requires a numerical response. Most printers have a platen width of 8″. Yes, they'll accept 8.5″ wide paper, but the print head only travels 8″ from one end to the other. Similarly, so-called wide carriage printers may accept paper up to 15″ wide, but the actual platen width is only 13.2″. These two platen widths, 8.0″ and 13.2″, cover virtually all currently available printers. If you need to change the platen width, type the option number, 4, press RETURN, type the new platen width, and press RETURN.

INTERFACE CARD INITIALIZATION CODES

The **Interface cards** option only appears if you are running *AppleWorks* on an Apple IIGS or IIe computer. If you have an Apple IIGS or IIe, your printer is plugged into an interface card that is, in turn, plugged into one of the seven slots in your computer's motherboard (main circuit board)—probably slot 1. If this interface card is either an Apple Parallel Interface Card or an Apple Super Serial Card, you can leave the **Interface cards** option exactly as it is. If, however, you are using a non-Apple interface card (e.g., Grappler, Tymac, etc.), you will have to change the interface card initialization code so that it agrees with the code your card is expecting.

Look at Table 1-1. It shows the initialization code for most of the popular, non-Apple, parallel interface cards (as many as I could find).

TABLE 1-1

Interface Card	Initialization Code
Grappler Plus and compatibles	Control-I 0N
PKASO	Control-I 0N (the 0 is a zero)
Tymac or Microtek RV-611C	Control-I 255N
MPC AP Graph or Graphwriter	Control-I 255N
Practical Peripherals	Control-I N

If you have a non-Apple interface card that is not listed in Table 1-1, you can probably find the required initialization code in the manual that came with the card. In some cases, you may have to contact the card manufacturer to get this information.

To type in your specific code, select option 5, **Interface cards**, from the Add a Printer Menu, and your screen should look like Figure 1-15. You want to replace the list of characters already in the Interface Cards folder with the list of characters for your particular interface card. So

FIGURE 1-15 Using non-Apple interface cards

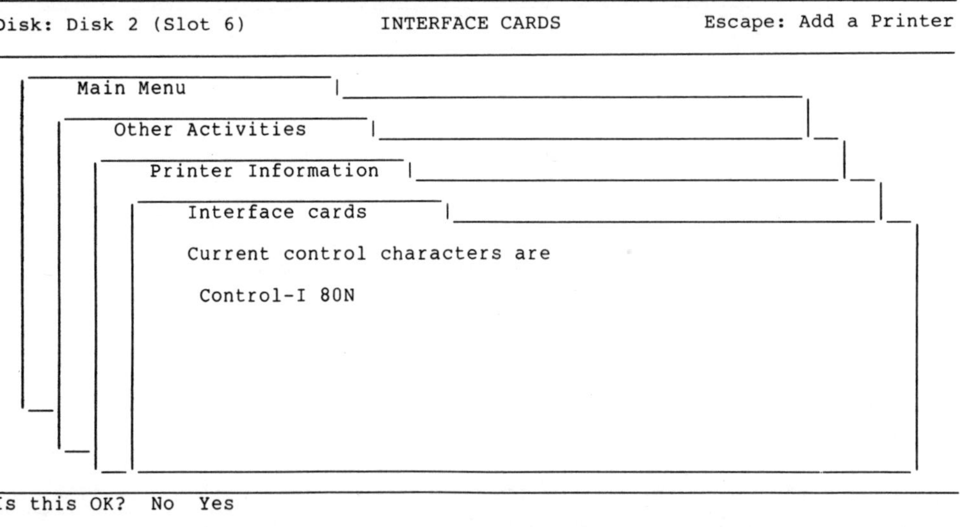

the first thing to do is to get rid of the string of characters already there. In response to the question at the bottom of the screen, **Is this OK?**, type the letter "N" (*don't* press RETURN).

Now your screen looks like Figure 1-16. Notice that all of the initialization codes in Table 1-1 begin with the character CONTROL-I. To type this character, hold the CONTROL key down while you type the letter "I." Now type the rest of the characters that make up your interface card's initialization code without pressing the CONTROL key. Note that while Table 1-1 shows a space between the CONTROL-I and the next character, this is only for the purpose of clarity. In other words, don't type any spaces. Also notice that the last character in the code is an upper-case (capital) "N."

When you have finished typing the initialization code, *do not* press the RETURN key. Instead, type a caret or circumflex character, "^" (SHIFT-6). This will bring you back to the Add a Printer Menu. If you make a mistake while typing in the initialization code, you won't be able to erase the wrong character with the DELETE key. You'll have to type the "^" character to get out of the Interface Cards folder and repeat the entire sequence beginning at the top of the previous paragraph.

CUSTOM PRINTER CODES

If you have selected "Custom printer" as your printer type because your printer wasn't among those listed, your Add a Printer menu also shows

FIGURE 1-16 Changing the interface card initialization code

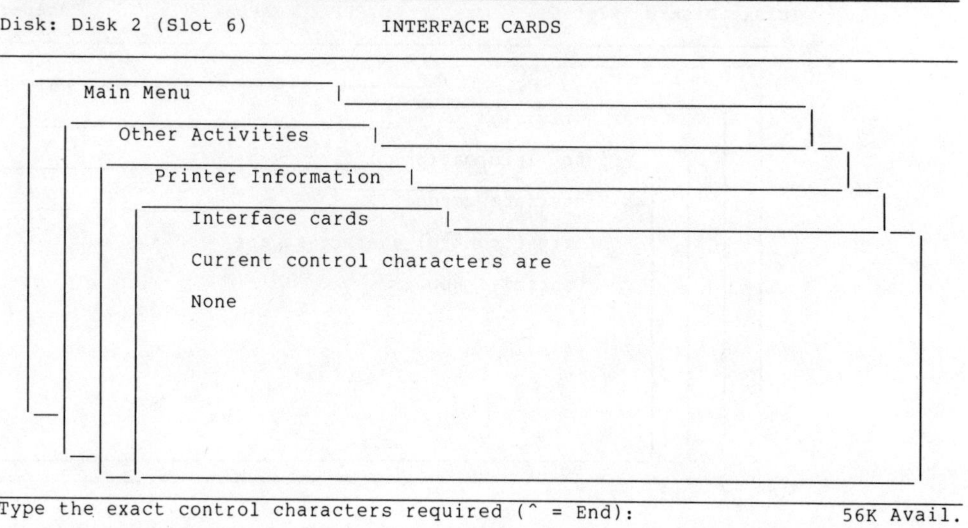

```
Disk: Disk 2 (Slot 6)          INTERFACE CARDS

   Main Menu
      Other Activities
         Printer Information
            Interface cards

            Current control characters are

            None

Type the exact control characters required (^ = End):        56K Avail.
```

the option for **Printer codes** (it may be numbered either 5 or 6). The reason for this option is that *AppleWorks* allows you to make use of many of the special features that most modern printers have, such as underlining, boldfacing, various print sizes and styles (pica, elite, etc.), superscripting and subscripting, and so forth. If your printer is one of those listed (e.g., Apple, Epson, Qume), *AppleWorks* automatically knows what commands have to be sent to your printer in order to produce a particular feature (such as underlining).

If you select Custom printer, *AppleWorks* doesn't know which features, if any, your printer supports. Nor does it know what commands are needed to achieve a particular feature on your printer. The **Printer codes** option lets you tell *AppleWorks* which features your printer supports and how to make them work.

Because entering special codes for your printer is a rather involved process, and because the codes are different for different printers, I have placed this part of the configuration process in Appendix B. If you have a custom printer, now is the time to go to Appendix B and complete the Printer codes section of the printer configuration.

RETURNING TO THE MAIN MENU

Finally, press the ESC key to go to the Printer Information folder, press ESC again to go to the Other Activities folder, and press ESC once more to return to the Main Menu. Your copy of the *AppleWorks* program has been configured for your computer system and is now ready to be used.

Common Features

As you might imagine, each of the three sections of *AppleWorks*—word processor, data base, and spreadsheet—has its own set of commands and features. Some commands, however, behave the same way in all three applications.

THE CURSOR MOVEMENT KEYS

The four arrow keys are used to move the cursor around the screen. The direction of the arrow on the key indicates the direction of movement of the cursor.

SCREEN PRINT OUT

AppleWorks allows you to print out on your printer whatever is on your screen at any moment. To do this, first make sure you have paper in your printer and that it is plugged in and turned on. Then type ⌘**H** (that is, hold down the OPEN-APPLE key while you type the letter "H"). Your printer should print out exactly what you're seeing on your screen.

HELP SCREENS

Because there are so many commands to remember, *AppleWorks* provides you with Help screens that list and briefly explain all the commands that *AppleWorks* currently accepts. To see the Help screen for the Main Menu, type ⌘**?** (Figure 1-17). You can use the up- and down-arrow keys to scroll through the list. Pressing ESC will return you to the application or menu screen you were looking at before you typed ⌘?.

SAVING YOUR DOCUMENT AS YOU WORK

You can save the current document you are working on at any time by typing ⌘S. *AppleWorks* will put a copy of your document on your data disk. If the document has been saved previously, *AppleWorks* will throw away the old version and replace it with the current version.

FIGURE 1-17 Opening the Help folder

```
Disk: Disk 2 (Slot 6)              HELP              Escape: Main Menu

       Main Menu
          Help

          Open-Apple:    This key is used in combination with
                         other keys to request many of the special
                         features of AppleWorks.  For example,
                         you can save the contents of any file by
                         pressing S while you hold down Open-Apple.
                         This example is shown below as ₫-S.

          ESC:           The Escape key will erase an entry or let
                         you leave what you are currently doing.

          DELETE:        This key will usually remove the character
                         preceding the cursor.

Use arrows to see remainder of Help                          56K Avail.
```

THE DELETE KEY

With the exception of Printer codes and Interface Card codes, the DELETE key can always be used to erase what you have just typed.

THE ESC KEY

If you press the ESC key while you are working in any section of *AppleWorks* (except Printer codes and Interface Card codes) you will be returned to the Main Menu. Depending on what you were doing at the time, you may have to press the ESC key more than once to get to the Main Menu.

Quitting *AppleWorks*

When you're ready to stop using *AppleWorks*, don't just turn off your computer. Press the ESC key to return to the Main Menu. Then select option 6, **Quit**. *AppleWorks* will ask you if you really want to quit. If you do, press the "Y" key. If there are any documents on your Desktop that have not been saved, *AppleWorks* will give you the opportunity to save them before the program terminates.

Now, on to word processing.

CHAPTER

2 THE WORD PROCESSOR

The term *word processing* usually refers to a computer program that assists you in writing various kinds of documents—personal letters, office memos, term papers, or even books such as *AppleWorks: The Program for the Rest of Us.* The assistance such a program provides varies from one word processor program to another but most of them offer the following features: full-screen editing, print formatting, and the ability to move sections of text from one point to another in the document.

Full-screen editing means that if you want to change something anywhere in your document, you can just move the cursor there and make the change. Print formatting refers to features such as margins, alignment, type size (pica, elite, etc.), and pagination (automatic page numbering).

I. CREATING A NEW WORD PROCESSOR DOCUMENT

The word processor section of *AppleWorks* performs all of these functions and several others as well. What we are going to do in this chapter is to create and format a word processor document from scratch. So that we're all working on the same document, Figure 2-1 shows an office memo from your company, Hot & Cold Inc., that I thought we'd use.

Using the Word Processor for the First Time

Before you start to type the memo, here are a few pointers to keep in mind.

1. Press the RETURN key only at the end of *paragraphs.* If you are used to typing on a typewriter, you may find this difficult to remember at first. But just keep typing until you reach the end of the paragraph. As you reach the end of a line, *AppleWorks* will automatically bring your cursor to the beginning of the next line on the screen. It will also bring whatever word you are currently typing to the beginning of the next line. In other words, *AppleWorks* will *not* break a word in the middle, leaving some of it at the end of one line and putting the rest at the beginning of the next. This process of bringing the entire word down to the beginning of the next line is called *word wraparound* and is a feature of most word processors.

FIGURE 2-1 Office Memo

To: Bill
Chuck
Penney

From: Mike

Subject: On Site Charges

As you know, for the past three years, Hot & Cold Inc. has been charging the same rate for on site labor, $40.00 per hour. While most of our competetors have adopted higher prices for both parts and labor, we have tried to "hold the line" in spite of our increasing costs. Unfortunately, I find it necessary to raise our labor charge from $40.00 to $45.00 per hour, effective immediately.

I want to be sure that our service policies are understood by all H & C employees so we can avoid customer misunderstandings. Here are some guidelines which should help you answer any service charge questions your on site customer might have.

1. Labor is billed at $45.00 per hour. Time starts when the service technician arrives at the customer's location.

2. There is a minimum one hour labor charge. If the job takes more than one hour, then time is billed by the quarter hour, rounded up to the nearest quarter hour. In other words, if the job takes one hour and twenty minutes, the customer is charged for an hour and a half.

3. If the job requires two men, the labor charge per hour will double.

4. We will not use customer purchased parts in our repairs because we cannot guarantee their quality.

5. A seven per cent state sales tax will be added to the cost of all parts, but not to labor.

6. We will be happy to estimate the cost of any job. Estimates are billed at a flat one hour charge, $45.00. If the customer elects to have us do the work, the $45.00 charge will be applied toward his final bill.

7. Payment is due upon completion of work unless the customer has an open account with us.

8. H & C guarantees its work, parts and labor, for a period of 90 days.

If we all understand and follow the above guidelines, there will be less chance for customer confusion. Keep this memo with you and feel free to show it to your customers, should there be any questions.

2. The cursor type that *AppleWorks* will choose for you is the *insert* cursor. This is the cursor that appears as a blinking underline symbol. If you place this cursor on top of an existing character on the screen (the arrow keys move the cursor around) and type, whatever you type will be inserted at the point on the screen where the cursor sits. All text to the right of the cursor will be "pushed" to the right as you type. The other cursor is the *overstrike* cursor, which you saw when you typed in the current date during the start-up process. It looks like a blinking box. If you place this cursor on top of an existing character on the screen and type, each character you type replaces a character on the screen. You can switch between cursor types by typing an ⌘E (hold the OPEN-APPLE key down while you type the letter "E"). I have found the insert cursor to be more useful in word processing (I usually do more inserting than correcting), so I usually leave the cursor in the insert mode—but you should try it both ways to see which cursor is more useful to you.
3. Use the DELETE key to erase mistyped characters. It's the easiest and fastest way to correct errors. Each time you press the DELETE key, the character immediately to the left of the cursor is erased.
4. Notice, in the numbered items in the memo, that there are *three* spaces between the period following the number and the first word of the item. I know it sounds like a picky point, but it will be important later.

Working with the Desktop

Let's start typing the memo. First, start up *AppleWorks*, if it's not already up and running. Next, from the Main Menu, select choice 1, **Add files to the Desktop**. (Your screen should look like Figure 2-2.) Because we're going to create a new word processor document, select option 3, **Make a new file for the: Word Processor**, from the Add Files Menu. From the Word Processor folder select choice 1, **From Scratch**. You will then be asked, at the bottom of the screen, to **Type a name for this new file:** (Figure 2-3). Type **Office Memo** and press RETURN.

Note: AppleWorks document names can be from 1 to 15 characters long. You may use any combination of letters (upper or lower case), numbers, periods, and spaces. The first character must be a letter.

FIGURE 2-2 Create a new word processor document

```
Disk: Disk 2 (Slot 6)        ADD FILES          Escape: Erase entry

   Main Menu
      Add Files

          Get files from:

       1. The current disk: Disk 2 (Slot 6)
       2. A different disk

          Make a new file for the:

       3. Word Processor
       4. Data Base
       5. Spreadsheet

Type number, or use arrows, then press Return 3        56K Avail.
```

FIGURE 2-3 Name the new document

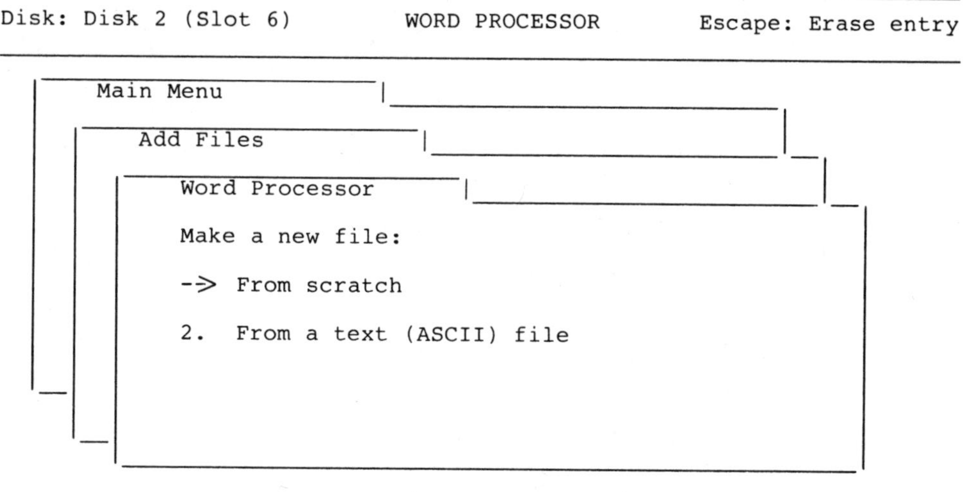

Typing Your Document

Figure 2-4 shows what *AppleWorks* calls its "Review/Add/Change" screen for the word processor. This is where you'll actually type your document. Type the memo, exactly as it appears in Figure 2-1. Remember to press the RETURN key at the end of paragraphs only. You probably noticed that once you began typing the first paragraph, your cursor never got beyond column 60 on the screen. Don't worry; this is normal. The explanation has to do with *AppleWorks*' choice of left and right page margins and its choice of pica type size. We'll go into this more deeply a little later in this chapter when we discuss print formatting. For now, just ignore it and keep typing.

FIGURE 2-4 Review/Add/Change for the word processor

```
File: Office Memo              REVIEW/ADD/CHANGE            Escape: Main Menu
=====|====|====|====|====|====|====|====|====|====|====|====|====|====|====|===










--------------------------------------------------------------------------------
Type entry or use ⌘ commands             Line  1   Column   1      ⌘-? for Help
```

Saving Your Document to Your Data Disk

Once you've finished typing the memo, you'll probably want to print it out. But before you do, it's a good idea to save the memo. In fact, it's a good idea to save your work every 5 minutes or so. My local power company has an annoying habit of momentarily interrupting service, and a momentary power failure is all it takes to wipe out your Apple's memory. This doesn't do any permanent damage, but whatever you were working on is gone! To limit the amount of loss, save your documents frequently.

AppleWorks makes it easy to save your work at any time. Just type ⌘**S** and your document is automatically saved onto your data disk. If your computer system has two drives, *AppleWorks* will save the memo to the data disk in drive 2 (the external drive on a IIc). If your computer system has one disk drive, *AppleWorks* will prompt you (after you type ⌘S) to remove the Program disk from your disk drive and insert your data disk. After *AppleWorks* is through saving your memo, you will be prompted to switch back to the Program disk.

Printing Your Document

When your memo has been saved, turn on your printer and get ready to print what you have typed. You're going to print out several versions of this memo, so I hope you have a good supply of paper handy. To print out the memo, type ⌘**P**.

AppleWorks wants to know how much of the document you want to print. It's asking *where* you want it to start printing. Since you want to print the entire document, you want it to start printing at the *beginning*. So press RETURN to accept the choice: **Print from? Beginning**. We'll talk about the two other options, **this page** and **cursor**, a little later.

Select your printer from the Print Menu. If you configured your printer in Chapter 1, your printer is named "My Printer" and is choice 1 (Figure 2-5).

FIGURE 2-5 Select your printer

```
File: Office Memo              PRINT MENU            Escape: Review/Add/Change
====|====|====|====|====|====|====|====|====|====|====|====|====|====|====|====




                     Where do you want to print the file?

                     1.  My Printer

                     2.  A text (ASCII) file on disk




--------------------------------------------------------------------------------
Type number, or use arrows, then press Return                        54K Avail.
```

Finally, press the RETURN key to accept the choice of 1 copy of the memo to be printed. (*Note:* You can print up to 9 copies of your *AppleWorks* documents at a time by changing the value of the number of copies option.)

Your printer should print out the memo exactly as you typed it. In fact, it should look just like Figure 2-1.

The Help Screen

By now, I think you can probably see that you'll be using a number of special commands to get *AppleWorks* to do what you want it to do (Ó S, Ó P, and Ó E, among others). To help you remember these commands, *AppleWorks* provides you with Help screens. Look at the bottom line on your monitor. At the left you see a general instruction: **Type entry or use Ó commands**. The apple symbol represents the OPEN-APPLE key (Ó). In the center of the bottom line is an indicator showing the current line and column position of your cursor. At the right is the instruction: **Ó? for Help**. Anytime you see this at the bottom of the screen, you can type Ó? and see a Help screen that will list all of the *AppleWorks* commands available to you. Try it! Type Ó**?** (don't use the SHIFT key) and look at the Help screen for the word processor section of *AppleWorks*. You can use the up- and down-arrow keys to scroll through the list of commands. Don't try to memorize them all at once; that's why *AppleWorks* has Help screens. When you want to return to your document, press ESC.

II. EDITING YOUR DOCUMENT

AppleWorks provides several ways to make changes in your word processor documents. These are discussed in the following sections.

Inserting Text

Suppose, for example, you wanted to insert the word "Service" just in front of the word "Charges" in the line near the top that reads "Subject: On Site Charges." Make sure that you are using the insert cursor (the one that looks like a blinking underline). Remember, Ó E changes the cursor type.

Next, use the arrow keys to position the insert cursor so that it is on top of the "C" in "Charges." Now type the word "Service" (don't forget the space that separates "Service" from "Charges"). That was easy, wasn't it?

Replacing Text

The correction of most misspellings, on the other hand, usually involves substituting one letter for another. You probably noticed that I misspelled the word "competitors" in the third line of the first paragraph. Let's correct it now. This time we'll use the *overstrike* (blinking box) cursor. Switch to the overstrike cursor by typing ⌘E. Move the overstrike cursor so that it sits on top of the second "e" in "competetors" and type an "i." That's all there is to it.

Resaving a Document

Save this version of the memo by typing ⌘**S**. You're going to mess up your memo a little, and I want you to be able to load back this version later. This time, when you type ⌘S, *AppleWorks* removes the old version of the memo that was saved earlier and replaces it with the current version. You'll see how to keep both the new and old versions of a document on your data disk later in the chapter.

The Delete Command

Let's suppose you wanted to delete one of the items in the memo—say, item 5. You could place the cursor at the end of item 5 and use the DELETE key to remove all the characters in item 5, one at a time. But there's a much faster way. Place the cursor on the number 5, and type ⌘**D**. Press the down-arrow key twice. Note that each time you press the down-arrow key, a whole line is highlighted. The highlighted lines indicate which text is about to be deleted. If you wanted to delete only part of a line, you could use the left- and right-arrow keys to select a portion of the line. When you've highlighted the portion of text you want to delete, press the RETURN key. Zap! There goes the text.

If you change your mind about deleting *before* you press the RETURN key, you can press the ESC key and abort the Delete command. But once you've deleted the text from your document, it's gone forever. If you want it back, you'll have to type it in again.

The Replace Command

One of the most remarkable features of any word processor is its ability to perform what is called *global search and replacement*. Suppose you had used the word "salesman" in a number of places in a document, and you wanted to replace each instance with the word "salesperson." The Replace command will search through the entire document (global) looking for instances of the word "salesman." Each time "salesman" is found, it replaces that string of characters with "salesperson." You could just as easily have *AppleWorks* search an entire document and replace every occurrence of the word "he" with the word "she."

Let's try using this command in your memo. Suppose you wanted to replace every occurrence of "H & C" with "Hot & Cold." To do this, position the cursor at the very beginning of the document because the search process always begins from the current cursor position and continues to the end of the document. A quick way of moving the cursor to the beginning of your memo is to type **1**. (More about 1 through 9 later.) Now type the Replace command, **R**.

If you look down at the bottom line on your screen, you'll see you have a choice of **Text** or **Case sensitive text**.

AppleWorks is asking whether it should pay attention to the case (upper or lower) of the text it's searching for. If you choose "Text" and tell it to search for "H & C" then it will find occurrences of "H & C," "H & c," or "h & c." If, however, you choose **Case sensitive text**, then a search for "H & C" will only find "H & C." For our example, choose "Text" by pressing RETURN. (You could also have just typed the letter "T" without pressing RETURN.)

You are asked: **Replace what?** Type the five characters **H & C** and press RETURN. *AppleWorks* now asks: **Replace with what?** Type **Hot & Cold** and press RETURN. Finally, you are asked if you want to replace **All** occurrences at once, or just **One at a time**. If you select **One at a time**, you will have to respond "Yes" or "No" at each occurrence in your document to indicate whether you want to replace that particular instance of "H & C."

For this exercise, type **A** (don't press RETURN) to indicate All occurrences. Scroll through your document with the up- and down-arrow keys and look at the effect of using Replace. Amazing, isn't it?

Cut and Paste: The Move Command

There is one more way you can edit text, and that is by copying or moving sections of text. Suppose, for instance, that you wanted to move up the second paragraph in your memo so that it becomes the first paragraph. *AppleWorks* makes this easy.

First, move the cursor so that it sits on top of the first letter in the second paragraph, the letter "I." Type the Move command, ⌘**M**. At the bottom of your screen, *AppleWorks* is asking you where you want to move the text. Choose **Within document** by pressing the letter "W" (don't press RETURN). (*Note:* You'll learn about the two other options, **To clipboard** and **From clipboard**, in Chapter 5.)

AppleWorks now asks you to indicate by using the arrow keys which text you want to move. (*Note:* The section of text you want to move *begins* at the current cursor position. That's why you have to place the cursor at the beginning of the text you want to move *before* you type ⌘M.)

Press the down-arrow key five times to highlight the entire second paragraph, including the blank line below the paragraph. Press RETURN to indicate that you have completed selecting the lines you want to move. Now move the cursor to the point in the document where you want the selected text to be moved—the first letter of paragraph 1, the letter "A"—and press RETURN. Presto!

The Copy Command

The Copy command, ⌘C, works almost exactly like the Move command. The only difference is that the original text is left in place. The text is "copied" instead of "moved."

Restoring the Original Memo

Now that you've messed up the original memo, let's throw away this version and load back the "good" version from your data disk.

REMOVING FILES FROM THE DESKTOP

To remove the current version of the memo, press ESC to go to the Main Menu. Select option 4, **Remove files from the Desktop**. *AppleWorks* allows you to have several files on the Desktop at the same time, and you'll use this feature later on. Right now, the only file listed should be Office Memo. (See Figure 2-6.) Press the right-arrow key to select this document to be removed. If you had several documents on the Desktop, they would all be listed, and you could use the down-arrow key to move through the list and the right-arrow key to select those you wanted to

FIGURE 2-6 Removing a document from the Desktop

```
Disk: Disk 2 (Slot 6)              REMOVE FILES              Escape: Main Menu

  Main Menu
      Remove Files
      Name              Status         Document type        Size
      ==========================================================
    ->Office Memo       Changed        Word Processor        3K

Use Right Arrow to choose files, Left Arrow to undo             54K Avail.
```

remove from the Desktop. If you were to select a document by mistake, you could use the left-arrow key to cancel the selection.

Press RETURN to indicate you're through selecting the documents you want to remove. *AppleWorks* wants to know if you want to save the document to disk, before it removes the document from the Desktop. Because you don't care about this version of the memo, select option 3, **Throw out the changes to the file**. And when you're asked **Do you really want to do this?**, press the "Y" key to indicate "Yes." *AppleWorks* will then throw away the file and return you to the Main Menu.

LOADING A FILE FROM THE DATA DISK

You now want to retrieve the version of the memo you last saved. To do this, select option 1, **Add files to the Desktop**, from the Main Menu. This is the same Add Files Menu you saw earlier (Figure 2-2), but this time you will choose option 1, **Get files from: The current disk: Disk 2 (Slot 6)** or **Ext. disk //c**. (*Note:* Those of you with one-drive systems will see: **The current disk: Disk 1 (Slot 6)** or **Built-in disk** and, when you select this option, you'll be prompted to remove your *AppleWorks* Program disk from your disk drive and insert your data disk.)

Figure 2-7 shows what your screen should look like. You'll see that your Office Memo document is the only file on your data disk.

Look at the second line in the AppleWorks Files folder, the one that says **Disk volume /DATA has 133K available**. The first thing you should

FIGURE 2-7 Adding a saved document to the Desktop

```
Disk: Disk 2 (Slot 6)            APPLEWORKS FILES            Escape: Add Files

   Main Menu
      Add Files
         AppleWorks files
         Disk volume /DATA has 133K available
             Name        Type of file    Size    Date       Time
         ======================================================
       -->Office Memo  Word Processor     3K    1/28/87   10:26 am

Use Right Arrow to choose files, Left Arrow to undo                56K Avail.
```

notice is that your data disk's name is listed by *AppleWorks* as "/DATA" even though, when you formatted it, you called it "DATA." Don't worry, this is normal and has to do with the way ProDOS (*AppleWorks*' disk operating system) names disks and files. There is a discussion of ProDOS disk and file names in Chapter 6, in the section on using *AppleWorks* with a hard disk drive.

The second thing to notice is that *AppleWorks* is telling you how much blank space is left on your data disk for saving other documents: 133K. (*Note:* If your data disk is a 3.5" disk, your disk will have 793K of blank space remaining.)

As you save more and more documents to your data disk, the space remaining will, of course, decrease. Even though *AppleWorks* will warn you if there isn't enough room on your data disk to save a document, don't try to use every available bit of space on your data disk. When the space available decreases below 10K or so, format a new data disk (you can give it the same name, "DATA," or a different one) and begin using it.

If you had several documents on your data disk, the AppleWorks Files folder would show you the entire list and you could scroll through the list using the up- and down-arrow keys. You could indicate which file(s) you wanted to load onto the Desktop by pressing the right-arrow key as your choice is highlighted.

With only one file on your data disk, the Office Memo, you can just press the RETURN key to choose it. Your Office Memo should now be loaded and your screen should look like Figure 2-8. (*Note:* If your

FIGURE 2-8 The saved memo is back on your screen

```
File: Office Memo               REVIEW/ADD/CHANGE               Escape: Main Menu
=====|====|====|====|====|====|====|====|====|====|====|====|====|====|====|===
To:        Bill
           Chuck
           Penney

From:      Mike

Subject:   On Site Service Charges


As you know, for the past three years, Hot & Cold Inc. has
been charging the same rate for on site labor, $40.00 per
hour. While most of our competitors have adopted higher
prices for both parts and labor, we have tried to "hold the
line" in spite of our increasing costs. Unfortunately, I
find it necessary to raise our labor charge from $40.00 to
$45.00 per hour, effective immediately.

I want to be sure that our service policies are understood
by all H & C employees so we can avoid customer
misunderstandings. Here are some guidelines which should
--------------------------------------------------------------------------------
Type entry or use  commands            Line 1  Column  1          -? for Help
```

computer system has one disk drive, you will be prompted to remove your data disk from the drive, insert the *AppleWorks* Program disk, and press RETURN.)

III. MOVING AROUND IN YOUR DOCUMENT

AppleWorks provides several ways to move your cursor within your document.

The Arrow Keys

You already know how to move the cursor using the four arrow keys, but each of the arrow keys can be used in *two* ways. If you press either the left- or right-arrow key by itself, the cursor moves left or right one character. But, if you hold down the key while you press the left-or right-arrow keys, the cursor moves left or right one *word*. Similarly, the up- and down-arrow keys by themselves move the cursor up or down one line. If you hold down the key, the up- and down-arrow keys move the cursor a whole screen at a time.

1 through 9

Another way of moving the cursor is to use 1 through 9. As you saw earlier, 1 always moves the cursor to the beginning of the document. And, that's right, 9 moves the cursor to the end of the document. The other number keys move the cursor proportionally through the document. For example, 5 moves the cursor to the halfway point in your document. These keys perform the same way in all three *AppleWorks* applications: word processor, data base, and spreadsheet.

The Find Command

AppleWorks allows you to find a particular word or phrase in your document. All you do is tell *AppleWorks* what you're looking for and your document is searched until the specified word or phrase is found (or the end of the document is reached). Let's try it. First, type **1**. You want your cursor at the beginning of your memo because the Find command starts looking from the current position of the cursor. Now, type **F**.

While the Find command becomes more useful as the size of your document increases, you can see most of its features with your Office Memo. At the bottom of the screen, you'll see five options for Find: **Text**, **Page**, **Marker**, **Case sensitive text**, and **Options for printer**. You select which one you want by typing the first letter of the option: T, P, M, C, or O. (You can also make the selection by using the right-arrow key to highlight your choice and pressing RETURN.) Three of these Find options are discussed in the following section. I'm going to put off discussing **Marker** and **Options for printer** until after you learn about document formatting.

FIND TEXT

Let's try out some of these Find options. Type **T** (for Text) and you'll be prompted by the message **Find what text?**. Type **h & c** in lower case and press RETURN. *AppleWorks* finds the first occurrence of the five characters, "h & c", and highlights them for you. You are then asked if you want to find the next occurrence. Type **Y** for "Yes," **N** for "No." If the Find command cannot find what you've told it to look for, it will beep at you and tell you: **Not found, press Space Bar to continue**. Notice that while you specified the search string as "h & c", *AppleWorks* found occurrences of "H & C." In other words, the Find Text option doesn't pay attention to case.

FIND CASE SENSITIVE TEXT

Now let's try the **Case sensitive text** option. Type **1**,**F**, **C** (don't press RETURN). *AppleWorks* remembered the "h & c" from the last Find Text search. Erase these characters by typing CONTROL-Y. (Hold down the CONTROL key while you type a "Y.") Typing CONTROL-Y is a quick way of erasing a line of text.

Now, type **h & c** and press RETURN. This time, using Find Case sensitive text, *AppleWorks* couldn't find a match for "h & c"—at least it shouldn't have. Press the Space Bar, as directed. When you use the **case sensitive** option, matching text must agree in capitalization as well as identical characters. If you were to ask it to Find Case sensitive text "H & C", it *would* be successful.

FIND PAGE

Let's try to use the Find Page feature, and don't worry if it doesn't work the first time. Type**1**, to go to the beginning of your memo, and then, **F**, **P**. In response to **Page number?**, type **1** and press Return. What happened? Your Apple beeped at you and at the bottom of your screen you see the message: **Not found. Press Space Bar to continue**. Press the Space Bar and let's see what the problem is.

You are asking *AppleWorks* to find the end of page 1 of your document. *AppleWorks* is telling you that it couldn't find the end of page 1. The reason *AppleWorks* couldn't find page 1 is that you didn't tell *AppleWorks* to calculate where the page breaks (where one page ends and the next one begins) occurred in your memo.

CALCULATE PAGE NUMBERS

This calculation of page breaks is performed automatically when you print your document, but we can have *AppleWorks* calculate page breaks without printing, by using the Calculate command, K. Type **K**, select your printer from the displayed list, and see what *Apple-Works* does.

As you scroll through your memo, you'll see a dashed line labeled "End of Page 1" and, a bit further on, another dashed line labeled "End of Page 2" (see Figure 2-9). These page break indicators will remain until you make any change to your document. While they're still there, let's try the Find Page feature again. Type**1**,**F**, and **P** and again respond **1**

FIGURE 2-9 Page breaks

```
File: Office Memo              REVIEW/ADD/CHANGE              Escape: Main Menu
=====|====|====|====|====|====|====|====|====|====|====|====|====|====|====|===

6.   We will be happy to estimate the cost of any job.
Estimates are billed at a flat one hour charge, $45.00. If
the customer elects to have us do the work, the $45.00
charge will be applied toward his final bill.

7.   Payment is due upon completion of work unless the
customer has an open account with us.

8.   H & C guarantees its work, parts and labor, for a
period of 90 days.

If we all understand and follow the above guidelines, there
will be less chance for customer confusion. Keep this memo
- - - - - - - - - - - - - - - - - End of Page 1 - - - - - - - - - - - - - - - - -
with you and feel free to show it to your customers, should
there be any questions.
- - - - - - - - - - - - - - - - - End of Page 2 - - - - - - - - - - - - - - - - -


--------------------------------------------------------------------------------
Type entry or use  commands            Line 41  Column  1       -? for Help
```

to **Page number?**. This time, *AppleWorks* had no trouble finding the end of page 1.

I'll bet you're wondering what those strange squares at the end of each paragraph are. For the moment, just ignore them (the explanation involves the Zoom command). If you want to make them disappear, type **Z**.

The Tab Command

There is one other way to move your cursor to a desired place on the screen, and that's with the Tab command, T. If you have used a typewriter, you are probably familiar with tabs. Tabs are positions on the 80-column line to which you can move your cursor by pressing a single key, the TAB key. Let's take a practical example. Suppose you wanted to indent the first line of each paragraph in a document 6 spaces. You could, of course, hit the Space Bar 6 times whenever you started a new paragraph, but there is an easier way to do this using tabs.

At the top of your screen (second line), you'll see a line of "=" symbols interspersed with "|" characters. This is called the Tab Line. Each "|" represents a tab stop. When you begin a new word processor document, *AppleWorks* automatically sets tabs at columns 6, 11, 16, 21, etc. To see how this works, try pressing the TAB key on your keyboard a few times.

Now let's change the default tab settings. Type ⌘**T**. At the bottom of the screen, you see that the Tab command recognizes only three characters: "S" for Set, "C" for Clear, and "R" for Remove all. At the far right is an indicator showing the horizontal position of the cursor. Type **R** and see that all of the "|" characters disappear from the Tab Line. You have just removed all of the preset tabs.

You can use the left- and right-arrow keys to move the cursor back and forth along the Tab Line. To set a tab at a particular position, move the cursor to the position you want, column 6, for example. (Looking at the cursor indicator on the bottom line will help you to accurately place the cursor). Type **S** to set the tab. If you make a mistake and want to clear a single tab, place the cursor over the "|" character and type **C**. When you're through setting your tabs, press the ESC key. Now, any time you want to move to a tab position to the right of your cursor's position, just press the TAB key. If you want to "back up" to a tab to the left of your cursor, hold down the OPEN-APPLE key while you press TAB. *Note:* You can only tab as far to the right as your right margin will allow (more about margins in a moment).

IV. PRINT FORMATTING

AppleWorks has a large variety of print formatting options. These allow you to "dress up" your documents and make them look more professional.

The Printer Options Screen

Type ⌘**O** and look at Figure 2-10. The screen display for Printer Options occupies the lower 11 lines on the screen. (*Note:* If you're not using version 2.0 of *AppleWorks*, your Printer Options screen won't show the last printer option, "MM.")

All printer options are selected by typing the two-character code, which appears to the left of each option, and pressing RETURN. Some options, such as margins, require a numerical value to be typed in immediately after the two-character option code. Pressing ESC, instead of typing an option code, returns you to your document.

FIGURE 2-10 Printer Options

```
File: Office Memo              PRINTER OPTIONS           Escape: Review/Add/Change
=====|====|====|====|====|====|====|====|====|====|====|====|====|====|====|===
To:        Bill
           Chuck
           Penney

From:      Mike

Subject:   On Site Service Charges


As you know, for the past three years, Hot & Cold Inc. has
been charging the same rate for on site labor, $40.00 per
    PW=8.0  LM=1.0  RM=1.0  CI=10  UJ  PL=11.0  TM=0.0  BM=2.0  LI=6  SS
Option:                 UJ: Unjustified     GB: Group Begin     BE: Boldface End
                        CN: Centered        GE: Group End       +B: Superscript Beg
PW: Platen Width        PL: Paper Length    HE: Page Header     +E: Superscript End
LM: Left Margin         TM: Top Margin      FO: Page Footer     -B: Subscript Begin
RM: Right Margin        BM: Bottom Margin   SK: Skip Lines      -E: Subscript End
CI: Chars per Inch      LI: Lines per Inch  PN: Page Number     UB: Underline Begin
P1: Proportional-1      SS: Single Space    PE: Pause Each page UE: Underline End
P2: Proportional-2      DS: Double Space    PH: Pause Here      PP: Print Page No.
IN: Indent              TS: Triple Space    SM: Set a Marker    EK: Enter Keyboard
JU: Justified           NP: New Page        BB: Boldface Begin  MM: Mail Merge
```

You should keep one thing in mind whenever you use a printer option. *Every option takes effect at the point in your document where your cursor was sitting when you typed ⌘O.* Most options continue in effect until the end of the document. There are two exceptions. Boldface printing and underlining remain "on" only until the end of the paragraph or until they are turned "off," whichever comes first.

The Printer Options Status Line

If you're in Printer Options, ESC out to your memo. Type ⌘**1**, to move your cursor to the top, and type ⌘**O** to get into Printer Options again. Look at the highlighted line on the screen. This is the Status Line for Printer Options. It tells you the current value of the following format options: Platen Width (PW), Left Margin (LM), Right Margin (RM), Characters per Inch (CI), Alignment (UJ, JU, or CN), Paper Length (PL), Top Margin (TM), Bottom Margin (BM), Lines per Inch (LI), and Line Spacing (SS, DS, or TS).

When you begin a new word processor document, *AppleWorks* chooses values for each of these format options. As you learned earlier, these prechosen values are called *default* values and, though you can change any or all of them, each *new* document will start out with the defaults listed in Table 2-1.

TABLE 2-1 Printer Option defaults

Printer Option	Default Value
Platen Width	8.0″
Left Margin	1.0″
Right Margin	1.0″
Characters per Inch	10
Alignment	UJ (unjustified)
Paper Length	11.0″
Top Margin	0.0″
Bottom Margin	2.0″
Lines per Inch	6
Line Spacing	SS (single spaced)

Margins

Now you can understand why, when you were typing your memo, the cursor never got beyond column 60. Because *AppleWorks* sets Platen Width to 8″ and Left and Right Margins to 1″ each, only 6″ of space are left on each line for your text. And, because the default for Characters per Inch is 10, a 6″ line with 10 characters per inch gives 60 characters per line. Here's a simple formula that calculates the number of characters per line your printer will print out:

Characters per Line = (PW − LM − RM) × CI

You noticed that even with a Left Margin of 1″, *AppleWorks* displayed your text starting in column 1, rather than in column 11. This is just the way *AppleWorks* chooses to display your document on the screen. Line length is "shortened" by both left and right margins, but text is always shown starting in column 1 (unless you use more than one value for Left Margin in your document).

However, when you print your document, it will show a 1″ margin at both left and right edges.

LEFT AND RIGHT MARGINS

Let's change the Left Margin in the middle of your Office Memo so that each line of the eight numbered items starts half an inch further to the right. First, ESC out of Printer Options and place the cursor on top of the number 1 of the first item. (You have to get out of Printer Options in order to move the cursor, and you have to move the cursor to the point in your document where you want the new printer option to take effect.)

Reenter Printer Options (type ⌘**O**) and change the Left Margin to 1.5″. To do this, type **LM** and press RETURN; then type **1.5** and press RETURN. (Remember, the original Left Margin value was 1.0″.)

Now, ESC back to your memo and look at the effect of your Left Margin change (see Figure 2-11). The other three margins, Right, Top, and Bottom, can all be changed the same way.

FIGURE 2-11 Changing the left margin

```
File: Office Memo              REVIEW/ADD/CHANGE              Escape: Main Menu
=====|====|====|====|====|====|====|====|====|====|====|====|====|====|====|===
I want to be sure that our service policies are understood
by all H & C employees so we can avoid customer
misunderstandings. Here are some guidelines which should
help you answer any service charge questions your on site
customer might have.

     1.   Labor is billed at $45.00 per hour. Time starts
     when the service technician arrives at the customer's
     location.

     2.   There is a minimum one hour labor charge. If the
     job takes more than one hour, then time is billed by
     the quarter hour, rounded up to the nearest quarter
     hour. In other words, if the job takes one hour and
     twenty minutes, the customer is charged for an hour and
     a half.

     3.   If the job requires two men, the labor charge per
     hour will double.

-------------------------------------------------------------------------------
Type entry or use ⌘ commands        Line 25  Column  6           ⌘-? for Help
```

Let's try one more change. Leaving your cursor at the same place in your memo (over the "1"), go back to Printer Options (⌘O) and change the value of Right Margin to 1.5″. Type **RM** and press RETURN; then type **1.5** and press RETURN. ESC out and compare your memo to Figure 2-12.

There is one small problem. Scroll down and look at the last paragraph in your memo. You'll see that it, too, has been affected by the changes in the Left and Right Margin values. What you ought to do is to change the margins back to their original values for the last paragraph. To do this, place the cursor over the first letter of the first word in the last paragraph, the letter "I." Now, enter Printer Options and change the Left Margin to 1″ and the Right Margin to 1″. ESC back to your memo and compare it with Figure 2-13.

FIGURE 2-12 Changing the right margin

```
File: Office Memo                 REVIEW/ADD/CHANGE                Escape: Main Menu
=====|====|====|====|====|====|====|====|====|====|====|====|====|====|====|===
I want to be sure that our service policies are understood
by all H & C employees so we can avoid customer
misunderstandings. Here are some guidelines which should
help you answer any service charge questions your on site
customer might have.

     1.   Labor is billed at $45.00 per hour. Time
     starts when the service technician arrives at the
     customer's location.

     2.   There is a minimum one hour labor charge. If
     the job takes more than one hour, then time is
     billed by the quarter hour, rounded up to the
     nearest quarter hour. In other words, if the job
     takes one hour and twenty minutes, the customer is
     charged for an hour and a half.

     3.   If the job requires two men, the labor charge
     per hour will double.

--------------------------------------------------------------------------------
Type entry or use ⌘ commands          Line 26  Column  6             ⌘-? for Help
```

FIGURE 2-13 Reset the margins for the last paragraph

```
File: Office Memo                 REVIEW/ADD/CHANGE                Escape: Main Menu
=====|====|====|====|====|====|====|====|====|====|====|====|====|====|====|===
     do the work, the $45.00 charge will be applied
     toward his final bill.

     7.   Payment is due upon completion of work unless
     the customer has an open account with us.

     8.   H & C guarantees its work, parts and labor,
     for a period of 90 days.

If we all understand and follow the above guidelines, there
will be less chance for customer confusion. Keep this memo
with you and feel free to show it to your customers, should
there be any questions.

--------------------------------------------------------------------------------
Type entry or use ⌘ commands              Line 61  Column  1         ⌘-? for Help
```

TOP AND BOTTOM MARGINS

Usually, if Top and Bottom Margins are altered, the change is made at the top of the document so that all pages of the document have the same Top and Bottom Margins. You might wonder why the default value for Top Margin is 0" while the Bottom Margin is set to 2.0". These values are intended to give a 1″ margin at the top *and* bottom of each printed page according to the following logic. With most printers, it is easier to establish the line where the document will begin by physically adjusting the paper in the printer. Generally, you would want the first line of text about 1″ from the top of the page. With a Paper Length of 11″ and a Bottom Margin of 2″, your printer will type 9″ of text (11 − 2 = 9) and stop 1″ from the bottom of the page. The reason it stops 1″ from the bottom rather than 2″ is that you have already advanced the paper 1″ at the top. When your printer reaches the end of the page, *AppleWorks* automatically advances the paper 2″. If you are using tractor-feed paper, this action positions your printer 1″ from the top of the second sheet.

The maximum number of lines of text that will be typed on a single page by your printer is determined by the values of four Printer Options: Paper Length, Top Margin, Bottom Margin, and Lines per Inch. The "formula" to compute the number of lines per page is:

$$\textbf{Lines per Page} = (\textbf{PL} - \textbf{TM} - \textbf{BM}) \times \textbf{LI}$$

If you plug in the default values you get:

$$\textbf{Lines per Page} = (11 - 0 - 2) \times 6 = 54$$

Indent

The Indent option doesn't quite operate the way you probably imagine it does. It is *not* used to indent the first line of paragraphs; you have to do that yourself (see the discussion about the Tab command). Instead, the Indent option is used to indent all the lines *except* the first line in a paragraph. The reason for this can best be understood by using the option with your memo. Look at the eight numbered items. Each one begins with a number, a period, and three spaces, before the first word of the item. What we would like to do is to "hang" these five characters to the left of the paragraph.

Look at Figure 2-14 and you'll see what I mean. Paragraphs formatted like those in the figure are sometimes called "bulleted" or "hanging" paragraphs.

Place your cursor back on top of the number "1" in the first item. Enter Printer Options (ƆO) and change the Indent to 5 characters. To do this, type **IN** and RETURN; then type **5** and RETURN. ESC out, and your memo should look *almost* like Figure 2-14. The only difference is that last paragraph, again. It was affected by the Indent option along with the numbered items. To correct this, we'll change the value of the

FIGURE 2-14 Set the indent for hanging paragraphs

```
File: Office Memo              REVIEW/ADD/CHANGE             Escape: Main Menu
=====|====|====|====|====|====|====|====|====|====|====|====|====|====|====|===
     5.    A seven per cent state sales tax will be
           added to the cost of all parts, but not to
           labor.

     6.    We will be happy to estimate the cost of any
           job. Estimates are billed at a flat one hour
           charge, $45.00. If the customer elects to
           have us do the work, the $45.00 charge will
           be applied toward his final bill.

     7.    Payment is due upon completion of work unless
           the customer has an open account with us.

     8.    H & C guarantees its work, parts and labor,
           for a period of 90 days.

If we all understand and follow the above guidelines, there
will be less chance for customer confusion. Keep this memo
with you and feel free to show it to your customers, should
there be any questions.
-------------------------------------------------------------------------------
Type entry or use Ć commands          Line 46  Column  1          Ć-? for Help
```

Indent back to 0 at the point where the last paragraph begins. So, first move your cursor to the "I" in "If." Then go to Printer Options, change Indent to 0 (type **IN** and RETURN; type **0** and RETURN), and ESC out. Now your memo should look exactly like Figure 2-14.

Changing the Name of a Document

I think it's a good idea to save what you've done so far. But rather than replace the original memo with this formatted memo, we'll keep the old version on the disk and add this new version. Normally, when you save a document that has already been saved on disk, the current version *replaces* the older version on the disk. (And, normally, that's what you want it to do.) To prevent this replacement, you have to change the *name* of your document. Type Ć **N** and look at the bottom line. You are being prompted to: **Type filename:**. And the current file name, "Office Memo," is being displayed. Type **CONTROL-Y** to erase the current file name (hold down the CONTROL key while you type a "Y"). The CONTROL-Y command erases all the characters from the cursor to the end of the line. Let's rename the memo, "Formatted Memo." Type **Formatted Memo** and press RETURN.

Save the new, renamed version of the memo by typing Ć **S**. *Note:* The next time you see a list of the documents on your data disk, you'll see both Office Memo *and* Formatted Memo.

Alignment

The term alignment refers to *how* a line of text is printed relative to the left and right margins. *AppleWorks* provides three alignment options.

UNJUSTIFIED

The first option is called Unjustified (UJ) and is the default setting. Unjustified prints each line starting at the left margin and ending either at or before the right margin, depending on the length of the last word on the line (see a discussion of "word wraparound" at the beginning of this chapter). The right edge of the printed document is ragged because some lines will "come out even" with the last word extending exactly to the right margin, while other lines will stop short of the right margin because the next word was so long that it was wrapped around to the next line.

JUSTIFIED

The second alignment option is Justified (JU). When Justified is selected, lines of text are printed starting at the left margin and ending at the right margin. How do the lines always "come out even," you ask? Simple. *AppleWorks* adds enough extra spaces between words to make each line extend all the way from the left to the right margin. Let's see how this works.

First, print out the Formatted Memo just as it is. (Type ⌘**P**, press RETURN to have your memo start printing from the beginning, select your printer from the list, and accept 1 copy by pressing RETURN again.)

Now let's change the alignment. Move the cursor to the top of your memo (⌘1) and enter Printer Options (⌘O). Select the Justified option by typing **JU** and pressing RETURN. ESC back to your document. Notice that the change in alignment doesn't alter how the document appears on your screen. But print it out again and compare this printed version with the previous one. (See Figure 2-15.)

CENTERED

The third alignment option is Centered. Here, lines of text are printed so that they are centered between the left and right margins. This option is often used when typing titles.

FIGURE 2-15 Justified printing

To: Bill
Chuck
Penney

From: Mike

Subject: On Site Service Charges

As you know, for the past three years, Hot & Cold Inc. has been charging the same rate for on site labor, $40.00 per hour. While most of our competitors have adopted higher prices for both parts and labor, we have tried to "hold the line" in spite of our increasing costs. Unfortunately, I find it necessary to raise our labor charge from $40.00 to $45.00 per hour, effective immediately.

I want to be sure that our service policies are understood by all H & C employees so we can avoid customer misunderstandings. Here are some guidelines which should help you answer any service charge questions your on site customer might have.

1. Labor is billed at $45.00 per hour. Time starts when the service technician arrives at the customer's location.

2. There is a minimum one hour labor charge. If the job takes more than one hour, then time is billed by the quarter hour, rounded up to the nearest quarter hour. In other words, if the job takes one hour and twenty minutes, the customer is charged for an hour and a half.

3. If the job requires two men, the labor charge per hour will double.

4. We will not use customer purchased parts in our repairs because we cannot guarantee their quality.

5. A seven per cent state sales tax will be added to the cost of all parts, but not to labor.

6. We will be happy to estimate the cost of any job. Estimates are billed at a flat one hour charge, $45.00. If the customer elects to have us do the work, the $45.00 charge will be applied toward his final bill.

7. Payment is due upon completion of work unless the customer has an open account with us.

8. H & C guarantees its work, parts and labor, for a period of 90 days.

If we all understand and follow the above guidelines, there will be less chance for customer confusion. Keep this memo with you and feel free to show it to your customers, should there be any questions.

To demonstrate Centered alignment, let's add today's date to the top of the memo. Make sure that the cursor is at the top of the memo and then enter Printer Options. Type **CN**, press RETURN, and ESC. Now your document looks like Figure 2-16. What happened? The whole document is centered, but don't worry. We'll fix it in a moment.

Press the RETURN key twice and then press the up-arrow key twice. (This allows you to type above the top line of your document.) Now type today's date and *press RETURN*. Notice that your cursor automatically jumps to a position halfway between the left and right margins so that as you type the date, it is centered.

FIGURE 2-16 Centered alignment

```
File: Formatted Memo           REVIEW/ADD/CHANGE              Escape: Main Menu
=====|====|====|====|====|====|====|====|====|====|====|====|====|====|====|===
                       To:        Bill
                                 Chuck
                                 Penney

                       From:      Mike

             Subject:  On Site Service Charges


As you know, for the past three years, Hot & Cold Inc. has
 been charging the same rate for on site labor, $40.00 per
  hour. While most of our competitors have adopted higher
prices for both parts and labor, we have tried to "hold the
 line" in spite of our increasing costs. Unfortunately, I
find it necessary to raise our labor charge from $40.00 to
          $45.00 per hour, effective immediately.

I want to be sure that our service policies are understood
      by all H & C employees so we can avoid customer
 misunderstandings. Here are some guidelines which should
------------------------------------------------------------------------------
Type entry or use 𝄞 commands            Line  3   Column  1       𝄞-? for Help
```

What we have to do now is to "undo" the centering effect for the rest of the document. Enter Printer Options (⌘O), type **JU** or **UJ** (whichever format you like best), press RETURN, and ESC. The rest of your memo is back to normal and your date is still centered, as in Figure 2-17.

Making Printer Options Visible

There are times when it would be nice to see what printer options have been embedded in your document. *AppleWorks* allows you to see these options by pressing ⌘Z, the Zoom command. Try it (Figure 2-18).

FIGURE 2-17 Reset the rest of the memo to unjustified alignment

```
File: Formatted Memo          REVIEW/ADD/CHANGE          Escape: Main Menu
=====|====|====|====|====|====|====|====|====|====|====|====|====|====|====|===
                              September 15

To:         Bill
            Chuck
            Penney

From:       Mike

Subject:    On Site Service Charges

As you know, for the past three years, Hot & Cold Inc. has
been charging the same rate for on site labor, $40.00 per
hour. While most of our competitors have adopted higher
prices for both parts and labor, we have tried to "hold the
line" in spite of our increasing costs. Unfortunately, I
find it necessary to raise our labor charge from $40.00 to
$45.00 per hour, effective immediately.

--------------------------------------------------------------------------------
Type entry or use ⌘ commands            Line  5   Column  1        ⌘-? for Help
```

FIGURE 2-18 Viewing Printer Options

```
File: Formatted Memo          REVIEW/ADD/CHANGE          Escape: Main Menu
=====|====|====|====|====|====|====|====|====|====|====|====|====|====|====|===
--------Justified
--------Centered
                              September 15
--------Justified

To:         Bill
            Chuck
            Penney

From:       Mike

Subject:    On Site Service Charges
As you know, for the past three years, Hot & Cold Inc. has
been charging the same rate for on site labor, $40.00 per
hour.  While most of our competitors have adopted higher
prices for both parts and labor, we have tried to "hold the
line" in spite of our increasing costs. Unfortunately, I
--------------------------------------------------------------------------------
Type entry or use ⌘ commands            Line  5   Column  1        ⌘-? for Help
```

Not only do you see all your printer options, but those strange-looking squares (remember them?) indicate each place in your memo where you pressed the RETURN key. If you press ⌘ Z a second time, the printer options are hidden again.

Deleting a Printer Option

Suppose you wanted to delete one of the printer options. This is a little hard to do because, normally, you can't see them. However, as you found out in the section above, the Zoom command makes printer options visible. Once you can see them, all you have to do to delete one is to move your cursor to the line the option is on, type ⌘D, and press RETURN.

Let's delete the unnecessary Justified option at the very top of the memo (Figure 2-18). Type ⌘ **Z** to Zoom in on the printer options. Move your cursor to the top line (the Justified printer option), type ⌘ **D**, and press RETURN.

Line Spacing

Changing the line spacing from single spaced (the default) to double or triple spaced is easy. Just remember to move your cursor to the point in your document where you want the change to begin. From Printer Options, type the two-character code for the kind of spacing you want—SS, DS, or TS—and press RETURN.

Lines per Inch

Many printers support more than one value of vertical distance between lines. All printers provide 1/6" distance between lines; this, of course, gives 6 lines per inch. Some printers also provide 1/8" movement (8 lines per inch) as well as other values. The printer option Lines per Inch (LI) allows you to select either 6 or 8 lines per inch.

You might wonder what *AppleWorks* would do if you selected a value for this option (or any other printer option) that your printer *didn't* support. The answer is that *AppleWorks* simply ignores printer options that don't apply to your printer.

Printer Type Sizes and Styles

Most dot matrix printers provide several different type sizes. Some also provide for proportional printing. Apple's ImageWriter printer, for example, features printing at 4, 5, 6, 9, 10, 12, 13, 15, and 17 characters per inch, as well as two sizes of proportional printing. The manual that came with your printer will have a list or chart of the various type sizes that it uses. (If your printer was installed as a "custom printer," you had to type in the printer command codes for each different type size.)

If you use a daisy wheel printer, the print wheel determines the type size and, unless you change the print wheel, you'll have to make do with a single type size.

MONOSPACED PRINTING

Changing the number of characters per inch for your printer is easy. From Printer Options, you type **CI** and RETURN, then the value you want (5, 12, 17, etc.) and press RETURN. You can change the value for Characters per Inch at the beginning of any paragraph in your document, but *AppleWorks* will not let you change the number of characters per inch in the middle of a paragraph.

PROPORTIONAL PRINTING

When your printer is printing, say, 10 characters per inch, its print head is moving to the right exactly 1/10 of an inch after every character it types, regardless of the width of the character. Some printers, however, have a printing mode in which they move their print head a *variable* amount of distance, depending on the width of the character. In other words, the print head would move further to the right after typing the letter "w" than it would after typing the letter "i," because a "w" is wider than an "i." This mode of printing is called *proportional* printing, and *AppleWorks* has two Printer Option commands (P1 and P2) to allow you to make use of this printer feature. The reason for two proportional printing commands is that some printers (Apple's ImageWriter, for one) have two *sizes* of proportional printing. *Note:* If your printer was installed as a "custom printer," the proportional printing commands P1 and P2 will have no effect on your printer.

One caution. Don't use proportional printing when you're printing columns of information, such as a table. You'll find that, even though the columns appear to be aligned on the screen, they won't be aligned when you print the document, if you print proportionally.

Page Breaks

As your printer prints out your document, *AppleWorks* counts the lines of typing. After a certain number of lines have been printed (depending on the values of Page Length, Top and Bottom Margins, and Lines per Inch), *AppleWorks* automatically directs your printer to move to the top of the next piece of paper.

Sometimes this break occurs at an inconvenient place in your document—in the middle of a paragraph or a table, for example. *AppleWorks* provides two ways of dealing with this problem.

NEW PAGE

The first is the New Page (NP) command. If you insert this command into your document, *AppleWorks* will tell your printer to begin a new page at this point. Let's see how this works.

When you printed out your "Formatted Memo," you saw that it was a two-page memo, and that page 2 began with instruction number 8. Suppose you wanted page 2 to begin with instruction number 5 instead of number 8. To do this, move your cursor to the "5" character in your memo, enter Printer Options (🍏O), type **NP** and press RETURN, and ESC. Now print out your memo again and see the difference (Figure 2-19). *Note:* I've indicated where page 1 ends on Figure 2-19 with a row of # characters.

GROUP BEGIN AND END

The second way *AppleWorks* controls page breaks is with the Group Begin (GB) and Group End (GE) commands. These two printer options allow you to indicate, in your document, the beginning and end of a block of text. If a page break would normally occur within the block, *AppleWorks* will automatically start a new page at the *beginning* of the block of text.

Before we try out this feature, you should delete the New Page marker you inserted above. Type🍏 **Z** so that you can see the printer options in your memo. Move your cursor to the New Page indicator, type 🍏**D**, and press RETURN.

Now, suppose you wanted to keep all eight items in your memo together on one page. What you would do is to indicate the beginning of a group of text at the start of item 1, and the end of the group at the line following the end of item 8. So, move your cursor to the "1" in item 1, enter Printer Options (🍏O), type **GB** (Group Begin), press RETURN, and ESC.

Next, move your cursor to the blank line following item 8, enter Printer Options, type **GE** (Group End), press RETURN, and ESC. Print out your memo and see where the page break occurs now (Figure 2-20).

FIGURE 2-19 Forcing a page break

```
To:       Bill
          Chuck
          Penney

From:     Mike

Subject:  On Site Service Charges
```

As you know, for the past three years, Hot & Cold Inc. has been charging the same rate for on site labor, $40.00 per hour. While most of our competitors have adopted higher prices for both parts and labor, we have tried to "hold the line" in spite of our increasing costs. Unfortunately, I find it necessary to raise our labor charge from $40.00 to $45.00 per hour, effective immediately.

I want to be sure that our service policies are understood by all H & C employees so we can avoid customer misunderstandings. Here are some guidelines which should help you answer any service charge questions your on site customer might have.

1. Labor is billed at $45.00 per hour. Time starts when the service technician arrives at the customer's location.

2. There is a minimum one hour labor charge. If the job takes more than one hour, then time is billed by the quarter hour, rounded up to the nearest quarter hour. In other words, if the job takes one hour and twenty minutes, the customer is charged for an hour and a half.

3. If the job requires two men, the labor charge per hour will double.

4. We will not use customer purchased parts in our repairs because we cannot guarantee their quality.

##

5. A seven per cent state sales tax will be added to the cost of all parts, but not to labor.

6. We will be happy to estimate the cost of any job. Estimates are billed at a flat one hour charge, $45.00. If the customer elects to have us do the work, the $45.00 charge will be applied toward his final bill.

7. Payment is due upon completion of work unless the customer has an open account with us.

8. H & C guarantees its work, parts and labor, for a period of 90 days.

If we all understand and follow the above guidelines, there will be less chance for customer confusion. Keep this memo with you and feel free to show it to your customers, should there be any questions.

FIGURE 2-20 Grouping text

```
To:        Bill
           Chuck
           Penney

From:      Mike

Subject:   On Site Service Charges
```

As you know, for the past three years, Hot & Cold Inc. has been charging the same rate for on site labor, $40.00 per hour. While most of our competitors have adopted higher prices for both parts and labor, we have tried to "hold the line" in spite of our increasing costs. Unfortunately, I find it necessary to raise our labor charge from $40.00 to $45.00 per hour, effective immediately.

I want to be sure that our service policies are understood by all H & C employees so we can avoid customer misunderstandings. Here are some guidelines which should help you answer any service charge questions your on site customer might have.

###

1. Labor is billed at $45.00 per hour. Time starts when the service technician arrives at the customer's location.

2. There is a minimum one hour labor charge. If the job takes more than one hour, then time is billed by the quarter hour, rounded up to the nearest quarter hour. In other words, if the job takes one hour and twenty minutes, the customer is charged for an hour and a half.

3. If the job requires two men, the labor charge per hour will double.

4. We will not use customer purchased parts in our repairs because we cannot guarantee their quality.

5. A seven per cent state sales tax will be added to the cost of all parts, but not to labor.

6. We will be happy to estimate the cost of any job. Estimates are billed at a flat one hour charge, $45.00. If the customer elects to have us do the work, the $45.00 charge will be applied toward his final bill.

7. Payment is due upon completion of work unless the customer has an open account with us.

8. H & C guarantees its work, parts and labor, for a period of 90 days.

If we all understand and follow the above guidelines, there will be less chance for customer confusion. Keep this memo with you and feel free to show it to your customers, should there be any questions.

Automatic Page Numbering

AppleWorks will automatically number your pages for you, either at the top of each page or at the bottom. You can also control whether the page number appears on the first page or begins on the second page with "page 2." Your page numbers don't even have to start with "1." You can start numbering at any value.

PAGE HEADER

Setting up your document for page numbering involves the use of the Page Header (HE) or Page Footer (FO) commands. The two commands operate almost the same way. The Page Header (or Page Footer) command repeats the line *immediately below* the command in your document at the top (or bottom) of every page, when you print out the document.

Let's demonstrate this feature. Type ⌘**1** to move your cursor to the top of your memo. Enter Printer Options (⌘O) and type **HE** to set a Page Header, press RETURN, and ESC. Hit the RETURN key once and the up-arrow key so that your cursor is on a blank line just under the Page Header indicator. Anything you type on this line will be used as the page header and will be the first line typed on every page in your document. Type **This is the header**. (Don't worry if this line is affected by the Centered alignment command that you inserted for your date line, earlier. See Figure 2-21.) Now, print out your memo and look at the top of *both* pages. The line "This is the header" is at the top of both pages and is followed by two blank lines. *AppleWorks* automatically inserts two blank lines following the header and preceding the footer.

Suppose you didn't want the header to be printed on the first page, but you wanted it on all the remaining pages of your document. The trick here is *where* in your document you place the Page Header. You placed the header at the very top of your memo. Suppose you move it between the first and second paragraphs of the memo. To do this, place your cursor on the beginning of the Page Header line. Type ⌘**M** and press the RETURN key to accept the "Within document" option. Press the down-arrow key twice and the left-arrow key once, to highlight the Page Header line *and* the line below it, and press RETURN. Move the cursor to the line between the first and second paragraphs, and press RETURN again. The two lines, the Page Header indicator and the "This is the header" line, should have moved to the space between the first and second paragraphs of the memo (Figure 2-22). Print out the memo again and see that the header skipped page 1 but appears on page 2.

FIGURE 2-21 Inserting a page header

```
File: Formatted Memo           REVIEW/ADD/CHANGE              Escape: Main Menu
=====|====|====|====|====|====|====|====|====|====|====|====|====|====|====|===
--------Page Header
                    This is the header
                       September 15


To:       Bill
          Chuck
          Penney

From:     Mike

Subject:  On Site Service Charges

As you know, for the past three years, Hot & Cold Inc. has
been charging the same rate for on site labor, $40.00 per
hour. While most of our competitors have adopted higher
prices for both parts and labor, we have tried to "hold the
line" in spite of our increasing costs. Unfortunately, I
find it necessary to raise our labor charge from $40.00 to
-------------------------------------------------------------------------------
Type entry or use ⌘ commands             Line 3  Column 40        ⌘-? for Help
```

FIGURE 2-22 The header will skip the first page

```
File: Formatted Memo           REVIEW/ADD/CHANGE              Escape: Main Menu
=====|====|====|====|====|====|====|====|====|====|====|====|====|====|====|===

From:     Mike

Subject:  On Site Service Charges


As you know, for the past three years, Hot & Cold Inc. has
been charging the same rate for on site labor, $40.00 per
hour. While most of our competitors have adopted higher
prices for both parts and labor, we have tried to "hold the
line" in spite of our increasing costs. Unfortunately, I
find it necessary to raise our labor charge from $40.00 to
$45.00 per hour, effective immediately.
--------Page Header
This is the header

I want to be sure that our service policies are understood
by all H & C employees so we can avoid customer
misunderstandings. Here are some guidelines which should
help you answer any service charge questions your on site
-------------------------------------------------------------------------------
Type entry or use ⌘ commands             Line 22  Column 41       ⌘-? for Help
```

PAGE FOOTER

The Page Footer command works the same way. The only difference is that if you want the footer to skip page 1, insert it in your document after the end of page 1. (Note: You can use ⌘K to show where the page breaks occur and insert the footer after the page break for page 1.)

PRINTING PAGE NUMBERS IN THE HEADER OR FOOTER

What has all this to do with automatic page numbering? One of the printer options is Print Page No. (PP), and, if you insert this command on the line following either the Page Header or the Page Footer indicator, your pages will be numbered automatically.

Let's delete the Page Header from your document and work with the Page Footer. Move your cursor to the beginning of the Page Header line and type **D**. Press the down-arrow key twice and the left-arrow key once, to highlight the two lines you wish to delete, and press RETURN.

Leave the cursor where it is, on the blank line between the first and second paragraphs, and enter Printer Options (O). Type **FO** and RETURN to insert a Page Footer. Then type **PP**, press RETURN, and ESC back to your document. Now that you're back in your memo, press the RETURN key.

Do you see the caret symbol, "^", on the line just below the Page Footer indicator? Move your cursor so that it "sits" on top of that caret and look at the bottom line on your screen. In the middle of that line, where the Line/Column indicator usually is, you'll see **Print Page No.** (see Figure 2-23). *AppleWorks* represents the page number indicator (and several other special printer features) with a caret. If you move the cursor over the caret and watch the Line/Column indicator at the bottom of your screen, *AppleWorks* will tell you what that caret represents.

FIGURE 2-23 Inserting a page footer

```
File: Formatted Memo            REVIEW/ADD/CHANGE              Escape: Main Menu
=====|====|====|====|====|====|====|====|====|====|====|====|====|====|====|===

As you know, for the past three years, Hot & Cold Inc. has
been charging the same rate for on site labor, $40.00 per
hour. While most of our competitors have adopted higher
prices for both parts and labor, we have tried to "hold the
line" in spite of our increasing costs. Unfortunately, I
find it necessary to raise our labor charge from $40.00 to
$45.00 per hour, effective immediately.
--------Page Footer
^

I want to be sure that our service policies are understood
by all H & C employees so we can avoid customer
misunderstandings. Here are some guidelines which should
help you answer any service charge questions your on site
customer might have.

      1.    Labor is billed at $45.00 per hour. Time
            starts when the service technician arrives at
            the customer's location.
--------------------------------------------------------------------------------
Type entry or use  commands            Print Page No.           -? for Help
```

Let's "dress up" your page number indicator. With the insert cursor on top of the caret, press the Space Bar enough times to move the caret about halfway across the screen. Now, type a dash, "-", on either side of the caret (Figure 2-24). Print out your memo and you should see page numbers at the bottom of both pages.

FIGURE 2-24 Printing page numbers in the footer

```
File: Formatted Memo          REVIEW/ADD/CHANGE          Escape: Main Menu
=====|====|====|====|====|====|====|====|====|====|====|====|====|====|====|===

As you know, for the past three years, Hot & Cold Inc. has
been charging the same rate for on site labor, $40.00 per
hour. While most of our competitors have adopted higher
prices for both parts and labor, we have tried to "hold the
line" in spite of our increasing costs. Unfortunately, I
find it necessary to raise our labor charge from $40.00 to
$45.00 per hour, effective immediately.
--------Page Footer
                                -^-

I want to be sure that our service policies are understood
by all H & C employees so we can avoid customer
misunderstandings. Here are some guidelines which should
help you answer any service charge questions your on site
customer might have.

    1.    Labor is billed at $45.00 per hour. Time
          starts when the service technician arrives at
          the customer's location.

--------------------------------------------------------------------------------
Type entry or use ♂ commands          Line 23  Column 33        ♂-? for Help
```

CHOOSING A STARTING PAGE NUMBER

If you should ever want your page numbers to start with some number other than 1, you can use the Page Number (PN) printer option to select whatever starting value for page number you wish. Just be sure that your cursor is at the top of your document before you enter Printer Options to invoke the Page Number command. *AppleWorks* has to see the Page Number command before it sees the PP indicator in order for the Page Number command to have any effect.

Print Enhancements

AppleWorks allows you to do some special kinds of printing: boldface, underlining, subscripting, and superscripting—providing your printer supports these features. All four features are selected the same way.

UNDERLINING

Suppose, for example, you wanted to underline the subject of your memo: "On Site Service Charges." To do this, first place your cursor on top of the "O" in "On." Enter Printer Options (⌘O), type **UB** for Underline Begin, press RETURN, and ESC. Next, move the cursor so that it sits on the space to the right of the "s" in "Charges." Again enter Printer Options, type **UE** for Underline End, press RETURN, and ESC. Note that *AppleWorks* indicates the beginning and ending of underlining with caret, "^", symbols.

If you run your cursor over the carets, you'll see that the first caret represents "Underline Begin," while the second caret represents "Underline End" (Figure 2-25). Now, print out your memo and see the effect.

FIGURE 2-25 Underlining text

```
File: Formatted Memo              REVIEW/ADD/CHANGE              Escape: Main Menu
=====|====|====|====|====|====|====|====|====|====|====|====|====|====|====|===
                              September 15


To:        Bill
           Chuck
           Penney

From:      Mike

Subject:   ^On Site Service Charges^


As you know, for the past three years, Hot & Cold Inc. has
been charging the same rate for on site labor, $40.00 per
hour. While most of our competitors have adopted higher
prices for both parts and labor, we have tried to "hold the
line" in spite of our increasing costs. Unfortunately, I
find it necessary to raise our labor charge from $40.00 to
$45.00 per hour, effective immediately.
--------Page Footer
                                  -^-
--------------------------------------------------------------------------------
Type entry or use ⌘ commands              Underline End              ⌘-? for Help
```

There is an easier way to underline text in your document. Suppose you wanted to underline the next-to-the-last word in the memo, "any." The easy way to do this is to move the cursor on top of the "a" in "any" and type **CONTROL-L** (hold down the CONTROL key while you type an "L"). *AppleWorks* inserts a caret. Then, move the cursor so that it is just to the right of the last character you want to underline, the "y" in "any." You don't want the cursor to be on top of the "y," you want it, in this case, to be on the space between "any" and "questions." Again type

CONTROL-L, and again *AppleWorks* inserts a caret. Print out the memo again.

This method of typing CONTROL-L at the beginning and ending of text you want to underline is much faster than entering Printer Options twice to type "UB" and "UE" and accomplishes exactly the same thing.

BOLDFACE PRINTING

The Boldface printer option works the same way that underlining works. You can either use "BB" (Boldface Begin) and "BE" (Boldface End) from Printer Options or you can type CONTROL-B at the beginning and ending of text you want to print boldface. As an example, let's print the word "three," in the first line of the first paragraph, in boldface. Move the cursor to the "t" in "three" and type **CONTROL-B**. Now move your cursor to the right of the word "three" and again type **CONTROL-B**. The first CONTROL-B begins boldface printing; the second one ends it.

If you forget to turn off boldface printing (or underlining), *AppleWorks* automatically turns off the option at the end of the paragraph. Print out your memo again to see the effect of boldface printing.

SUBSCRIPTING AND SUPERSCRIPTING

Subscripting and superscripting must be selected from Printer Options. Otherwise, they operate the same way as boldface and underlining. Your cursor is placed at the beginning of text to be sub- or superscripted. You enter Printer Options, select either "+B" for Superscript Begin or "-B" for Subscript Begin, press RETURN, and ESC. Then you move the cursor one character to the right of the end of the text you want sub- or superscripted, reenter Printer Options, type either "+E" for Superscript End or "-E" for Subscript End, press RETURN, and ESC. That's all there is to it. (*Note:* If you use tractor-feed paper and want to do subscripting or superscripting, you may have to use the pinch roller in addition to the tractors to ensure proper paper movement.)

More Options for the Find Command

Back in the section on editing, you learned how to use three of the options in the Find command. Here, you'll learn how to use the two remaining Find options, **Marker** and **Options for printer**.

SETTING MARKERS

The Set a Marker (SM) printer option allows you to insert numbered markers in your document. The markers are not printed and, in fact, don't even appear unless you use the Zoom command, ⌘Z. They can only be used with the Marker option in the Find command.

To set a marker, move your cursor to the place in your document you wish to be able to find later. Enter Printer Options, type **SM**, and press RETURN. *AppleWorks* will ask you for a number for your marker. This can be any number between 0 and 254. Type the number, press RETURN, and ESC.

FINDING A MARKER

If you want to find the place in your document where you set a marker, type ⌘**1** to go to the top of your document. Then type ⌘**F** for Find. Press **M** for Marker, type the number of the marker, press RETURN, and *AppleWorks* will find the place in your text where that marker was inserted. Press the RETURN key again to exit the Find command. (*Note:* When you use Find Marker, *AppleWorks* automatically invokes the Zoom command so that you can see the marker in your document. You can type ⌘Z to cancel the Zoom feature.)

FINDING A PRINTER OPTION

You can also use the Find command to locate hidden printer options. Just type ⌘**F** and then **O** for Options for printer. *AppleWorks* will show you the Printer Options chart. Type the two-character code for the printer option you want *AppleWorks* to find, press Return, and *AppleWorks* will find that option.

Special Printer Commands

There are four special printer commands that you may find useful: Skip Lines (SK), Pause Each Page (PE), Pause Here (PH), and Enter Keyboard (EK).

SKIP LINES

The Skip Lines command allows you to leave a specified number of blank lines when you print your document. You might use this option if you wanted to leave space for a drawing to be inserted after you print.

Suppose you measured the length of the drawing and found that it needed 3.5″ of space. With the standard line spacing of 6 lines per inch, that drawing would occupy the equivalent of 21 lines of text. You could then place your cursor at the point in your document where the drawing would be inserted, enter Printer Options, type **SK** and RETURN, type **21** in response to the prompt **Lines:**, press RETURN, and ESC. When your document is printed, 21 lines will be left blank, starting at the marked point in your text.

PAUSE EACH PAGE

In Chapter 1 when you configured your printer for *AppleWorks*, do you remember the printer setup option: **Stop at the end of each page**? I suggested that if you planned to use tractor-feed paper, you should answer "No" to this question.

While you may plan to use tractor-feed paper most of the time, you might occasionally want to use single sheets of paper. Instead of going back to the printer configuration section and changing the **Stop at the end of each page** option, you can use the **Pause Each page** (PE) printer option. This lets you tell *AppleWorks* to stop printing at the end of each page and wait until you press the Space Bar before it continues printing the next page.

If you use this printer option, your cursor should be at the top of your document so that the entire document is affected by the option.

PAUSE HERE

Suppose you were using a daisy wheel printer and you wanted to change the print wheel to a different style—italics, for example—in the middle of printing your document. The **Pause Here** (PH) printer option lets you do this. You simply move your cursor to the place in the text where you want your printer to pause, enter Printer Options, type **PH**, RETURN, and ESC. When your printer reaches that place in the document, *AppleWorks* will stop and wait for you to press the Space Bar. You can use the Pause Here option as often as you like in a document.

ENTER KEYBOARD

AppleWorks not only allows you to pause your printer and restart it, but it also will let you type in text while your printer waits for you. That's the function of the Enter Keyboard (EK) command.

Suppose you wanted to send your memo to each of the three service technicians in your company, Hot & Cold Inc., with just that person's name on the memo. One copy of the memo would say

"To: Bill"

another copy would say

"To: Chuck"

and so forth.

The Enter Keyboard command makes this kind of "personalizing" easy. First, you will replace the three names in your memo with an Enter Keyboard indicator. To do this, move your cursor so that it sits on the "B" in "Bill." Enter Printer Options, type **EK**, press RETURN, and ESC. You'll see a caret has been inserted to the left of "Bill." Next, without moving the cursor, type **D**. Press the down-arrow key twice and the right-arrow key five times (this will highlight all three names). Press the RETURN key and the three names will be deleted (see Figure 2-26).

You can now print out three copies of the memo, inserting a different name each time. Type **P**. Press RETURN to accept printing from the beginning of your memo. Select your printer from the list and when you are asked, **How many copies:**, type **3** and press RETURN. As your printer starts to type the first copy of your memo, you will be prompted at the bottom of the screen for **Information** to be inserted in place of the Enter Keyboard caret (Figure 2-27). Type **Bill** and press RETURN. The first copy of the memo will be printed with Bill's name on it. You will then be prompted for the next name ("Chuck") to be inserted into the second copy of the memo, and so on.

You can use the Enter Keyboard command as many times as you like in the same document. *AppleWorks* will prompt you for each piece of information as the document is being printed.

Form Letters

You're probably thinking, "What about producing form letters?" *AppleWorks* 2.0 *has* a mail merge utility. It's one of the major enhancements this version of *AppleWorks* has over earlier versions. Creating a form letter uses the MM (Mail Merge) feature in Printer Options. But, because the mail merge utility combines information from a data base file with a word processor document, I'm going to postpone this exercise until Chapter 5. By then, you'll know all about data base files.

FIGURE 2-26 The Enter Keyboard option

```
File: Formatted Memo          REVIEW/ADD/CHANGE          Escape: Main Menu
=====|====|====|====|====|====|====|====|====|====|====|====|====|====|====|===
                         September 15


To:       ^

From:     Mike

Subject:  ^On Site Service Charges^


As you know, for the past three years, Hot & Cold Inc. has
been charging the same rate for on site labor, $40.00 per
hour. While most of our competitors have adopted higher
prices for both parts and labor, we have tried to "hold the
line" in spite of our increasing costs. Unfortunately, I
find it necessary to raise our labor charge from $40.00 to
$45.00 per hour, effective immediately.
--------Page Footer
                               -^-

------------------------------------------------------------------------------
Type entry or use ⌘ commands         Line 2  Column  1          ⌘-? for Help
```

FIGURE 2-27 Entering text as the memo is printed

```
File: Formatted Memo             PRINT MENU        Escape: Review/Add/Change
=====|====|====|====|====|====|====|====|====|====|====|====|====|====|====|===
                         September 15


To:       ^






                    You can type information to be placed
                    at the point marked above.






------------------------------------------------------------------------------
Information?                                                    53K Avail.
```

The Sticky Space

Finally, there is the Sticky Space feature. Sticky Spaces are used in place of ordinary spaces when you want to prevent two (or more) words from being split at the end of a line. For example, suppose you were typing the name "Mr. Smith" in a letter. You wouldn't want to have "Mr." printed at the end of one line and "Smith" printed at the beginning of the next. So, instead of typing an ordinary space between the period and the "S," you would hold down the OPEN-APPLE key while you press the Space Bar (🍏 Space Bar). This results in a caret (representing the Sticky Space) showing up between the "." and the "S." Now, no matter how you move your text around, "Mr." and "Smith" will always be printed on the same line.

Quitting *AppleWorks*

Save your document one more time with the 🍏 S command. Then press ESC to return to the Main Menu. Quit *AppleWorks* by typing a **6** and pressing RETURN. When *AppleWorks* asks you if you really want to quit, press the "Y" key.

Always use this technique to quit *AppleWorks*. Don't just turn off your computer. When you choose the Quit option, *AppleWorks* checks to see if you've made any changes to the documents on the Desktop since the last time you saved them. If you have, *AppleWorks* gives you the opportunity to save the changes before you leave the program. If you just turn off your computer without going through the Quit procedure, any unsaved changes to your files will be lost.

Final Comments

We've covered a lot of material in this chapter on word processing: commands, features, options, and the like. I hope you have been actually *doing* the exercises with the sample memo and not just reading the chapter and looking at the figures. Start using the word processor for your own letters and memos. You'll find that the more you use it, the easier it will be to use.

CHAPTER

3 THE DATA BASE

The data base section of *AppleWorks* is designed to help you enter, organize, and print out what are called "related sets of information." For example:

1. An address book, which might contain the following information for every person listed in the book:
   first name
   last name
   street address
   city
   state
   zip code
   telephone number
2. A repair shop inventory list, which might contain the following information for each part:
   part number
   description
   manufacturer
   cost
   quantity on hand
   quantity on order
3. A repair person's time sheet, which might list the following data for each service call:
   repair person's name
   date of service call
   customer
   billed time
   hourly rate
   parts cost
   total charge to customer

Do you see what I mean about related sets of information? In all three examples, specific kinds of information are required for each entry. Anytime you have data organized in this fashion, you can use a data base to store them. You can arrange the data in any order you wish (for example, by zip code, in the case of the address book). And you can print out reports containing some or all of the data.

Data base users have special terms for talking about their data bases. Each type of information (first name, city, part number, hourly rate, etc.) is called a *field*. (In your *AppleWorks* manual, these fields are called *categories*; to avoid confusion, I'll use the term category from now on.) One set of data for these categories—in the address book example, an entry for first name, last name, street address, and so on—is called a *record*. And if you lump together all of these records of the same type, you have a *file*.

In this chapter, you will create two different data base files, arrange the records in a useful, logical order (data base users call this *sorting* the file), and print out two different types of reports.

I. EXAMPLE 1: THE CUSTOMER LIST

Your first data base file will be a list of customers for a company called "Hot & Cold Inc.," a heating and air conditioning company.

Creating the File

Start up *AppleWorks* and from the Main Menu select option 1, **Add files to the Desktop**. Next, choose option 4, **Make a new file for the: Data Base**. The Data Base folder will ask you where this new file is coming from. Choose option 1, **From scratch**, and when you're prompted, **Type a name for this new file:**, type **Customer List** and press RETURN.

You should now be looking at the Change Name/Category screen (Figure 3-1). *AppleWorks* has chosen the first category name for you

FIGURE 3-1 Creating a new data base

```
File: Customer List          CHANGE NAME/CATEGORY     Escape: Review/Add/Change



Category names
================================================================================
Category 1                                  |
                                            | Options:
                                            |
                                            | Change category name
                                            | Up arrow    Go to filename
                                            | Down arrow  Go to next category
                                            | ⌘-I         Insert new category
                                            |
                                            |
                                            |
                                            |
                                            |
                                            |
                                            |
--------------------------------------------------------------------------------
Type entry or use ⌘ commands                                          56K Avail.
```

called "Category 1." Let's delete Category 1 and replace it with the first category name in your file. Type **CONTROL-Y** (hold down the CONTROL key while you type a "Y") to erase Category 1.

Table 3-1 is a list of the seven category names you will use for this file. Type in the seven category names. Press the RETURN key after each name, including the last one, so that each name is on its own line (Figure 3-2). And that's all there is to creating a data base file in *AppleWorks*.

Before we go on, though, I'd like to say a few words about planning your data base files. When you're creating your own data base files, it's a very good idea to stop and think about the information you want your file to contain. *AppleWorks* will allow up to 30 categories per record, so

TABLE 3-1 Category names for Example 1

Category Names
Customer Name
Address
City
State
Zip
Phone
Acct. No.

FIGURE 3-2 Adding categories

```
File: Customer List          CHANGE NAME/CATEGORY     Escape: Review/Add/Change



Category names
==============================================================================
Customer Name                                    |
Address                                          | Options:
City                                             |
State                                            | Type category name
Zip                                              | Up arrow    Go to previous category
Phone                                            |
Acct. No.                                        |
                                                 |
                                                 |
                                                 |
                                                 |
                                                 |
                                                 |
------------------------------------------------------------------------------
Type entry or use ♂ commands                                        56K Avail.
```

make sure you've thought of all the things you want each record to contain. While it is possible to add new categories later on, it's an awkward process.

If you need more than 30 categories, you may have to look for a different data base program. Before you do, see if there isn't a way to merge two or more categories into one. In this Customer List file, for example, you have separate categories for City, State, and Zip. I set up the file this way because you might want to sort the records in the file according to their zip codes. To do this, you would need to have the zip code information by itself, in its own category. But, if you never intended to sort the file by zip code, you could have included City, State, and Zip all in one category.

As I mentioned earlier in Chapter 1, *AppleWorks* holds all your data in your Apple's internal memory. Most other data base programs keep all the file's data stored on disk so that every time you want to look at a different record, the program has to go out to the disk and copy the record into the computer. The advantage of a memory-based data base program like *AppleWorks* is that searching a file for particular information or sorting a file takes practically no time. *AppleWorks* can put a file of 500 records in numerical order by zip code, for example, in less than 10 seconds. That same sorting process done by a disk-based data base program might take 15 minutes or more.

The disadvantage of a memory-based program is that the maximum size of a file, which means the maximum number of records in the file, is limited by the amount of available internal memory. Disk-based programs are limited by the amount of storage space available on a disk. Since *AppleWorks* is memory-based, there is a limit to the number of records you can type into your file. This limit is not a fixed number. It depends on the average amount of information typed in per record and the amount of memory you have in your Apple. The larger the average record size, the fewer records your file can hold. *AppleWorks* keeps track of the size of your file and continually tells you how much of its memory is available for more records.

Here is a guideline that will help you decide whether your data base application will "fit" in one *AppleWorks* file. If you type in about 75 characters per record, *AppleWorks* will have room for about 750 records. (*Note:* This assumes that your Apple computer has 128K of internal memory. See Chapter 6 for a discussion of add-on memory.)

This means that if, for example, you have a mailing list of 20,000 names and you want to put them all in a single data base file, *AppleWorks* is the *wrong* program to use. If, however, you're willing to split your information into several parts, each of which is small enough for *AppleWorks* to handle, *AppleWorks* is an excellent choice.

Entering Records to a New File

If you look at the upper right corner of the screen, you'll see that pressing the ESC key will take you to Review/Add/Change. The data base portion of *AppleWorks* consists of two parts: the data entry part and the report generator. In Review/Add/Change (the data entry part), you'll be able to add new records and to review and change old, previously entered records. Press ESC and look at Figure 3-3.

FIGURE 3-3 No records in the file

```
File: Customer List            REVIEW/ADD/CHANGE            Escape: Main Menu

==============================================================================

                        This file does not yet contain
                        any information.  Therefore, you
                        will automatically go into the
                        Insert New Records feature.

------------------------------------------------------------------------------
Press Space Bar to continue                                        56K Avail.
```

AppleWorks is letting you know that this is a new file without any records in it. Down in the lower right corner, *AppleWorks* tells you how much memory is available for your data base file. Press the Space Bar and you'll see the Insert New Records screen (Figure 3-4).

AppleWorks has taken the seven category names you typed in earlier and arranged them, one under the other. This is *AppleWorks*' default Insert New Records screen. In a moment, you'll see how to set up the Insert New Records screen the way you want it to look.

Notice that *AppleWorks* has added a colon, ":", after each category name and has placed a dash, "-", as a default entry in each category. The dash is what *AppleWorks* has chosen to be the **Standard Value** for all categories. The Standard Value is what would be the entry for a category if you were just to press the RETURN key, without typing any data. Later on you'll see how to change the Standard Value for any category.

FIGURE 3-4 Adding the first record

```
File: Customer List           INSERT NEW RECORDS     Escape: Review/Add/Change



Record 1 of 1
==============================================================================
Customer Name: -
Address: -
City: -
State: -
Zip: -
Phone: -
Acct. No.: -








------------------------------------------------------------------------------
Type entry or use ⌘ commands                                        56K Avail.
```

Let's enter a few records. You can make up data to type into this sample file, but if you'd rather not be bothered thinking up your own, Table 3-2 has some sample records for you to use.

Type the first category entry, the Customer Name: **Mr. & Mrs. Rob Smith**. Then press RETURN to move your cursor to the next category, Address. Type the address, press RETURN, and continue entering the data for the remaining categories that comprise the first record. If you make a mistake, press the DELETE key to erase one character at a time, or press the ESC key to erase the entire entry.

If you need to correct an entry *after* you've pressed RETURN, you can use the up- and down-arrow keys to move your cursor from one category to the next. (*Note:* The up- and down-arrow keys won't work once you begin typing an entry. They only work just after you press RETURN. Remember, you can erase an entire entry by moving the cursor to the first character of the entry and typing CONTROL-Y.)

TABLE 3-2 Sample records for Example 1

Customer Name	Address	City	State	Zip	Phone	Acct. No
Mr. & Mrs. Rob Smith	1423 First Ave.	Meadowbrook	IL	60099	555-3562	84-104
Mr. Steve Miller	573 W. Elm St.	Meadowbrook	IL	60099	555-6342	83-282
Ms. Gail Dooley	512 E. Main St.	East Meadowbrook	IL	60098	555-8211	85-103
Ms. D. McMullen	1615 Ninth Ave.	Bayshore	IL	60990	555-0593	84-220
Mr. & Mrs. Terry Dethloff	R.R. 1	Farmtown	IL	60095	555-3961	84-109

As you finish typing the entry for the last category of the first record, the entire record will disappear. Don't worry, your data isn't lost. It's just been moved off the screen. A new, blank record is displayed so that you can enter the next set of data.

Just above the double line on the screen is the record counter. It tells you how many records there are in the file and which one you are currently looking at. While you were typing the first record, the record counter indicated: **Record 1 of 1**. After you finished the first record and went on to the second, the record counter changed to: **Record 2 of 2**. Right now, each new record is being added to the end of your file. Later you will see how to insert new records at any point in your file, not just at the end.

Finish typing the second record. Your record counter should have just changed to: **Record 3 of 3**. Before you start typing the third record, press ESC. Then type ⌘**Z**.

This takes you out of the Insert New Records mode and puts you into one of the two record display formats of the Review/Add/Change screen: the **multiple record format** (Figure 3-5). This format shows you the first five categories of both of the records you typed in.

Moving around Your File

As you can see, there is space on the screen to display up to 15 records. When your file contains more than 15 records, you can scroll through the file in several different ways.

USING THE ARROW KEYS

The up- and down-arrow keys can be used to move the cursor up and down, one record at a time. If you hold down the OPEN-APPLE key as you press either the up-arrow or down-arrow keys, your cursor will move up or down one whole screen (15 records) at a time. (I know this isn't very useful with only two records, but when your data base holds several dozen or several hundred records, you'll need to know how to move quickly within the file.)

USING ⌘1 Through ⌘9

You can also use ⌘1 through ⌘9. They work the same way they did in the word processor section of *AppleWorks*. ⌘1 moves your cursor to the

FIGURE 3-5 The multiple record format screen

```
File: Customer List              REVIEW/ADD/CHANGE                 Escape: Main Menu

Selection: All records

Customer Name    Address           City              State              Zip
===============================================================================
Mr. & Mrs. Rob   1423 First Ave.  Meadowbrook        IL                 60099
Mr. Steve Mille  573 W. Elm St.   Meadowbrook        IL                 60099










-------------------------------------------------------------------------------
Type entry or use ⌘ commands                                       ⌘-? for Help
```

first record in your file, ⌘9 to the last record, ⌘5 to the middle record, and so on.

The Zoom Command: ⌘Z

The second display format (the multiple record format was the first) is called the *single record format*. It displays *all* the information in a single record. Your cursor is probably on the first record; if it isn't, move it there by pressing the up-arrow key. Now type ⌘ **Z**, the Zoom command. This command lets you zoom in on whichever single record your cursor was pointing to (Figure 3-6). If you press ⌘ Z again, you'll zoom back out to the multiple record format (Figure 3-5).

The Help Screen: ⌘?

On the bottom line of the screen, in either display format, you'll see that there is a Help screen available when you want it. Pressing ⌘? will display the Help screen (Figure 3-7), a summary of all the commands that are effective at this point in the *AppleWorks* program. The up and down-arrow keys will allow you to scroll through the command listing. You press ESC to return to the Review/Add/Change screen.

FIGURE 3-6 The single record format screen

```
File: Customer List          REVIEW/ADD/CHANGE          Escape: Main Menu

Selection: All records

Record 1 of 2
================================================================================
Customer Name: Mr. & Mrs. Rob Smith
Address: 1423 First Ave.
City: Meadowbrook
State: IL
Zip: 60099
Phone: 555-3562
Acct. No.: 84-104




--------------------------------------------------------------------------------
Type entry or use 🍏 commands                                      🍏-? for Help
```

FIGURE 3-7 The data base Help screen

```
File: Customer List                HELP           Escape: Review/Add/Change


================================================================================
                     🍏-A   Arrange (sort) on this category

                     🍏-C   Copy records (includes cut and paste)

                     🍏-D   Delete records

                     🍏-F   Find all records that contain.....

                     🍏-I   Insert new records before the
                            current record

                     🍏-L   Change record layout

                     🍏-M   Move records (cut and paste)
--------------------------------------------------------------------------------
Use arrows to see remainder of Help                                  56K Avail.
```

Changing Record Layouts: ⌘L

Now I'd like you to practice changing the layout of both record format displays, single and multiple.

CHANGING THE SINGLE RECORD FORMAT

Let's start by changing the single record format display. The arrangement of the categories on the screen is called the *layout*. When you change the layout of the single record format, you will also change the layout of the Insert New Records screen. You'll remember that *AppleWorks* chose a default layout for this screen. You're about to change it.

Zoom in (⌘Z) to the single record format and type the Change Record Layout command, ⌘L (Figure 3-8).

The only keys that have any effect in changing the record layout are the arrow keys, used either by themselves or with the OPEN-APPLE key. You're going to move the categories around the screen to improve the "look" of the single record format screen.

Those seven categories can be moved anywhere on the screen by placing the cursor on the first letter of the category name, and then holding down the OPEN-APPLE key while you press the arrow keys.

FIGURE 3-8 Changing the single record layout

```
File: Customer List          CHANGE RECORD LAYOUT     Escape: Review/Add/Change

                        Return or arrows     Move cursor
                        ⌘ and arrows         Move category location

===============================================================================
Customer Name: Mr. & Mrs. Rob Smith
Address: 1423 First Ave.
City: Meadowbrook
State: IL
Zip: 60099
Phone: 555-3562
Acct. No.: 84-104




-------------------------------------------------------------------------------
Use options shown above to change record layout.                    56K Avail.
```

The category will be moved in the direction of the arrow—up, down, left, or right. The only move you can't make is to move one category "through" another. If a category lies between the one you want to move and the place you want to move it, you'll have to move your category around the one that's in the way. Let's try it.

Place your cursor on the "A" in Acct. No. Hold down the OPEN-APPLE key and press the down-arrow key a few times. Try the other arrow keys while you're still holding down the OPEN-APPLE key. Fun, isn't it? When you want to leave a category in a particular spot, release the OPEN-APPLE key and move the cursor elsewhere.

I suggested that you start with the Acct. No. category because the remaining six categories could not be moved vertically since other categories were in the way. It's generally a good idea to start moving the bottom category first, then the next-to-the-bottom, and so forth.

Look at Figure 3-9 and move your categories around until your screen resembles it. When it does, press the ESC key and you'll be back at the Review/Add/Change single record format display.

FIGURE 3-9 The new single record layout

```
File: Customer List           CHANGE RECORD LAYOUT    Escape: Review/Add/Change

                      Return or arrows    Move cursor
                      ⌘ and arrows        Move category location

================================================================================
Customer Name: Mr. & Mrs. Rob Smith

Address: 1423 First Ave.

City: Meadowbrook                        State: IL          Zip: 60099

Phone: 555-3562                          Acct. No.: 84-104



--------------------------------------------------------------------------------
Use options shown above to change record layout.                     56K Avail.
```

CHANGING THE MULTIPLE RECORD DISPLAY

You can also change the layout of the multiple record display. Zoom out (⌘Z) and press ⌘L again (Figure 3-10). Press the right-arrow key once, by itself. Each time you press either the left- or right-arrow keys the cursor will move one category to the left or right. Press the right-arrow

FIGURE 3-10 Changing the multiple record layout

```
File: Customer List           CHANGE RECORD LAYOUT    Escape: Review/Add/Change




==============================================================================

                   --> or <--   Move cursor
                    >    <    Switch category positions
                   -->  <--   Change column width
                   -D          Delete this category
                   -I          Insert a previously deleted category

------------------------------------------------------------------------------

Customer Name   Address         City            State           Zip
--------------- --------------- --------------- --------------- ---------------
Mr. & Mrs. Rob  1423 First Ave. Meadowbrook     IL              60099
Mr. Steve Mille 573 W. Elm St.  Meadowbrook     IL              60099

---------------------------------------------------------------------- More -->
Use options shown above to change record layout.                    56K Avail.
```

key a few more times. See, the Phone and Acct. No. categories weren't thrown away. There just wasn't room on the 80-column screen to display them. With the multiple record layout you can decide *which* categories will be displayed, their *order* left to right, and *how wide* each displayed category will be.

Suppose you wanted the multiple record format to display the following categories: Acct. No., Customer Name, Address, City, and Phone, in that order.

The first thing you would want to do is to delete the two categories you didn't want to display: State and Zip. Don't worry. You're not throwing away any data. You're just altering the way the data is being displayed. Move your cursor to the State category and type **D** to delete it. Your cursor will now be on the Zip category, so type **D** again to delete it, too.

There are two ways of changing the order of the categories. One way is to use the > and < keys to switch adjacent categories. You'll use this technique when you design your first Tables report in a little while.

The second way to change the position of a category is to delete it and then insert it in a different position. This is the technique you'll use here. In order to move the Acct. No. category from its place at the far right to the leftmost position, move your cursor to Acct. No., and type **D** once more.

Move your cursor to the Customer Name category. This is where you want to insert Acct. No. Type **I** (to Insert a deleted category), and you'll see a list of the three categories you've just deleted. Select Acct. No. (it should be choice 3) by typing **3** and RETURN.

Now that you've got your choice of categories in the order you want, you can control how wide each category will be by moving your cursor to the category and pressing either left-arrow to shorten it or right-arrow to widen it. Look at Figure 3-11 and adjust your category widths so that they look something like the figure.

When you're finished adjusting the widths of the categories, press the ESC key, and *AppleWorks* will ask you which direction you want the cursor to move (in the multiple record format display) when you press the RETURN key. Press RETURN to accept choice 1, **Down (standard)**, and you'll be back at the multiple record display with your new layout.

FIGURE 3-11 The new multiple record layout

```
File: Customer List          CHANGE RECORD LAYOUT    Escape: Review/Add/Change



==============================================================================

                    -->or<--   Move cursor
                    >     <   Switch category positions
                    --><--   Change column width
                    -D        Delete this category
                    -I        Insert a previously deleted category

------------------------------------------------------------------------------

Acct.  Customer Name              Address                City         Phone
------ -------------------------- ---------------------- ------------ --------
84-104 Mr. & Mrs. Rob Smith       1423 First Ave.        Meadowbrook  555-3562
83-282 Mr. Steve Miller           573 W. Elm St.         Meadowbrook  555-6342

--------------------------------------------------------------------- More -->
Use options shown above to change record layout.                    56K Avail.
```

Setting Standard Values: V

You're going to type in the remaining three records (and as many others as you like) in a moment, but before you do, did you notice that all the customers listed in Table 3-2 live in Illinois? This value for the State category never changes, at least it doesn't in the five sample records. Why don't you let *AppleWorks* supply this constant value instead of typing it yourself for each record?

Type ⌘**V** to access Set Standard Values (Figure 3-12). The up- or down-arrow key will move your cursor to the State category. Type **IL** and press RETURN. Now ESC back to Review/Add/Change. It doesn't look as if anything has been accomplished, but wait until you enter the remaining records.

FIGURE 3-12 Setting a standard value

```
File: Customer List          SET STANDARD VALUES      Escape: Review/Add/Change


Record
==============================================================================

Customer Name: -

Address: -

City: -                                   State: -          Zip: -

Phone: -                                  Acct. No.: -


------------------------------------------------------------------------------
Type standard category values                                       54K Avail.
```

Inserting New Records

To insert the remaining records, type ⌘**I**. This calls up the Insert New Records screen—but with a difference. Notice that *AppleWorks* now supplies the name of the state automatically. Enter the remaining three records, but when you reach the State category, accept the standard value "IL" by pressing the RETURN key. (*Note:* You can override the standard value by typing CONTROL-Y to erase the entry, and then typing your own value. The next new record will again show the standard value, which you can either accept or replace.)

When you've finished typing the last record (and have gone on to the next blank record), press ESC to leave Insert New Records and return to Review/Add/Change (Figure 3-13). Note that your new records were inserted *above* the first two records. New records are inserted

FIGURE 3-13 All five records have been entered

```
File: Customer List           REVIEW/ADD/CHANGE               Escape: Main Menu

Acct.  Customer Name                Address                  City            Phone
=====================================================================================
85-103 Ms. Gail Dooley              512 E. Main St.          East Meadowb  555-8211
84-220 Ms. D. McMullen              1615 Ninth Ave.          Bayshore      555-0593
84-109 Mr. & Mrs. Terry Dethloff    R.R. 1                   Farmtown      555-3961
84-104 Mr. & Mrs. Rob Smith         1423 First Ave.          Meadowbrook   555-3562
83-282 Mr. Steve Miller             573 W. Elm St.           Meadowbrook   555-6342






-------------------------------------------------------------------------------
Type entry or use  commands                                       -? for Help
```

above the record your cursor was sitting on when you typed I. Because you can arrange your records in any order you like, the order in which you enter them doesn't matter.

Arranging (Sorting) Your Records

AppleWorks allows you to arrange your records in ascending or descending order using any category. You should be looking at the multiple record format screen. If you're not, type **Z**.

Let's arrange the records in alphabetical order according to City. First, you have to move the cursor to the City column. Don't try to use the arrow keys to move the cursor. They won't move the cursor to a different column. Pressing the TAB key moves the cursor one column to the right, as long as the cursor was sitting on the first character of the entry. (TAB moves the cursor one column to the left.) Use the TAB key to move the cursor to the City column and then type **A**, the Arrange command (Figure 3-14).

You want a standard alphabetic sort, **From A to Z**, so type **1** and press RETURN. That's all there is to sorting a file. You can see the results of the sort in Figure 3-15.

FIGURE 3-14 Arranging the data base file

```
File: Customer List           ARRANGE (SORT)        Escape: Review/Add/Change
Selection: All records


================================================================================
                    This file will be arranged on
                    this category: City

                    Arrangement order:

                          1.  From A to Z
                          2.  From Z to A
                          3.  From 0 to 9
                          4.  From 9 to 0


--------------------------------------------------------------------------------
Type number, or use arrows, then press Return                         54K Avail.
```

FIGURE 3-15 Records are arranged alphabetically by city

```
File: Customer List          REVIEW/ADD/CHANGE                 Escape: Main Menu

Selection: All records

Acct.  Customer Name                 Address                City          Phone
================================================================================
84-220 Ms. D. McMullen               1615 Ninth Ave.        Bayshore      555-0593
85-103 Ms. Gail Dooley               512 E. Main St.        East Meadowb  555-8211
84-109 Mr. & Mrs. Terry Dethloff     R.R. 1                 Farmtown      555-3961
84-104 Mr. & Mrs. Rob Smith          1423 First Ave.        Meadowbrook   555-3562
83-282 Mr. Steve Miller              573 W. Elm St.         Meadowbrook   555-6342




--------------------------------------------------------------------------------
Type entry or use  commands                                         -? for Help
```

Record Selection: R

Suppose you wanted to look at only those records whose Acct. No. began with "84." *AppleWorks* has a special command called Record Selection that makes this easy. Type **R** (Figure 3-16). You're looking at

FIGURE 3-16 Choose a field for record selection

```
File: Customer List              SELECT RECORDS              Escape: Erase entry

Selection:
================================================================================
 1.  Customer Name
 2.  Address
 3.  City
 4.  State
 5.  Zip
 6.  Phone
 7.  Acct. No.







--------------------------------------------------------------------------------
Type number, or use arrows, then press Return  7                     54K Avail.
```

a list of your category names. Because you want to select records based on the data in their Acct. No. category, type **7** and press RETURN.

AppleWorks has a number of ways to compare your choice of "84" with data in the Acct. No. category, as you will see in Figure 3-17. Some of the comparisons (the first four) are mathematical comparisons. The others are used in comparing nonnumerical data. You want to select those records with Acct. No. *beginning* with "84", so your comparison choice is number 8, **begins with**. Press **8** and RETURN.

AppleWorks then asks: **Type comparison information:**. Type **84** and press RETURN.

You are now given additional options that would allow you to select records based on more than one comparison. Because you've already set up the one comparison you wanted, press the ESC key to leave the Record Selection function.

As you can see, *AppleWorks* has selected and displayed only those records (three of them) with Acct. No. data beginning with "84" (Figure 3-18). Note the **Selection:** line near the top of your screen. It indicates whether you have used the Record Selection function, and if so, what the Record Selection comparison is.

Suppose you want to display all the records again. No problem. Type ⌘**R** again and at the bottom of the screen you'll be asked: **Select all records?** Just press the "Y" key and *AppleWorks* displays all the records (Figure 3-15).

FIGURE 3-17 Choose a comparison for record selection

```
File: Customer List                SELECT RECORDS       Escape: Review/Add/Change

Selection: Acct. No.

===============================================================================
 1.  equals
 2.  is greater than
 3.  is less than
 4.  is not equal to
 5.  is blank
 6.  is not blank
 7.  contains
 8.  begins with
 9.  ends with
10.  does not contain
11.  does not begin with
12.  does not end with

-------------------------------------------------------------------------------
Type number, or use arrows, then press Return                        54K Avail.
```

FIGURE 3-18 Only selected records are displayed

```
File: Customer List             REVIEW/ADD/CHANGE                Escape: Main Menu

Selection: Acct. No. begins with 84

Acct.  Customer Name                 Address                 City          Phone
================================================================================
84-220 Ms. D. McMullen               1615 Ninth Ave.         Bayshore      555-0593
84-109 Mr. & Mrs. Terry Dethloff     R.R. 1                  Farmtown      555-3961
84-104 Mr. & Mrs. Rob Smith          1423 First Ave.         Meadowbrook   555-3562







--------------------------------------------------------------------------------
Type entry or use ⌘ commands                                       ⌘-? for Help
```

Deleting Records: ⌘D

Deleting records is even easier than deleting text was in the word processor. Just move the cursor to the record you want to delete, type ⌘**D**, and press RETURN. If you want to delete more than one adjacent record, you can use the up- or down-arrow key to highlight the ones you want to delete, before you press the RETURN key. **Warning:** *Once you have deleted a record, it is gone forever.* So, if you press ⌘D by mistake, you can avoid deleting any records by pressing ESC. (You'll have a chance to delete some records in a moment.)

Finding a Record

Suppose your file contained 500 records and you wanted to a find one particular record. Suppose that all you remembered about the record was that the customer lived on Elm Street. The Find command was designed with just this situation in mind. Type ⌘**F** and you will be prompted to **Type comparison information:**. Respond with **Elm** and press RETURN. *AppleWorks* displays the record (or records) that have the three letters "ELM" in *any* of their categories. So, if one of the customers lived in the city of "Elmhurst" or one of the customers were named "Elmer," that record would be displayed also. *Note:* The case of the letters (whether the letters were capitalized or small) does not matter. Nor do the searched-for characters have to be at the beginning of the entry. Even if the entry containing the characters was not displayed on the multiple record screen, the record would still be found.

Press ESC to return to Review/Add/Change.

Making Copies of Records

There may be times when you'll want to duplicate a record. The Copy command, ⌘C, lets you do this automatically so that you don't have to type in the same record over and over. Let's try it.

COPYING A SINGLE RECORD

Move your cursor to the fourth record, the one with the Customer Name of "Mr. & Mrs. Rob Smith," and type ⌘**C**. Press the RETURN key to accept the choice of Current Record. *AppleWorks* now asks you how many copies you want. Type **5** and press RETURN (Figure 3-19).

Now that you've made those five extra copies of the "Mr. & Mrs. Rob Smith" record, use the Delete command to remove them from your file. Place your cursor on the first of the five duplicate records. Type ⌘**D**, and use the down-arrow key to select all five records. Then press RETURN.

FIGURE 3-19 Copying a single record

```
File: Customer List            REVIEW/ADD/CHANGE            Escape: Main Menu

Selection: All records

Acct.  Customer Name                 Address                 City          Phone
===============================================================================
84-220 Ms. D. McMullen               1615 Ninth Ave.         Bayshore      555-0593
85-103 Ms. Gail Dooley               512 E. Main St.         East Meadow   555-8211
84-109 Mr. & Mrs. Terry Dethloff     R.R. 1                  Farmtown      555-3961
84-104 Mr. & Mrs. Rob Smith          1423 First Ave.         Meadowbrook   555-3562
84-104 Mr. & Mrs. Rob Smith          1423 First Ave.         Meadowbrook   555-3562
84-104 Mr. & Mrs. Rob Smith          1423 First Ave.         Meadowbrook   555-3562
84-104 Mr. & Mrs. Rob Smith          1423 First Ave.         Meadowbrook   555-3562
84-104 Mr. & Mrs. Rob Smith          1423 First Ave.         Meadowbrook   555-3562
84-104 Mr. & Mrs. Rob Smith          1423 First Ave.         Meadowbrook   555-3562
83-282 Mr. Steve Miller              573 W. Elm St.          Meadowbrook   555-6342



-------------------------------------------------------------------------------
Type entry or use Ć commands                                      Ć-? for Help
```

COPYING MULTIPLE RECORDS

You can also duplicate several records at the same time using the same Copy command, ĆC. Suppose you wanted to copy all five records in your file. TypeĆ **1** to move your cursor to the top of your file. Next, type Ć**C**. But, instead of accepting the choice of Current Record, press the letter "T" to select **To clipboard** and don't press the RETURN key. Use the down-arrow key to highlight all five of your records and then press RETURN.

It looks as if nothing has happened, right? But something has. You have copied those five records to a place in your Apple's memory that *AppleWorks* calls the *Clipboard*. These records are there now and will remain there until you either put something else in the Clipboard (other records, for example) or quit *AppleWorks*. You can copy the records that are in the Clipboard back into your file as many times as you wish. Your cursor's location determines *where* in your file the copied records will be inserted. They will be inserted just *above* the record your cursor is sitting on. This means that you cannot Copy records to the end of your file.

Leave your cursor at the top of your file and type Ć**C** again. This time press the "F" key to select **From clipboard**. *AppleWorks* immediately copies the records in the Clipboard to your file (Figure 3-20). And you can transfer as many copies of the Clipboard records to your file as

FIGURE 3-20 Copying several records

```
File: Customer List            REVIEW/ADD/CHANGE            Escape: Main Menu

Selection: All records

Acct.  Customer Name                  Address                 City          Phone
=================================================================================
84-220 Ms. D. McMullen                1615 Ninth Ave.         Bayshore      555-0593
85-103 Ms. Gail Dooley                512 E. Main St.         East Meadow   555-8211
84-109 Mr. & Mrs. Terry Dethloff      R.R. 1                  Farmtown      555-3961
84-104 Mr. & Mrs. Rob Smith           1423 First Ave.         Meadowbrook   555-3562
83-282 Mr. Steve Miller               573 W. Elm St.          Meadowbrook   555-6342
84-220 Ms. D. McMullen                1615 Ninth Ave.         Bayshore      555-0593
85-103 Ms. Gail Dooley                512 E. Main St.         East Meadow   555-8211
84-109 Mr. & Mrs. Terry Dethloff      R.R. 1                  Farmtown      555-3961
84-104 Mr. & Mrs. Rob Smith           1423 First Ave.         Meadowbrook   555-3562
83-282 Mr. Steve Miller               573 W. Elm St.          Meadowbrook   555-6342


---------------------------------------------------------------------------------
Type entry or use  commands                                           -? for Help
```

you want by repeatedly choosing the **From clipboard** option in the Copy command.

The Clipboard feature of *AppleWorks* has many uses, and you'll see more of them in Chapter 5. But for now, let's go on. Use the Delete command, D, to remove all but the original five records.

Moving Records in Your File

Suppose you wanted to move the fourth and fifth records in your file up to the top. The Move command, M, does this. It works in much the same way as the Copy command works in that it uses the Clipboard to store the records that you want to move.

To move records four and five to the top of your file, place your cursor on record four, type **M**, and press the "T" key, **To clipboard**. Press the down-arrow key once so that both the fourth and fifth records are highlighted, and then press RETURN. Both records have disappeared from the screen, but don't worry, they're on the Clipboard. Now move your cursor to the top of your file, type **M**, and press the "F" key, **From clipboard** (Figure 3-21). Presto!

FIGURE 3-21 Moving records

```
File: Customer List          REVIEW/ADD/CHANGE              Escape: Main Menu

Selection: All records


Acct.   Customer Name                 Address                  City          Phone
===================================================================================
84-104 Mr. & Mrs. Rob Smith         1423 First Ave.          Meadowbrook   555-3562
83-282 Mr. Steve Miller             573 W. Elm St.           Meadowbrook   555-6342
84-220 Ms. D. McMullen              1615 Ninth Ave.          Bayshore      555-0593
85-103 Ms. Gail Dooley              512 E. Main St.          East Meadow   555-8211
84-109 Mr. & Mrs. Terry Dethloff    R.R. 1                   Farmtown      555-3961

--------------------------------------------------------------------------------
Type entry or use ⌘ commands                                        ⌘-? for Help
```

Printing Mailing Labels

There are two kinds of reports that *AppleWorks* can print out using your data base file. One of them is called a *Tables* report and prints out your records, one record per line, similar to the multiple record layout display. You'll use this kind of report with the second data base example in this chapter.

The second type of report is the *Labels* report and it's the one you'll use with the Customer List file. Imagine that as the owner of Hot & Cold Inc. (the name of your company, remember?), you would like to send out a mailing to all of your customers announcing a special, pre-summer, air conditioning "tune-up." You've made up a flyer and had it copied at the printer's. Now you're faced with having to address all of the flyers individually to your customers. Wouldn't it be nice if your computer could print out mailing labels and save you the time and trouble? That's what the Labels report format is designed to do.

By the way, don't worry if you haven't bought any tractor-feed labels yet. You can still do the exercise and use ordinary paper for the output. When you actually get ready to print labels, though, you must run the labels through the tractor of your printer. Using the pinch-roller on the platen won't do because your labels will gradually slip out of alignment. The tractor ensures that your labels stay aligned.

Type ⌘**P** to go to the Report Menu (Figure 3-22).

CREATING A NEW LABELS REPORT

Select option 3, **Create a new "labels" format**, by typing **3** and pressing RETURN. Type **Mailing Labels** as the name for your report and press RETURN.

AppleWorks now shows you a standard Labels report format (Figure 3-23). (Notice that you have a new Help screen available to you.) While there are seven categories listed, you won't need all seven for your mailing labels. I have in mind a four-line label. The first line would be the Acct. No.; the second line, the Customer Name. Address would go on the third line, and City, State, and Zip would make up line four.

This means that the first thing you should do is delete the Phone category from the report format. Again, don't worry. You're not throwing away any data; you're just affecting how the data will be printed out. Place your cursor (use the down-arrow key) on the "P" in Phone and type ⌘**D** (don't press RETURN). The Phone category is erased; in its place is a blank line. If you accidentally erase a category and you want to put it back, use the Insert command, ⌘I.

Using the same technique you used when you changed the single record display format, move the Zip category down one line. (Remember, place the cursor on the first character of the category name. Then hold

FIGURE 3–22 Creating a report

```
File: Customer List              REPORT MENU          Escape: Review/Add/Change
Report: None

===============================================================================

                       1.  Get a report format
                       2.  Create a new "tables"format
                       3.  Create a new "labels" format
                       4.  Duplicate an existing format
                       5.  Erase a format

-------------------------------------------------------------------------------
Type number, or use arrows, then press Return                         54K Avail.
```

FIGURE 3-23 The new labels report

```
File: Customer List              REPORT FORMAT              Escape: Report Menu
Report: Mailing Labels
Selection: All Records


===============================================================================
Customer Name
Address
City
State
Zip
Phone
Acct. No.
-----------------------Each record will print  7 lines-----------------------





------------------------------------------------------------------------------
Use options shown on Help Screen                                  ⌘-? for Help
```

down the OPEN-APPLE key while you press one of the arrow keys, and the category will move in the direction of the arrow on the key.

Similarly, move the rest of the categories down one line so that there is a blank line at the top (Figure 3-24).

Drop your cursor down to Acct. No., and, using a combination of OPEN-APPLE arrow keys, move Acct. No. to the right, up to the top, and back left, so that it occupies the top line spot (Figure 3-25).

Your top three lines are just the way you want them. All you have to do is to move the State and Zip categories so that they are on the same line as City. Go ahead and do that (Figure 3-26).

Now it's beginning to look like a mailing label. You have one more thing to change in the report format. When you buy tractor-feed labels, there is a fixed distance between the top of one label and the top of the next. Usually this distance, measured in lines, is 6 lines. Label sizes are sometimes measured by inches (1″ labels, 1½″ labels, and so forth). Recalling that your printer normally prints 6 lines to the inch, 1″ labels are really 6-line labels, 1½″ labels are really 9-line labels, etc.

Suppose you had 6-line labels. Do you see the dashed line on your screen that says: **Each record will print 7 lines**? In order that the four lines of your label will always be printed in the same place on each and every label, that dashed line's value *must* be the same as your label size.

FIGURE 3-24 Move the categories down

```
File: Customer List              REPORT FORMAT              Escape: Report Menu
Report: Mailing Labels
Selection: All Records

================================================================================

Customer Name
Address
City
State
Zip
Acct. No.
-------------------------Each record will print  7 lines------------------------




--------------------------------------------------------------------------------
Use options shown on Help Screen                                    ♂-? for Help
```

FIGURE 3-25 Move Acct. No. to the top

```
File: Customer List              REPORT FORMAT              Escape: Report Menu
Report: Mailing Labels
Selection: All Records

================================================================================
Acct. No.
Customer Name
Address
City
State
Zip

-------------------------Each record will print  7 lines------------------------




--------------------------------------------------------------------------------
Use options shown on Help Screen                                    ♂-? for Help
```

With 6-line labels, the dashed line has to read: **Each record will print 6 lines**. To decrease the number of lines in your label, move your cursor to a blank line and type ♂ **D**. Do this enough times to get the dashed line value to 6 lines (Figure 3-27). If you need more lines for your label, press the RETURN key and keep pressing it until you get the number of lines you want.

FIGURE 3-26 Place City, State, and Zip on the same line

```
File: Customer List                  REPORT FORMAT              Escape: Report Menu
Report: Mailing Labels
Selection: All Records


===================================================================================
Acct. No.
Customer Name
Address
City                        State        Zip


-----------------------Each record will print  7 lines------------------------




-----------------------------------------------------------------------------------
Use options shown on Help Screen                                     ♂-? for Help
```

FIGURE 3-27 Reduce the number of lines to 6

```
File: Customer List                  REPORT FORMAT              Escape: Report Menu
Report: Mailing Labels
Selection: All Records


===================================================================================
Acct. No.
Customer Name
Address
City                        State        Zip

-----------------------Each record will print  6 lines------------------------




-----------------------------------------------------------------------------------
Use options shown on Help Screen                                     ♂-? for Help
```

FAMILIAR COMMANDS

Two of the commands you used in the Review/Add/Change section of the data base are available to you here, in the report format section, and the Help screen (♂?) lists them. They are Arrange (♂A) and Record Selection (♂R).

Zoom (♂Z) is also available, but it works a bit differently here. If you type ♂Z, the category names in your report format will be replaced with actual record entries. Try it (Figure 3-28). This is what the label will really look like when it is printed. You can look at other records as well. Pressing> (without pressing the SHIFT key) will show you the next record. And,< will display the previous record. You can also use 1 through9 to move quickly through your file.

Pressing Z will switch the display back to category names, but, for the moment, leave the record entry displayed.

FIGURE 3-28 Use Zoom to see data

```
File: Customer List                  REPORT FORMAT                 Escape: Report Menu
Report: Mailing Labels
Selection: All Records



==================================================================================
84-104
Mr. & Mrs. Rob Smith
1423 First Ave.
Meadowbrook                IL            60099

-----------------------Each record will print  6 lines-----------------------





----------------------------------------------------------------------------------
Use options shown on Help Screen                                         -? for Help
```

PRINTING BOTH CATEGORY NAME AND ENTRY

Suppose you wanted the category name, Acct. No., to be printed on the label in front of the entry value. You can do this with the Print Category Name and Entry command: V. Move your cursor to the first character of the Acct. No. entry (the number 8) on the top line and type**V** (Figure 3-29). Now every label will show the category name, Acct. No., next to the number itself.

PRINTER OPTIONS

The data base section of *AppleWorks* has a Printer Options page, similar to Printer Options in the word processor. Type**O** and let's take a look at it (Figure 3-30).

The first four options, grouped under **Left and right margins**, can be pretty much left alone. The only change you may want to make is to

FIGURE 3-29 Print both category name and data

```
File: Customer List              REPORT FORMAT           Escape: Report Menu
Report: Mailing Labels
Selection: All Records


===============================================================================
Acct. No: 84-104
Mr. & Mrs. Rob Smith
1423 First Ave.
Meadowbrook                IL          60099

------------------------Each record will print  6 lines------------------------





-------------------------------------------------------------------------------
Use options shown on Help Screen                                    ♂-? for Help
```

FIGURE 3-30 Printer Options for the data base

```
File: Customer List              PRINTER OPTIONS          Escape: Report Format
Report: Mailing Labels
===============================================================================

-------Left and right margins--------      ------Top and bottom margins-------
PW: Platen Width              8.0 inches   PL: Paper Length        11.0 inches
LM: Left Margin               0.0 inches   TM: Top Margin           0.0 inches
RM: Right Margin              0.0 inches   BM: Bottom Margin        0.0 inches
CI: Chars per Inch           10            LI: Lines per Inch       6

    Line width                8.0 inches       Printing length     11.0 inches
    Char per line (est)      80                Lines per page      66

          --------------------Formatting options---------------------
          SC:  Send Special Codes to printer                        No
          PD:  Print a Dash when an entry is blank                  No
          PH:  Print report Header at top of each page              Yes
          OL:  Omit Line when all entries on line are blank         Yes
          KS:  Keep number of lines the Same within each record     Yes


-------------------------------------------------------------------------------
Type a two letter option code                                       54K Avail.
```

change the Right Margin to 4.0" (because your labels aren't 8" wide). To change any of the first four options (or the next four, grouped under **Top and bottom margins**, for that matter), you type the two-letter code that's to the left of the option and press RETURN. Then you type the new value you want and press RETURN. So, to change the Right Margin to 4.0", type **RM**, RETURN, **4**, and RETURN.

If you discovered when you printed out your labels that one or more lines had so many characters that it was running off the right edge of the label, you could change the number of Characters per Inch (CI) that your printer prints to a higher value. Most dot matrix printers support CI values of 12 and/or 17.

There are two printer options you *must* change. The first is Paper Length (PL). For 1″ labels, change it to 1″. Each of your 6-line labels is considered to be a separate, 1″ "piece of paper." (*Note:* If your label height is greater than 1″, enter its height instead of 1″.)

The other option that must be changed is **Print report Header at top of each page** (PH). A Report Header consists of the file name, report name, page number, date, and record selection rules. And, since every label is a separate "page," you certainly don't want this Report Header to print on every label! PH is one of the last five options, grouped under **Formatting options**. These five have only "Yes" or "No" values. Every time you type one of their option codes, the option's value changes from "Yes" to "No" or from "No" to "Yes." The default value for Print Header is "Yes," so type **PH** and press RETURN to change it to "No."

Compare your altered Printer Options page with Figure 3-31. They should be the same. Press ESC to return to the Report Format page.

PRINTING LABELS TO THE SCREEN

Let's print out the labels and take a look at them. Type ⌘**P** and you should see a list of from five to seven (depending on how many printers you have configured, 1, 2, or 3) choices of where you can print your

FIGURE 3-31 Printer Options for labels

```
File: Customer List                PRINTER OPTIONS           Escape: Report Format
Report: Mailing Labels
===============================================================================

-------Left and right margins--------         ------Top and bottom margins-------
PW: Platen Width             8.0 inches       PL: Paper Length          1.0 inches
LM: Left Margin              0.0 inches       TM: Top Margin            0.0 inches
RM: Right Margin             4.0 inches       BM: Bottom Margin         0.0 inches
CI: Chars per Inch          10                LI: Lines per Inch        6

    Line width               4.0 inches           Printing length       1.0 inches
    Char per line (est)     40                    Lines per page        6

          ---------------------Formatting options---------------------
          SC:  Send Special Codes to printer                        No
          PD:  Print a Dash when an entry is blank                  No
          PH:  Print report Header at top of each page              No
          OL:  Omit Line when all entries on line are blank         Yes
          KS:  Keep number of lines the Same within each record     Yes


-------------------------------------------------------------------------------
Type a two letter option code                                        54K Avail.
```

labels. Find the one that says **The screen** (probably choice 2), choose it, and press RETURN. Your screen should look like Figure 3-32. Press the Space Bar to see the rest of your records. (*Note:* You could have pressed ESC instead of the Space Bar to abort further printing and immediately return to the Report Format page.)

Look at the fourth line of one of the labels. Do you see how far to the right the State is from the City? The problem is that you don't know how long the City entry is going to be.

The report format has a feature that solves this problem neatly. Press the Space Bar once more to return to the Report Format screen.

FIGURE 3-32 Printing labels to the screen

```
Acct. No: 84-104
Mr. & Mrs. Rob Smith
1423 First Ave.
Meadowbrook                IL          60099


Acct. No: 83-282
Mr. Steve Miller
573. W. Elm St.
Meadowbrook                IL          60099


Acct. No: 84-220
Ms. D. McMullen
1615 Ninth Ave.
Bayshore                   IL          60990





Press Space Bar to continue                                    54K Avail.
```

JUSTIFYING A CATEGORY

Move your cursor so that it sits on the first character of the State category. Type **J** and a "<" symbol will appear to the left of the category. Now, when you print out your labels, the State entry will be printed right next to the City entry with one space separating them. You could do the same thing to the Zip category, if you wanted to, and the Zip entry would print just to the right of the State entry.

PRINTING LABELS TO THE PRINTER

Now let's see what your labels look like when they're printed out on your printer. Type **P** and select your printer from the list. When you're asked **How many copies**?, just press the RETURN key to accept one copy. Your entire file, all five records, should be printed out for you.

If *AppleWorks* keeps asking you to press the Space Bar after each label is printed, go back to the Printer Options for your printer (see Chapter 1) and change the option **Stop at end of each page** from "Yes" to "No." You should also be sure that the printer option **Accepts top-of-page commands** is set to "No." This is necessary if you want your labels to be properly spaced.

There is one other thing that could interfere with proper label spacing. Some printers have a feature that allows them to skip over the perforation in tractor-feed paper automatically. If your printer has this feature, make sure it's turned *off*. There should be a switch inside the printer to control this feature, and your printer's manual should tell you where it is.

SAVING YOUR DATA BASE FILE

Save your data base file to your data disk by typing ⌘S. When *AppleWorks* saves your data base file, it also saves your screen layouts and your report formats. When you load back the file, your layouts and formats are there, too.

If you want to use a previously created report format, choose option 1, **Get a report format**, when you see the Report Menu. Then, select the report format you want to use from the Report Catalog. *AppleWorks* allows you to create a maximum of eight report formats per file.

After you've saved your data base file, ESC to the Main Menu of *AppleWorks* (you'll have to press ESC several times). Then, either quit the program by choosing option 6 or, if you're continuing with the second data base example, use option 4 to remove the current data base from your Desktop.

II. EXAMPLE 2: THE WEEKLY REPAIR CALL REPORT

Your business, Hot & Cold Inc., employs three service technicians who perform on-site repairs for your customers. You would like to prepare a weekly report that will list all of the service calls your techs made. You want to keep track of which tech performed the job, the number of hours each job took, the cost of any parts (including sales tax), and who the customer was.

You would like the report to compute the cost of the repair time to the customer (based on $45 per hour) and the total cost of each job (the sum of the charge for time and the charge for parts). You would like weekly totals on repair time (hours), cost of parts, and total job cost. You also would like subtotals for each technician. Sounds like a tall order but that's just what you're going to do in this exercise.

Creating the File

Table 3-3 is a list of category names for this file. Use it to create your file in the same way you created the Customer List file in Example 1. Call this new file "Repair Calls."

Type **CONTROL-Y** to erase the default name for the first category. Then type in the category names from Table 3-3—one name per line. Press RETURN after each category name, including the last name.

Because you also want your report from this file to give you the labor cost and the total cost for each repair job, you might wonder why categories for these items have not been included in Table 3-3. The answer is that when you prepare your report, you will be able to *create* these two categories based on the data in your file.

Press ESC and then the Space Bar to move to the Insert New Records screen.

TABLE 3-3 Category names for Example 2

Category Names
Technician
Acct. No.
Hours Billed
Parts Cost

Table 3-4 contains ten records for the file. I know it seems like a lot of work to type in all ten records, but please do it anyway. It's hard to show group totals if you only have a couple of records in your file and, if you type in all ten records, your totals will match mine.

When you're through typing the tenth record, ESC out to the multiple record format display of Review/Add/Change and compare your screen with Figure 3-33.

TABLE 3-4 Sample records for Example 2

Technician	Acct. No.	Hours Billed	Parts Cost
Chuck	83-211	1.5	120.75
Penney	85-109	1	0
Penney	84-142	1.75	79.40
Bill	83-115	2	55.20
Chuck	85-114	1	0
Chuck	83-121	2.5	248.75
Bill	84-200	1	.85
Penney	83-101	1.5	110.95
Chuck	85-147	1.25	45.30
Bill	84-138	1.5	67.35

FIGURE 3-33 All ten records have been added to the new data base

```
File: Repair Calls              REVIEW/ADD/CHANGE              Escape: Main Menu

Selection: All records

Technician       Acct. No.          Hours Billed   Parts Cost
==============================================================================
Chuck            83-211             1.5            120.75
Penney           85-109             1              0
Penney           84-142             1.75           79.40
Bill             83-115             2              55.20
Chuck            85-114             1              0
Chuck            83-121             2.5            248.75
Bill             84-200             1              .85
Penney           83-101             1.5            110.95
Chuck            85-147             1.25           45.30
Bill             84-138             1.5            67.35



------------------------------------------------------------------------------
Type entry or use ⌘ commands                                      ⌘-? for Help
```

Adding a Category to a File

Now that you've typed in all the record data, you've just had a brainstorm. You've decided that you want to include as a category the *date* the service call was made. Is it too late? Do you have to start over? No, to both questions. With many data base programs, once you've set up the categories for a file, you're stuck with them. *AppleWorks*, however, allows you to add or remove categories whenever you want. There is a penalty, and you'll see what it is in a minute.

Type ⌘N. *AppleWorks* takes you back to the Change Name/Category screen where you first entered category names for the file. Down at the bottom of the screen, *AppleWorks* is asking you whether you want to change the name of your data base file. Since you don't, just press the RETURN key (Figure 3-34).

You are now free to modify the list of category names any way you want. You can delete categories, change the name of existing categories, or add new ones. You want to add a new category called Date. You can insert this new category anywhere in the list or place it at the bottom. Suppose you wanted to insert it between Acct. No. and Hours Billed. Move your cursor down to the first letter of the Hours Billed category and type ⌘**I**, the Insert command.

FIGURE 3-34 Adding an extra category

```
File: Repair Calls            CHANGE NAME/CATEGORY    Escape: Review/Add/Change



Category names
==============================================================================
Technician                              |
Acct. No.                               | Options:
Hours Billed                            |
Parts Cost                              | Change category name
                                        | Up arrow   Go to previous category
                                        | Down arrow Go to next category
                                        | ⌘-I        Insert new category
                                        | ⌘-D        Delete this category
                                        |
                                        |
                                        |
                                        |
                                        |
                                        |
                                        |
------------------------------------------------------------------------------
Type entry or use ⌘ commands                                        53K Avail.
```

Here comes the penalty I warned you about earlier. Over on the right side of the screen (Figure 3-35), *AppleWorks* is telling you that if you add or delete categories, any report formats you have created and any record layouts you have changed for this file will be thrown away. (*Note:* If you haven't changed a record layout and/or you haven't created a report format, you won't see the warnings shown in Figure 3-35. You can't lose what you don't have. If you *did* see the warning message on your screen, press the "Y" key and don't press RETURN.)

AppleWorks has inserted a blank line for you to type in the new category. Type **CONTROL-Y** to erase the default dash, then type **Date**, and press RETURN (Figure 3-36). Now ESC back to Review/Add/Change.

FIGURE 3-35 Warning messages

```
File: Repair Calls              CHANGE NAME/CATEGORY    Escape: Review/Add/Change


Category names
==============================================================================
Technician                                    |
Acct. No.                                     |
Hours Billed                                  | If you add or delete category
Parts Cost                                    | names at this point...
                                              |
                                              | Report formats for this file
                                              | will be erased.
                                              |
                                              | Custom record layouts, made
                                              | using ♂-L, will be set back
                                              | to standard.
                                              |
                                              |
                                              |
                                              |
------------------------------------------------------------------------------
Do you really want to do this?  No  Yes
```

FIGURE 3-36 Insert the new Date category

```
File: Repair Calls              CHANGE NAME/CATEGORY    Escape: Review/Add/Change


Category names
==============================================================================
Technician                                    |
Acct. No.                                     | Options:
Date                                          |
Hours Billed                                  | Change category name
Parts Cost                                    | Up arrow   Go to previous category
                                              | Down arrow Go to next category
                                              | ♂-I        Insert new category
                                              | ♂-D        Delete this category
                                              |
                                              |
                                              |
                                              |
                                              |
                                              |
                                              |
------------------------------------------------------------------------------
Type entry or use ♂ commands                                          51K Avail.
```

Changing Data in the Multiple Record Format

Your screen should look like Figure 3-37. *AppleWorks* has inserted your new Date category and has put a dash in each entry to show that no data has been entered. While you could Zoom (♂Z) to the single

FIGURE 3-37 All entries for Date are blank

```
File: Repair Calls              REVIEW/ADD/CHANGE           Escape: Main Menu

Selection: All records

Technician     Acct. No.       Date            Hours Billed   Parts Cost
==========================================================================
Chuck          83-211          -               1.5            120.75
Penney         85-109          -               1              0
Penney         84-142          -               1.75           79.40
Bill           83-115          -               2              55.20
Chuck          85-114          -               1              0
Chuck          83-121          -               2.5            248.75
Bill           84-200          -               1              .85
Penney         83-101          -               1.5            110.95
Chuck          85-147          -               1.25           45.30
Bill           84-138          -               1.5            67.35

--------------------------------------------------------------------------
Type entry or use ⌘ commands                                  ⌘-? for Help
```

record format and enter data for the Date category in each record, it is easier if you stay in the multiple record format.

DATE CONVERSION

Type ⌘**1** to move your cursor to the first record in the file, then use the TAB key to move the cursor over to the Date column. Suppose the first service call occurred on June 24. Type **6/24** and watch what happens when you press the RETURN key. *AppleWorks* converted your "6/24" to "Jun 24." Why did this happen? It's because the category was named "Date." Anytime a category is named "Date" or contains the word "date" in it (for example, Birth Date), *AppleWorks* will try to convert what you enter into the Month-and-Day or Month-Day-and-Year format. (*Note: AppleWorks* performs a similar conversion when a category is named, or contains the word, "Time.")

DITTOING ENTRIES

Suppose the next four service calls all occurred on the same day, June 24. You could type in "6/24" four more times, but there is an easier way. To duplicate a category entry in the multiple record display, just type ⌘", the Dittoing command. (*Note:* Don't use the SHIFT key.) Type ⌘" a total of four times.

Now let's say that the remaining five service calls occurred the next day, June 25. Type **6/25**, press RETURN, and use the Dittoing command to fill in the remaining records (Figure 3-38).

FIGURE 3-38 Add the dates

```
File: Repair Calls                REVIEW/ADD/CHANGE              Escape: Main Menu

Selection: All records

Technician      Acct. No.          Date              Hours Billed   Parts Cost
==============================================================================
Chuck           83-211             Jun 24            1.5            120.75
Penney          85-109             Jun 24            1              0
Penney          84-142             Jun 24            1.75           79.40
Bill            83-115             Jun 24            2              55.20
Chuck           85-114             Jun 24            1              0
Chuck           83-121             Jun 25            2.5            248.75
Bill            84-200             Jun 25            1              .85
Penney          83-101             Jun 25            1.5            110.95
Chuck           85-147             Jun 25            1.25           45.30
Bill            84-138             Jun 25            1.5            67.35



------------------------------------------------------------------------------
Type entry or use ₲ commands                                      ₲-? for Help
```

Creating a Tables Report

It's now time to prepare your weekly service call report. While this is a somewhat involved process, keep in mind that you only have to do this one time. Once you have created a report format, you can use it week after week. Remember, the report format is saved along with the rest of your file.

Type ₲**P** to leave Review/Add/Change and go to the Report Menu (Figure 3-22). This time, select option 2, **Create a new "tables" format**, and name it "Weekly Report." Your screen should look like Figure 3-39.

THE REPORT FORMAT SCREEN

In the middle section of the screen, you'll see a list of all the commands that work in the Tables report format. (That's why you don't have a special Help screen available here. All the commands are displayed all the time.)

Below the list of commands, you'll see all of the data in the first three records in your file along with the category names. This is *AppleWorks'* default report format. If you were to print your report now, it would look just the way those three records appear on the screen. Each record would be printed on a single line. All five categories would be printed in the order that you see them, and each category would be 12 spaces wide, with 1 space between adjacent categories.

FIGURE 3-39 A new Tables report

```
File: Repair Calls                  REPORT FORMAT            Escape: Report Menu
Report: Weekly Report
Selection: All records


================================================================================
--> or <--  Move cursor                         -J  Right justify this category
 >    <    Switch category positions           -K  Define a calculated category
-->  <--   Change column width                 -N  Change report name and/or title
-A  Arrange (sort) on this category            -O  Printer options
-D  Delete this category                       -P  Print the report
-G  Add/remove group totals                    -R  Change record selections rules
-I  Insert a prev. deleted category            -T  Add/remove category totals
--------------------------------------------------------------------------------

Technician  Acct. No.   Date        Hours Billed Parts Cost  L
-A--------- -B--------- -C--------- -D---------- -E--------- e
Chuck       83-211      Jun 24      1.5          120.75      n
Penney      85-109      Jun 24      1            0           6
Penney      84-142      Jun 24      1.75         79.40       5

--------------------------------------------------------------------------------
Use options shown above to change report format                  54K Avail.
```

If you look just to the right of the Parts Cost column, you'll see the Length Indicator. It's telling you that the total line length for all five categories is 65 characters. If you delete categories, create new categories, or adjust the width of one or more categories, the Length Indicator will change accordingly.

MOVING CATEGORIES AROUND

You *are* going to create new, calculated categories, but before you do, let's move the Date so that it will be the leftmost category. There is an easy way to do this. The left- and right-arrow keys will move your cursor from one category to the next. Press the right-arrow key twice so that your cursor is in column C, the Date column. (*Note:* The columns are labeled with letters on the dashed line below the category names.) With your cursor in column C, type < (hold down the OPEN-APPLE key while you type the "<" key; don't use the SHIFT key). Notice that the Date and Acct. No. categories have switched positions. Your cursor is still in the Date category but that category is now in column B. Press < again and the Date and Technician categories will switch (Figure 3-40). < causes a category to exchange positions with the one to its left; > swaps places with the category on the right. (*Note:* You can use this technique of switching category positions when you customize the multiple record format layout, too.)

FIGURE 3-40 Move the Date category to column A

```
File: Repair Calls                  REPORT FORMAT               Escape: Report Menu
Report: Weekly Report
Selection: All records


==================================================================================
-->or<--  Move cursor                         ♂-J  Right justify this category
 >  ♂  <  Switch category positions           ♂-K  Define a calculated category
-->♂<--   Change column width                 ♂-N  Change report name and/or title
♂-A  Arrange (sort) on this category          ♂-O  Printer options
♂-D  Delete this category                     ♂-P  Print the report
♂-G  Add/remove group totals                  ♂-R  Change record selections rules
♂-I  Insert a prev. deleted category          ♂-T  Add/remove category totals
----------------------------------------------------------------------------------

Date          Technician    Acct. No.      Hours Billed  Parts Cost  L
-A----------- -B----------- -C------------ -D----------- -E--------- e
Jun 24        Chuck         83-211         1.5           120.75      n
Jun 24        Penney        85-109         1             0           6
Jun 24        Penney        84-142         1.75          79.40       5

----------------------------------------------------------------------------------
Use options shown above to change report format                         54K Avail.
```

ADJUSTING COLUMN WIDTH

The width of a column can be increased or decreased by holding down the OPEN-APPLE key while pressing either the right- or left-arrow key, respectively. Since all dates will be six characters long, you can decrease the width of the Date column to as few as six characters without worrying about "chopping off" any of the data in that column. With your cursor in column A, type ♂ **left-arrow** five times until the width of column A has been reduced to 7 characters. (Leaving an extra space will improve the look of your report.) Notice that the Length Indicator now reads 60.

Experiment with adjusting the width of other columns. What you're trying to do is to create the nicest looking and easiest-to-read report possible.

RIGHT-JUSTIFYING NUMERICAL CATEGORIES

Two of your categories, Hours Billed and Parts Cost, contain numerical data. The problem is that *AppleWorks* doesn't know that this information should be treated as numbers. Look at the three entries in the Parts Cost column. The entries don't "line up" because *AppleWorks* hasn't been told that the entries are numbers. The Right-Justify command, ♂J, will print all the numbers in a category so that their decimal points line up.

Place your cursor in column D, Hours Billed, and type **J**. At the bottom of the screen, *AppleWorks* asks you **How many decimal places for this category:**. The default value is zero decimal places, but since the hours are given to the nearest hundredth (for example, 1.75 hours), you want the hours printed to two decimal places, so type **2** and press RETURN. *AppleWorks* then asks you for the number of **Blank spaces after this category:**. This is the number of spaces it will leave between this category and the one following it. The default value is three, and you can choose any value greater than zero. (I usually choose two blank spaces.)

After you have chosen the number of blank spaces you want and have pressed the RETURN key, you'll see that the three sample entries in column D have been replaced by a bunch of nines (Figure 3-41). This is *AppleWorks'* way of showing you that when this category is printed in your report, all of the entries will be printed with two decimal places. (*Note:* If you right-justify a category with nonnumerical data in it, *AppleWorks* will just print it flush with the right edge of the column.)

Now, move your cursor to column E, Parts Cost, and right-justify this category, too. Again choose two decimal places.

If you should want to *remove* the right-justify feature from a category, just place your cursor in that column and type J.

FIGURE 3-41 Define Hours Billed as a numerical category

```
File: Repair Calls                REPORT FORMAT              Escape: Report Menu
Report: Weekly Report
Selection: All records


==============================================================================
-->or<--    Move cursor                          -J  Right justify this category
>    <      Switch category positions            -K  Define a calculated category
--><--     Change column width                  -N  Change report name and/or title
-A  Arrange (sort) on this category             -O  Printer options
-D  Delete this category                        -P  Print the report
-G  Add/remove group totals                     -R  Change record selections rules
-I  Insert a prev. deleted category             -T  Add/remove category totals
------------------------------------------------------------------------------

Date    Technician  Acct. No.  Hours Billed   Parts Cost   L
-A----- -B--------- -C-------- -D-----------  -E---------- e
Jun 24  Chuck        83-211     999999999.99  120.75       n
Jun 24  Penney       85-109     999999999.99  0            5
Jun 24  Penney       84-142     999999999.99  79.40        7

------------------------------------------------------------------------------
Use options shown above to change report format                  54K Avail.
```

CREATING CALCULATED CATEGORIES

You are now ready to create the two categories that have been "missing" so far: Labor Cost and Total Cost. As I explained earlier, the reason you didn't set up separate categories for these items was that the categories already in your file could be used to create the two you needed. Why enter extra information when your computer can do it for you?

Before we create a column for Labor Cost, you have to decide two things. First, how are you going to calculate Labor Cost? Since Hot & Cold Inc. is your company, you can set any labor rate you wish. Let's suppose that you decide to charge $45.00 per hour. That means that the Labor Cost is computed by multiplying 45 times the number of hours in the Hours Billed column.

Your second decision is where in your report do you want the column for Labor Cost to appear. It makes sense to insert the column for Labor Cost after the Hours Billed column, so move your cursor to column E, the one that's just to the right of the Hours Billed column, and type **K**.

AppleWorks immediately inserts a column with the category name "Calculated." At the bottom of the screen you are asked to **Type a name for the calculated category:**. The default name "Calculated" is already listed, and you will want to replace it with your own choice for a category name. Type **CONTROL-Y** to erase "Calculated." Then type **Labor Cost** and press RETURN.

AppleWorks wants to know how it should calculate values for Labor Cost. That's what it's asking when it says **Type calculation rules:**. Let me give you some facts about these calculation rules before you go on. First, if you want to use an existing category (such as Hours Billed) in the calculation, use the column letter (D, for Hours Billed). Second, whatever calculation you decide on, *don't* type any spaces between the items. If you're adding columns A and B together, for example, type just three characters, A+B. Third, *AppleWorks* performs all calculations from left to right. It does *not* follow the rule of multiplying or dividing before adding or subtracting. And parentheses, "( )", are not allowed. Fourth, if *AppleWorks* doesn't understand your calculation, it will print a string of "#" characters in the calculated column when it prints your report. And fifth, only four mathematical operations can be performed: adding, subtracting, multiplying, and dividing. The four symbols representing these operations are, respectively: "+", "-", "*", and "/".

The calculation you want for the Labor Cost column is the product of 45 times the value in column D, so type **45*D** and press RETURN.

All calculated categories are automatically right-justified. So choose two decimal places and whatever value you want for blank spaces. Your screen should look like Figure 3-42.

Now do the whole process again and create another calculated category for Total Cost. You'll probably want Total Cost to be the last column in your report, so move your cursor as far to the right as it will go before you type ⌘K. Use "Total Cost" for the category name, and for your calculation rule use "E+F". (Yes, that's right. You *can* use the results of one calculated category in the calculation rules of another. Just be sure that the calculated category you're referring to lies to the *left* of the calculated category you're defining.)

FIGURE 3-42 Define Labor Cost as a calculated category

```
File: Repair Calls                    REPORT FORMAT            Escape: Report Menu
Report: Weekly Report
Selection: All records


=============================================================================
-->or<--  Move cursor                             ⌘-J  Right justify this category
 >  ⌘  <  Switch category positions               ⌘-K  Define a calcuated category
-->⌘<--   Change column width                     ⌘-N  Change report name and/or title
⌘-A  Arrange (sort) on this category              ⌘-O  Printer options
⌘-D  Delete this category                         ⌘-P  Print the report
⌘-G  Add/remove group totals                      ⌘-R  Change record selections rules
⌘-I  Insert a prev. deleted category              ⌘-T  Add/remove category totals
-----------------------------------------------------------------------------

Date     Technician  Acct. No.  Hours Billed  Labor Cost   Parts Cost  L
-A-----  -B--------- -C-------- -D----------  -E---------  -F-------   e
Jun 24   Chuck       83-211     999999999.99  99999999.99  9999999.99  n
Jun 24   Penney      85-109     999999999.99  99999999.99  9999999.99  7
Jun 24   Penney      84-142     999999999.99  99999999.99  9999999.99  0

-----------------------------------------------------------------------------
Use options shown above to change report format                   54K Avail.
```

Compare your screen to Figure 3-43 and notice that part of column G, the Total Cost column, is off the screen. If you move your cursor to the right, the columns will scroll to the left and you'll be able to see all of column G.

AppleWorks allows up to three calculated categories per report.

Individual values for calculated fields are computed as each line of your report is being printed. That's why you can't see values for your calculated categories in the report format. What this means is that you cannot Arrange (Sort) your file on a calculated category. Nor can you use Record Selection on a calculated category.

FIGURE 3-43 Define Total Cost as a calculated category, too

```
File: Repair Calls                REPORT FORMAT              Escape: Report Menu
Report: Weekly Report
Selection: All records

================================================================================
--> or <--  Move cursor                      -J  Right justify this category
>     <   Switch category positions         -K  Define a calcuated category
--> <--  Change column width                -N  Change report name and/or title
-A  Arrange (sort) on this category          -O  Printer options
-D  Delete this category                     -P  Print the report
-G  Add/remove group totals                  -R  Change record selections rules
-I  Insert a prev. deleted category          -T  Add/remove category totals
--------------------------------------------------------------------------------

Date    Technician  Acct. No.  Hours Billed  Labor Cost   Parts Cost  Total Cos
-A----- -B--------- -C-------- -D----------- -E---------- -F-------  -G-------
Jun 24  Chuck       83-211     999999999.99  99999999.99  999999.99  999999999
Jun 24  Penney      85-109     999999999.99  99999999.99  999999.99  999999999
Jun 24  Penney      84-142     999999999.99  99999999.99  999999.99  999999999

------------------------------------------------------------------------ More -->
Use options shown above to change report format                      54K Avail.
```

ADDING CATEGORY TOTALS

If you look back at your original plan for this report, you'll see that you wanted the report to print out column totals on the Hours Billed, Parts Cost, and Total Cost categories. To produce a total for a particular category, simply move your cursor to the category and type **T**, the Category Totals command. Accept the default value for number of decimal places and select a value for blank spaces. *AppleWorks* draws a double line on your screen at the bottom of the column to indicate that the category will be totaled at the end of the report.

Now add Category Totals to the Hours Billed, Parts Cost, and Total Cost columns and compare your screen with Figure 3-44. (*Note:* In Figure 3-44, column A has been scrolled off screen to the left.)

ADDING GROUP TOTALS

The last feature you wanted your report to have was to print subtotals (*AppleWorks* calls them group totals) for each technician so that you could see how many billable hours each technician worked, etc. Before you set up Group Totals, you had better Arrange your file by technician name so that all Bill's records print one after the other, followed by Chuck's records, and so forth.

Move your cursor to column B, Technician, and type **A**. Choose option 1, **From A to Z**, and press RETURN. Notice that the three records being displayed are all Bill's records.

FIGURE 3-44 Add category totals to numerical categories

```
File: Repair Calls                      REPORT FORMAT                 Escape: Report Menu
Report: Weekly Report
Selection: All records



==========================================================================================
--> or <--   Move cursor                             -J   Right justify this category
>    <      Switch category positions               -K   Define a calculated category
-->  <--    Change column width                     -N   Change report name and/or title
-A   Arrange (sort) on this category                -O   Printer options
-D   Delete this category                           -P   Print the report
-G   Add/remove group totals                        -R   Change record selections rules
-I   Insert a prev. deleted category                -T   Add/remove category totals
------------------------------------------------------------------------------------------

Technician   Acct. No.   Hours Billed   Labor Cost    Parts Cost   Total Cost    L
-B---------  -C--------  -D----------   -E---------   -F--------   -G----------  e
Chuck        83-211      999999999.99   99999999.99   9999999.99   999999999.99  n
Penney       85-109      999999999.99   99999999.99   9999999.99   999999999.99  8
Penney       84-142      999999999.99   99999999.99   9999999.99   999999999.99  3
                         ============                 ==========   ============
<--- More --------------------------------------------------------------------------------
Use options shown above to change report format                           54K Avail.
```

With your cursor still in column B, type **G**, to set up Group Totals in your report. *AppleWorks* asks if you want your report to print Group Totals only. If you say "Yes," your report won't print out individual records. It will only print the three Group Total lines and a final grand total. And it won't print out any entries at all for categories that weren't totaled. Since this isn't what you want, press the "N" key to respond "No" (don't press RETURN).

The second question you are asked is whether you want your report to start a new page every time there is a change in the Group Total category—in other words, every time the technician name changes. Answer "No" to this question, too, by pressing the "N" key.

It doesn't seem as if anything has changed in your report format, but if you look just above the double line on your screen (Figure 3-45) you'll see a new line that says **Group totals on: Technician**.

PRINTER OPTIONS

You're almost ready to print out your report. Before you do, though, you should look at the Printer Options page. Type **O** (Figure 3-46).

The commands for this Printer Options screen are almost the same as those in the Labels format. Notice the two lines, **Line width** and **Char per line (est)**. You can't change their values directly; they don't have two-character codes. But they're affected by the values of the four options above, Platen Width, Left and Right Margin, and Characters per

FIGURE 3-45 Perform Group Totals on Technician

```
File: Repair Calls                  REPORT FORMAT              Escape: Report Menu
Report: Weekly Report
Selection: All records

Group totals on: Technician
===============================================================================
-->or<--   Move cursor                         -J  Right justify this category
 >  <    Switch category positions            -K  Define a calculated category
--><--   Change column width                  -N  Change report name and/or title
-A  Arrange (sort) on this category           -O  Printer options
-D  Delete this category                      -P  Print the report
-G  Add/remove group totals                   -R  Change record selections rules
-I  Insert a prev. deleted category           -T  Add/remove category totals
-------------------------------------------------------------------------------
Technician  Acct. No.  Hours Billed  Labor Cost   Parts Cost  Total Cost   L
-B--------- -C-------- -D----------  -E---------  -F--------  -G---------- e
Bill        83-115     999999999.99  99999999.99  9999999.99  999999999.99 n
Bill        84-200     999999999.99  99999999.99  9999999.99  999999999.99 8
Bill        84-138     999999999.99  99999999.99  9999999.99  999999999.99 3
                       ============               ==========  ============
<--- More ---------------------------------------------------------------------
Use options shown above to change report format                     54K Avail.
```

FIGURE 3-46 Printer Options for Tables report

```
File: Repair Calls                 PRINTER OPTIONS           Escape: Report Format
Report: Weekly Report
===============================================================================

-------Left and right margins--------      ------Top and bottom margins-------
PW: Platen Width          8.0 inches       PL: Paper Length        11.0 inches
LM: Left Margin           0.0 inches       TM: Top Margin           0.0 inches
RM: Right Margin          0.0 inches       BM: Bottom Margin        2.0 inches
CI: Chars per Inch       10                LI: Lines per Inch       6

    Line width            8.0 inches           Printing length      9.0 inches
    Char per line (est)  80                    Lines per page      54

          --------------------Formatting options--------------------
          SC:  Send Special Codes to printer                      No
          PD:  Print a Dash when an entry is blank                No
          PH:  Print report Header at top of each of page         Yes
               Single, Double or Triple Spacing (SS/DS/TS)        SS


-------------------------------------------------------------------------------
Type a two letter option code                                        54K Avail.
```

Inch. Line Width is the result of subtracting Left Margin and Right Margin from Platen Width. And Characters per Line is the product of Line Width times Characters per Inch.

Do you remember how wide your report was? If you don't, ESC back to your report format, look at the Length Indicator (which is really a line width indicator), and then return to Printer Options (⌘O). Your Length Indicator probably shows a value of about 85 characters. The problem is that, according to the Char per Line value in Printer Options, your printer is only going to print 80 characters. This means that the last few characters of every line are going to be chopped off. So you're going to have to do something about it. You could try to shorten the width of some of the columns, but let's see how you can use Printer Options to solve the problem.

You can't change the Platen Width (unless you you have a wide-carriage printer), and the Left and Right Margins are already set to zero. That leaves only the number of characters per inch your printer will print. Most printers will print more than 10 characters per inch, and your printer's manual will tell you what values are supported. Try a value of 12 characters per inch. Type **CI**, RETURN, **12**, and RETURN. Notice that not only did the screen value for Characters per Inch change from 10 to 12, but estimated Characters per Line increased from 80 to 96. (*Note:* If your printer doesn't support 12 characters per inch, try 17.)

The four options listed under **Top and bottom margins** control printing down the page. **Printing length** is computed by subtracting Top Margin and Bottom Margin from Page Length. The number of **Lines per page** is the product of Lines per Inch times printing length.

The SC option, **Send Special Codes to printer**, allows you to give your printer one or more commands at the beginning of your report. Suppose, for example, you wanted your printer to print the entire report in boldface. SC lets you type in this command. Suppose your printer's command for boldface is the two characters: ESC ! (the ESC character followed by an exclamation point) as it is with Apple's ImageWriter printer. If you wanted your report done in boldface, you would type **SC** and press RETURN. You would then press the ESC key, type an exclamation point (SHIFT 1), and then type the caret or circumflex character (SHIFT 6) to indicate that you were through typing. (*Note:* Typing a caret is the only way to return to the Printer Options screen once you begin entering Special Codes.) If you want to remove any Special Codes you had previously typed in, type **SC** again and respond "No" (type **N**) to the question **Is this OK?** Then you can type the caret to return to Printer Options.

Print a Dash when an entry is blank (PD) actually serves two purposes. With nonnumerical data, such as technician names, the PD command does just what you think it will. If a particular entry was left blank, when the report is printed a dash will be printed if PD's value is "Yes." If PD's value is "No," the place in the report is left blank.

If a category has been chosen to be numerical, either with the Right-Justify (⌘J) command or the Category Total (⌘T) command, then PD works a little differently. If PD's value is "No" and an entry is either blank or has a value of zero, then the place in the report is left blank (in other words, a zero value won't print). If PD's value is "Yes," both blank entries and zero value entries will be printed as zeros. Since you have zero value entries in your Parts Cost category that you want to have printed as zeros, type **PD** and press RETURN. Notice PD's value changes from "No" to "Yes."

The Report Header consists of four lines. Line 1 contains the name of your file and the page number. (*AppleWorks* automatically numbers the pages of your report.) Line 2 has the name and date of your report. Category names are printed on line 3. And line 4 is a row of dashes. The default value is "Yes" and normally, for this kind of report, you will want a Report Header printed at the top of each page.

The last option allows you to choose single, double, or triple line spacing between records in your report. Selection is made by typing "SS," "DS," or "TS" and pressing RETURN. Let's choose to double space your report. Type **DS** and RETURN. By the way, the spacing option has no effect on the four-line header.

PRINTING THE REPORT

At last you're ready to print your report. ESC back to the Report Format screen and type ⌘**P**. Select your printer from the list. Type today's date and press RETURN. Then press RETURN once more to accept the default value of one copy. Compare your printed report with Figure 3-47.

Notice that every time the technician name changed, totals were printed for the records with that technician name. That's what the term Group Total means. At the bottom of your report are the totals of all the records for Hours Billed, Parts Cost, and Total Cost categories.

Save your data base file, and its report format, by typing ⌘**S**. Then ESC to the Main Menu, and Quit the program by selecting option 6.

Final Comments

While there were only two data base examples in this chapter, they encompassed virtually all of the available features and options. I

FIGURE 3-47 The printed report

File: Repair Calls Page 1
Report: Weekly Report

Date	Technician	Acct. No.	Hours Billed	Labor Cost	Parts Cost	Total Cost
Jun 24	Bill	83-115	2.00	90.00	55.20	145.20
Jun 25	Bill	84-200	1.00	45.00	.85	45.85
Jun 25	Bill	84-138	1.50	67.50	67.35	134.85
			4.50		123.40	325.90
Jun 24	Chuck	83-211	1.50	67.50	120.75	188.25
Jun 24	Chuck	85-114	1.00	45.00	0.00	45.00
Jun 25	Chuck	83-121	2.50	112.50	248.75	361.25
Jun 25	Chuck	85-147	1.25	56.25	45.30	101.55
			6.25		414.80	696.05
Jun 24	Penney	85-109	1.00	45.00	0.00	45.00
Jun 24	Penney	84-142	1.75	78.75	79.40	158.15
Jun 25	Penney	83-101	1.50	67.50	110.95	178.45
			4.25		190.35	381.60
			15.00*		728.55*	1403.55*

encourage you to create your own data bases and experiment with the two different report formats, Labels and Tables. Become familiar with the Record Selection function. It's really very versatile. Adjust the single and multiple record layouts to suit you. And, above all, keep at it. The more you use this and the other sections of *AppleWorks*, the easier it will be to make the program work for you.

CHAPTER

4 THE SPREADSHEET

Now that you're here in the spreadsheet section of *AppleWorks*, you may be wondering, "What do I do with a spreadsheet?" Or even, "What *is* a spreadsheet?" If you feel this way, don't worry. You've got a lot of company.

The spreadsheet application differs in a major way from word processor and data base applications. People wrote memos, letters, and books long before the existence of word processor programs. Word processing just makes writing and editing easier. Similarly, people kept information in files for centuries before there were data base programs to make that job easier. But, until microcomputers were available, the concept of an electronic spreadsheet did not exist—which means that spreadsheet programs have been around for less than 10 years.

A spreadsheet allows you to take any situation that can be expressed in numbers and set up a mathematical model of it. In this chapter, you will be creating several spreadsheets that will be used to demonstrate the various features and functions of this section of *AppleWorks*. You will be typing different kinds of data into the spreadsheet and will be using virtually all of its commands.

I. EXAMPLE 1: THE SALES FORECAST

Suppose you owned a company whose gross sales last year were $130,000. You've owned this company for a number of years, and, by observing the sales numbers for each month, you know what fraction of the total year's sales will be made each month (10 percent in January, 8 percent in February, and so forth). A spreadsheet allows you to express each of the 12 months' sales values as a fraction, or percentage, of a single yearly sales projection. You can then change just one number on your spreadsheet, the yearly sales projection, and all 12 monthly sales figures will change automatically.

This is a simple application, but let's use it as the first spreadsheet example.

Creating a New Spreadsheet

Start up *AppleWorks* and select option 1, **Add files to the Desktop**, from the Main Menu. Since you are creating a new spreadsheet, choose option 5, **Make a new file for the: Spreadsheet**. Select **From scratch** from the spreadsheet menu (Figure 4-1) and name your spreadsheet, "Sales Proj."

After you've named your spreadsheet and pressed RETURN, your screen should look like Figure 4-2. This is the Review/Add/Change screen for the spreadsheet. The top line of the screen contains the usual information: the name of your file ("Sales Proj."), the name of the activity (Review/Add/Change), and the place the program will go to if you press the ESC key (Main Menu).

The Spreadsheet Grid

The next line is a row of "=" symbols with letters ("A," "B," "C," etc.) interspersed. Running down the left side of the screen are the numbers 1 through 18. Those letters and numbers set up a grid pattern on the screen so that any position on the grid can be referred to by a letter/number combination. The letters refer to columns, while the numbers refer to rows.

The bright bar you see in the upper left corner is your cursor. It's sitting in column A, row 1, so its position is referred to as A1. If you look at the third line from the bottom of your screen, at the extreme left, you'll see the Cell Indicator.

The four arrow keys can move your cursor to other locations on the grid. Try it. As you move the cursor around, watch the Cell Indicator change.

The Spreadsheet Cell

Each one of those grid locations (A1, B6, etc.) is called a *cell*. All the cells are empty now because this is a new spreadsheet. But you are free to fill cells with any data you choose. Any cell can be filled with one of three types of data. You can put words in a cell; this is called *label data*. You can put numbers in a cell (*value data*). Or you can put a calculation in a cell and make its value the result of the values of one or more other cells.

You can't see all of the cells in your spreadsheet because they won't all fit on your screen at the same time. You can see, for example, columns A through H, but the columns actually range from A through DW, a total of 127 columns (A through Z, AA through AZ, BA through BZ, CA

FIGURE 4-1 Make a new spreadsheet

```
Disk: Disk 2 (Slot 6)              SPREADSHEET              Escape: Erase entry

      Main Menu
         Add Files
            Spreadsheet

            Make a new file:

            --> From scratch

            2.  From a DIF (TM) file

            3.  From a VisiCalc (R) file

Type a name for this new file: Sales Proj.                        56K Avail.
```

FIGURE 4-2 The new, blank spreadsheet

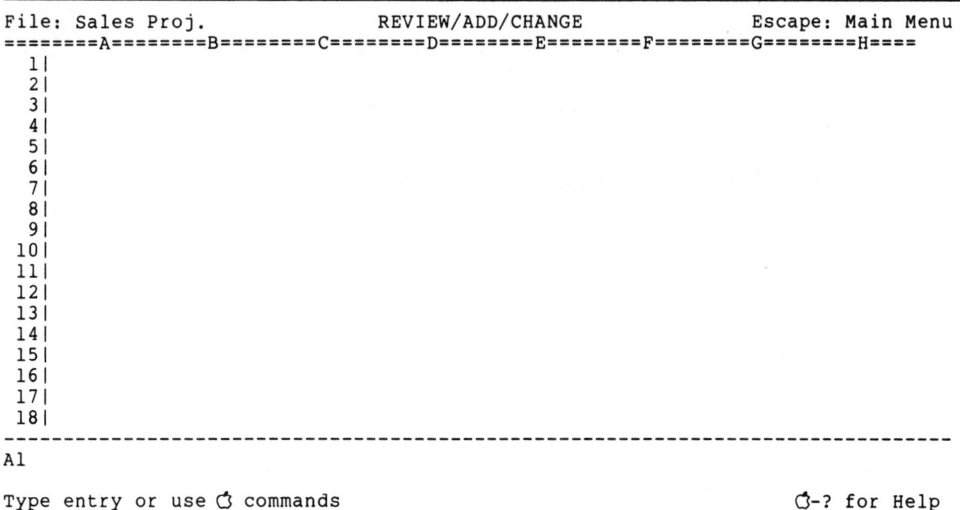

```
File: Sales Proj.              REVIEW/ADD/CHANGE              Escape: Main Menu
========A========B========C========D========E========F========G========H====
  1|
  2|
  3|
  4|
  5|
  6|
  7|
  8|
  9|
 10|
 11|
 12|
 13|
 14|
 15|
 16|
 17|
 18|
-----------------------------------------------------------------------------
A1

Type entry or use ⌘ commands                                    ⌘-? for Help
```

through CZ, and DA through DW). Similarly, there are more rows than the 18 you're looking at now. In fact, there are 999 rows. This gives you a total of 126,873 cells. (*Note:* You can't use them all in a single spreadsheet because of memory limitations. If your Apple has 128K of internal memory, you can fill about 6000 cells. See the discussion on add-on memory in Chapter 6.)

The Help Screen

Notice at the bottom right corner of your screen that you have a Help screen available. To see the screen, type ⌘**?**. As you might imagine, there are several special commands for the spreadsheet. After you learn how to use these commands, the Help screen can be used to aid you in recalling which keys to press to execute a particular command. Press the ESC key to return to the Review/Add/Change screen.

Typing Label Data into Cells

Let's begin your sales projection spreadsheet. The location of the cursor determines which cell you're going to be typing into. Move the cursor to cell B1 and type **Hot & Cold Inc.** As you start to type, two things happen. The characters that you type are placed directly in the cell your cursor is sitting on. And, on the second line from the bottom on your screen, you see the word **Label:** followed by the characters you type (Figure 4-3).

How did *AppleWorks* know that you were typing label data, instead of value data? It knew by the first character you typed. If the first character is a letter, *AppleWorks* assumes that the data is label data; if the first character in a cell is a number (or a "+," "-," "(," "." or "@" character), *AppleWorks* assumes the data to be value data. This brings up an interesting question. Suppose you wanted to put a label in a cell and the first character of the label was *not* a letter (for example, an address). How could you tell *AppleWorks* that you wanted your data to be treated as a label? The answer is to type a quote symbol (") before you begin typing the actual label. *AppleWorks* will treat whatever follows quotes as label data. The quote symbol itself is not displayed in the cell. (If you want the first character in a cell to be a quote symbol, you have to type *two* quote symbols.)

Here's something to keep in mind: Any time you're typing data into a cell and you want to erase what you've typed, just press the ESC key.

Continue typing the rest of **Hot & Cold Inc.** If you type the wrong character, use the DELETE key to erase your mistake. As you reach the end of the cell, *AppleWorks* automatically extends your label into the next cell, C1. All columns, and therefore all cells, have the default width of 9 characters. Later, you'll see how to change the width of columns.

When you complete the label, press the RETURN key. (*Note:* You must press the RETURN key whenever you are through typing the contents of a cell.) After you have pressed RETURN, look at the Cell

FIGURE 4-3 Entering a label

```
File: Sales Proj.              REVIEW/ADD/CHANGE             Escape: Erase entry
========A========B========C========D========E========F========G========H====
  1|         Hot
  2|
  3|
  4|
  5|
  6|
  7|
  8|
  9|
 10|
 11|
 12|
 13|
 14|
 15|
 16|
 17|
 18|
------------------------------------------------------------------------------
B1
Label: Hot
Complete the label                                                55K Avail.
```

Indicator. It not only shows that your cursor is on cell B1, but also shows that the cell contains label data and what the contents of the cell are.

Move your cursor to cell A3 and type the label, **Annual Sales Forecast =**. (See Figure 4-4.) Your label will extend from cell A3 to cell C3.

Typing Value Data into Cells

Move your cursor to cell D3. This is the cell that will contain the projected value for your company's annual sales. Let's choose a value of $150,000. Type **150000** without the dollar sign or the comma (don't forget to press RETURN). Notice that as you type the first digit, the "1," *AppleWorks* immediately recognizes that you are typing a value. Because the entry is a value, it won't appear in the cell until after you press the RETURN key. As with label data, you can use the DELETE key to erase mistakes (or the ESC key to erase everything you've typed into that cell), until you press the RETURN key (or an arrow key). Pressing RETURN or an arrow key indicates that you are through typing into that cell. You can make changes in a completed cell either by entering new data or by using the Edit command, ⌘U, which you'll learn about in a moment.

FIGURE 4-4 Extending a label into adjacent cells

```
File: Sales Proj.             REVIEW/ADD/CHANGE                Escape: Main Menu
========A========B========C========D========E========F========G========H====
  1|        Hot & Cold Inc.
  2|
  3|Annual Sales Forecast =
  4|
  5|
  6|
  7|
  8|
  9|
 10|
 11|
 12|
 13|
 14|
 15|
 16|
 17|
 18|
--------------------------------------------------------------------------------
A3: (Label) Annual Sa

Type entry or use ⌘ commands                                     ⌘-? for Help
```

Changing the Value Data Format

You would like that 150000 value in cell D3 to look like a dollar value. You'd like it to begin with a dollar sign and have commas appropriately placed. Because D3's entry is a value, you can't type in a dollar sign or commas, but you can change the display format, or Layout, of the cell. That way, *AppleWorks* will put in the dollar sign and commas for you.

Leave your cursor on cell D3 and type ⌘**L**, the Change Layout command. *AppleWorks* asks if you want to change the Layout of a single entry, one or more rows, one or more columns, or a block of cells. Type **E** (don't press RETURN) to select a single Entry. There are three types of Layouts: Value format, Label format, and Protection. Type the letter **V** to choose Value format. You now see six types of Value formats: Fixed, Dollars, Commas, Percent, Appropriate, and Standard. You'll learn about each of these formats later in this chapter. Right now, type **D** for Dollars format. The last question you have to answer is how many decimal places you want displayed. The default is zero decimal places, and for your $150,000 value, zero is a good choice. Press RETURN to accept zero decimal places. From now on, any value entered into cell D3 will be displayed in Dollars format (Figure 4-5). Look at the Cell Indicator again. It now shows cell D3's layout as well as its contents. "D0" means Dollars with 0 decimal places.

FIGURE 4-5 Changing a Value format to Dollars

```
File: Sales Proj.               REVIEW/ADD/CHANGE              Escape: Main Menu
========A========B========C========D========E========F========G========H====
  1|        Hot & Cold Inc.
  2|
  3|Annual Sales Forecast =     $150,000
  4|
  5|
  6|
  7|
  8|
  9|
 10|
 11|
 12|
 13|
 14|
 15|
 16|
 17|
 18|
---------------------------------------------------------------------------
D3: (Value, Layout-DO) 150000

Type entry or use ♂ commands                                ♂-? for Help
```

Changing the Label Data Format

Type the months of the year in cells A6 through A17. (Type **January** in A6, **February** in A7, and so forth.) If you want to save a little bit of time, you can press the down-arrow key instead of the RETURN key at the end of each label. Notice that *AppleWorks* normally left-justifies your label entries—that is, each label starts at the left edge of its cell. You can change this format for any cell or group of cells.

After you're through typing the label for the last month, December, move your cursor back to cell A6. Type ♂**L**, the Change Layout command. At the bottom of your screen, *AppleWorks* is asking you what portion of your spreadsheet you want to change. You can change the Layout (the way data is displayed) for a single cell, one or more rows of cells, one or more columns of cells, or a block of cells. You want to change the display format of the block of cells containing the 12 months, so type **B** for Block (*don't* press the RETURN key).

AppleWorks now tells you to use your cursor to highlight the block of cells whose format you want to change. Press the down-arrow key 11 times to highlight all 12 cells containing the names of the months, and then press RETURN.

This time, when *AppleWorks* shows you the three types of Layouts, type **L** for Label format and don't press RETURN. Now you see the four choices for Label format: Left-justify, Right-justify, Center, and Standard. Type **R** for Right-justify and compare your screen with Figure 4-6.

FIGURE 4-6 Changing a Label format to Right-justify

```
File: Sales Proj.              REVIEW/ADD/CHANGE              Escape: Main Menu
========A========B========C========D========E========F========G========H====
  1|        Hot & Cold Inc.
  2|
  3|Annual Sales Forecast =      $150,000
  4|
  5|
  6|   January
  7| February
  8|    March
  9|    April
 10|      May
 11|     June
 12|     July
 13|   August
 14|September
 15|  October
 16| November
 17| December
 18|
------------------------------------------------------------------------------
A6: (Label, Layout-R) January

Type entry or use ⌘ commands                                      ⌘-? for Help
```

Copying a Cell

You would like to add the label " Sales =" in each of the cells following the months. Move your cursor to cell B6. You want to start your labels in column B with a space because all the months are right-justified in column A. But, if you try to type a space as the first character in your label, your Apple will just beep at you. In order to begin your label with a space, you must first type the quote symbol. This tells *AppleWorks* you are typing a label, and you can then type the space, followed by **Sales =**. Try it (and don't forget to press RETURN).

You could type the same label 11 more times in cells B7 through B17, but there is a much faster way to do the same thing. Leave your cursor on cell B6 and type ⌘**C**, the Copy command.

Three options for the Copy command are shown on the bottom line of your screen. Type **W** to select **Within worksheet** (don't press the RETURN key yet). *AppleWorks* asks you to highlight the cell or cells you wish to copy *from*. Since you only want to copy from cell B6, and it's already highlighted, just press RETURN.

You are now asked to highlight the cell or cells you wish to copy *to*. This is a three-step process:

1. Use the arrow keys to move the cursor to the *first* of the cells you want to copy to. In this example, you would move your cursor to cell B7 by pressing the down-arrow key once.

2. Press the period (".") key, which tells *AppleWorks* that you are going to specify several cells (called a *range* of cells), instead of just one cell. (*Note:* if you were copying to only one cell, you would press the RETURN key at this point instead of the period key and ignore Step 3.)
3. Use the arrow keys to highlight *all* the cells you want to copy to. In this example, press the down-arrow key ten times so that cells B7 through B17 are highlighted. Finally, press the RETURN key. *AppleWorks* copies the contents of cell B6 into cells B7 through B17 as shown in Figure 4-7.

FIGURE 4-7 Copying a label cell

```
File: Sales Proj.                REVIEW/ADD/CHANGE                Escape: Main Menu
========A========B========C========D========E========F========G========H====
  1|         Hot & Cold Inc.
  2|
  3|Annual Sales Forecast =     $150,000
  4|
  5|
  6|   January Sales =
  7|  February Sales =
  8|     March Sales =
  9|     April Sales =
 10|       May Sales =
 11|      June Sales =
 12|      July Sales =
 13|    August Sales =
 14|September Sales =
 15|   October Sales =
 16|  November Sales =
 17|  December Sales =
 18|
--------------------------------------------------------------------------------
B6: (Label)  Sales =

Type entry or use Ó commands                                    Ó-? for Help
```

Typing Calculations into Cells

AppleWorks allows five kinds of mathematical operations: addition (23+652), subtraction (47-12), multiplication (4*15), division (73/1.2), and exponentiation or raising to a power (3 ^ 4). The first four operations are straightforward. In the exponentiation example, the value 3 is being raised to the fourth power (yielding 81).

The spreadsheet performs operations from left to right, so that the expression 2+4/3 ^ 5 evaluates to 32. You can use parentheses around a particular calculation to force *AppleWorks* to perform it first.

In your spreadsheet, the sales projection for January is calculated by multiplying the percentage of yearly sales for January times the projected annual sales value of $150,000. Table 4-1 shows the percentage of annual sales for each of the 12 months. To compute the sales projection for January, move your cursor to cell C6. From Table 4-1, you see that January's percentage of annual sales is 9.5 percent, or .095, of $150,000. But instead of multiplying .095 times 150000, you will tell *AppleWorks* to compute the value of cell C6 by multiplying .095 times the contents of cell D3—remember, D3 contains the 150000 value. The symbol *AppleWorks* uses for multiplication is the asterisk ("*"). With your cursor in cell C6, type **.095*D3**, and press RETURN. (*Note:* If you try to type D3*.095, *AppleWorks* will treat your entry as a *label*. The reason for this is that the first character is the letter "D," so *AppleWorks* thinks that you are typing a label. To avoid this misunderstanding, start your calculation with a plus sign, +D3*.095.)

AppleWorks computes the result of your calculation, 14250, and puts it in cell C6. Ignore the format of the value for the moment, and type in the calculations for the remaining 11 months in cells C7 through C17 (Figure 4-8).

Changing the Format for All Cells

When you begin a new spreadsheet, *AppleWorks* sets the layout for all cells to "Standard." At the same time, *AppleWorks* chooses certain "standard" settings for both label cells and value cells.

TABLE 4-1 Monthly sales percentages

Month	Percentage
January	9.5%
February	8.5%
March	5.0%
April	5.5%
May	6.5%
June	10.0%
July	11.5%
August	8.0%
September	6.0%
October	8.5%
November	10.5%
December	10.5%

FIGURE 4-8 Entering formulas

```
File: Sales Proj.              REVIEW/ADD/CHANGE              Escape: Main Menu
========A========B========C========D========E========F========G========H====
  1|         Hot & Cold Inc.
  2|
  3|Annual Sales Forecast =     $150,000
  4|
  5|
  6|  January Sales =      14250
  7| February Sales =      12750
  8|    March Sales =       7500
  9|    April Sales =       8250
 10|      May Sales =       9750
 11|     June Sales =      15000
 12|     July Sales =      17250
 13|   August Sales =      12000
 14|September Sales =       9000
 15|  October Sales =      12750
 16| November Sales =      15750
 17| December Sales =      15750
 18|
----------------------------------------------------------------------------
C17: (Value) .105*D3

Type entry or use ₲ commands                                    ₲-? for Help
```

The standard setting for label cells is Left-justified, while the standard setting for value cells is Appropriate. (*Note:* Appropriate format displays numbers, right-justified in their cells, with as many decimal places as you type in.) Unless you change the layout of a particular cell (with the ₲L command), every cell adopts the format of the standard setting. So, if you change the standard format setting for either labels or values, you'll change the format of all the cells in your spreadsheet at once. (*Note:* If you scroll to the end of the Help screen, you'll see a list of the current standard settings.)

Let's change the standard setting for values from Appropriate to Dollars. Type ₲ **V**, the Standard Values command. Type **V** to select Value format, then type **D** for Dollars. Press RETURN to accept zero decimal places, and all value cells in your spreadsheet will adopt this new standard format and display their numbers in Dollars format (Figure 4-9). If you decide later that you want a particular value cell to display a different format, you can use the Layout command (₲L) to change its format to something other than Standard, Fixed or Percent, for example.

Many *AppleWorks* users confuse the two cell format commands: Layout (₲L) and Standard Values (₲V). The Layout command is used to change the format of individual cells or groups of cells. But when you change the Standard Values, you affect every cell with a layout of Standard.

FIGURE 4-9 Changing the Standard Value to Dollars

```
File: Sales Proj.              REVIEW/ADD/CHANGE                Escape: Main Menu
========A========B========C========D========E========F========G========H====
  1|         Hot & Cold Inc.
  2|
  3|Annual Sales Forecast =       $150,000
  4|
  5|
  6|  January Sales =   $14,250
  7| February Sales =   $12,750
  8|    March Sales =    $7,500
  9|    April Sales =    $8,250
 10|      May Sales =    $9,750
 11|     June Sales =   $15,000
 12|     July Sales =   $17,250
 13|   August Sales =   $12,000
 14|September Sales =    $9,000
 15|  October Sales =   $12,750
 16| November Sales =   $15,750
 17| December Sales =   $15,750
 18|
--------------------------------------------------------------------------------
C17: (Value) .105*D3

Type entry or use ⌘ commands                                        ⌘-? for Help
```

Looking at Calculations

AppleWorks will show you the calculations you have entered in various cells. Type⌘**Z**, the Zoom command, and look at cells C6 through C17 (Figure 4-10).

The Purpose of It All

Right now, if you've never worked with a spreadsheet before, you're probably saying to yourself: "Interesting, but what's it all for?"

What you've done in this spreadsheet is to define each monthly sales value as a percentage of the Annual Sales Forecast, a value in cell D3. The power of a spreadsheet is that if you change that one value in cell D3, all 12 monthly sales values will change along with it.

If you're still looking at the calculations in cells C6 through C17, type⌘**Z** again so that those cells display dollar values (Figure 4-9). Move your cursor to cell D3, and type a different value for the Annual Sales Forecast, say **160000** (don't type a dollar sign or a comma). As you press the RETURN key, watch the values in cells C6 through C17 change automatically (Figure 4-11).

FIGURE 4-10 Use Zoom to see the formulas

```
File: Sales Proj.              REVIEW/ADD/CHANGE               Escape: Main Menu
========A========B========C========D========E========F========G========H====
  1|         Hot & Cold Inc.
  2|
  3|Annual Sales Forecast =    150000
  4|
  5|
  6|  January Sales = .095*D3
  7| February Sales = .085*D3
  8|    March Sales = .05*D3
  9|    April Sales = .055*D3
 10|      May Sales = .065*D3
 11|     June Sales = .1*D3
 12|     July Sales = .115*D3
 13|   August Sales = .08*D3
 14|September Sales = .06*D3
 15|  October Sales = .085*D3
 16| November Sales = .105*D3
 17| December Sales = .105*D3
 18|
--------------------------------------------------------------------------------
C17: (Value) .105*D3

Type entry or use ₵ commands                                    ₵-? for Help
```

FIGURE 4-11 Changing one value affects all the others

```
File: Sales Proj.              REVIEW/ADD/CHANGE               Escape: Main Menu
========A========B========C========D========E========F========G========H====
  1|         Hot & Cold Inc.
  2|
  3|Annual Sales Forecast =    $160,000
  4|
  5|
  6|  January Sales =  $15,200
  7| February Sales =  $13,600
  8|    March Sales =   $8,000
  9|    April Sales =   $8,800
 10|      May Sales =  $10,400
 11|     June Sales =  $16,000
 12|     July Sales =  $18,400
 13|   August Sales =  $12,800
 14|September Sales =   $9,600
 15|  October Sales =  $13,600
 16| November Sales =  $16,800
 17| December Sales =  $16,800
 18|
--------------------------------------------------------------------------------
D3: (Value, Layout-DO) 160000

Type entry or use ₵ commands                                    ₵-? for Help
```

Changing Column Width

With your cursor still in cell D3, type in a value of **1000000**, and see what happens (Figure 4-12). Cells C6 through C17 changed again, but instead of $1,000,000 appearing in cell D3, there is a row of "#" characters.

FIGURE 4-12 D3 isn't wide enough for its contents

```
File: Sales Proj.              REVIEW/ADD/CHANGE               Escape: Main Menu
========A========B========C========D========E========F========G========H====
  1|         Hot & Cold Inc.
  2|
  3|Annual Sales Forecast =     #########
  4|
  5|
  6|   January Sales =  $95,000
  7| February Sales =  $85,000
  8|    March Sales =  $50,000
  9|    April Sales =  $55,000
 10|      May Sales =  $65,000
 11|     June Sales = $100,000
 12|     July Sales = $115,000
 13|   August Sales =  $80,000
 14|September Sales =  $60,000
 15|  October Sales =  $85,000
 16| November Sales = $105,000
 17| December Sales = $105,000
 18|
--------------------------------------------------------------------------------
D3: (Value, Layout-Do) 1000000

Type entry or use ⌘ commands                                        ⌘-? for Help
```

AppleWorks is telling you that the formatted value in cell D3 requires more spaces to display than are available. The value, $1,000,000, is 10 characters wide (actually it requires 11 characters), and column D is only 9 characters wide. Rather than chop off characters from one end of the value, *AppleWorks* fills the cell with #########.

You need to increase the width of column D to at least 11 characters (10 characters for the formatted value plus one extra space). You can do this with the layout command, ⌘L. With your cursor in cell D3, type ⌘**L** and then type **C** to select Columns Layout. *AppleWorks* highlights all of column D and asks you to use the left- and right-arrow keys to highlight additional columns to the left or right of column D. Since you only want to change the width of one column, column D, just press the RETURN key.

AppleWorks now asks you to select the type of Layout you want to alter. Type **C** to select Column width (don't press RETURN yet). You can now change the width of column D by holding down the OPEN-APPLE key while you press either the left- or right-arrow keys. Pressing ⌘ left-arrow makes the column narrower; pressing ⌘ right-arrow makes it wider.

If you increase the width of column D to 11 spaces, or more, you'll see the string of ######### characters replaced by the actual value. When you've finished altering the width of column D, press RETURN.

Printing Your Spreadsheet

Before you print out your spreadsheet, I'd like you to look at the Printer Options for this application. Type **O** (Figure 4-13). All 11 options work exactly as they did in the data base Printer Options section (see Chapter 3). The Report Header consists of a line containing the spreadsheet name and the page number, an optional date line (you can enter a date when you actually print the spreadsheet), and a blank line.

FIGURE 4–13 Spreadsheet Printer Options

```
File: Sales Proj.              PRINTER OPTIONS        Escape: Review/Add/Change
===============================================================================


-------Left and right margins--------          ------Top and bottom margins-------
PW: PLaten Width           8.0 inches          PL: Paper Length       11.0 inches
LM: Left Margin            0.0 inches          TM: Top Margin          0.0 inches
RM: Right Margin           0.0 inches          BM: Bottom Margin       0.0 inches
CI: Chars per Inch        10                   LI: Lines per Inch      6

Line width                 8.0 inches              Printing length    11.0 inches
Char per line (est)       80                       Lines per page     66

      ------------------------Formatting options--------------------
      SC:  Send Special Codes to printer                       No
      PH:  Print report Header at top of each page             Yes
           Single, Double or Triple Spacing (SS/DS/TS)         SS



-------------------------------------------------------------------------------
Type a two letter option code                                       54K Avail.
```

You can leave the printer options as they are for this spreadsheet example, so press ESC to return to your spreadsheet. Type **P**, the Print command, and look at the bottom of your screen. *AppleWorks* is asking you which part of your spreadsheet you want to print. You can print all of it, one or more adjacent rows, one or more adjacent columns, or a block of adjacent cells. Type **A** for All.

The Print screen contains two useful pieces of information in addition to a list of places for you to print your spreadsheet (Figure 4-14). The first piece of information is that your spreadsheet is 38 characters wide. This number makes sense if you remember that the first three columns, A, B, and C, were each nine characters wide, while column D was increased to 11 characters wide.

FIGURE 4-14 How wide is the spreadsheet?

```
File: Sales Proj.                 PRINT                Escape: Review/Add/Change
================================================================================
                  The information that you identified
                  is 38 characters wide.

                  The Printer Options values allow
                  80 characters per line.

                  Where do you want to print the report?

                  1.  My Printer
                  2.  The clipboard (for the Word Processor)
                  3.  A text (ASCII) file on disk
                  4.  A DIF (TM) file on disk



--------------------------------------------------------------------------------

Type number, or use arrows, then press Return                        54K Avail.
```

The second piece of information is that your printer is currently set to print a maximum of 80 characters per line. This value is controlled by the first four Printer Options: **Left Margin**, **Right Margin**, **Platen Width**, and **Characters per Inch**. Since your printer can print up to 80 characters per line and your spreadsheet is only 38 characters wide, your printer won't have any problem printing out your entire spreadsheet.

Select your printer from the list (it's probably choice 1). Because you left the Report Header option as "Yes," *AppleWorks* will ask you to type in a report date. The report date is optional, so you can either type in a date or just press RETURN. Finally, *AppleWorks* asks you how many copies of the spreadsheet you want. Press RETURN again to accept the default value of one copy, and your report will be printed. Notice that column letters and row numbers do not appear in your printed spreadsheet.

You might wonder what you could do if your spreadsheet were wider than 80 characters. Of the four printer options that affect the maximum number of characters per line that your printer will print, only the **Characters per Inch** option will help you to increase the Characters per Line value beyond 80. This is because the Left and Right Margins are already set to zero, and, unless you have a wide carriage printer, the Platen Width cannot be changed. However, your printer probably *does* support type sizes other than 10 characters per inch. For example, most printers support 17 characters-per-inch printing (check your printer's manual for the type sizes that it supports).

Even with a value of 17 characters per inch, your printer, with a standard 8-inch platen, could only print a maximum of 136 characters per line. If you kept the column width for all columns in your spreadsheet set at 9 characters, that's about 15 columns (A through O). What happens if your spreadsheet is 20 columns wide, or more?

AppleWorks will automatically divide your spreadsheet into sections, with the width of each section determined by the maximum number of characters per line which, in turn, is controlled by the first four printer options. And before you start to worry, columns are never split between sections.

Save this spreadsheet to your data disk, and leave it on your *AppleWorks* Desktop as you continue with the second spreadsheet example.

II. EXAMPLE 2: A WEEKLY EXPENSE REPORT FORM

Suppose that employees of your company, Hot & Cold Inc., took business trips, and you wanted to keep a record of their expenses. The spreadsheet section of *AppleWorks* allows you to design an Expense Report Form that will give you daily expenses, weekly totals for transportation, food, lodging, etc., and special features such as the average daily expense and the maximum daily dinner cost for the week.

If you're continuing from Example 1, ESC to the Main Menu; otherwise, start up *AppleWorks*. Choose option 1, **Add files to the Desktop**, and make a new file for the spreadsheet. Name this new spreadsheet, "Expense Form."

Designing the Form

Your form needs separate columns for each day of the week, a column for weekly totals, a column for average daily expense, and a column for maximum daily expense.

You'll need to label rows for individual types of expenses such as Airfare, Taxi or Limousine, Car Rental, Lodging, Breakfast, Lunch, Dinner, etc. You'll also need a row for daily totals.

Figures 4-15 and 4-16 show rows and columns labeled in a typical expense report layout. While this is by no means the only way to display expense report data, it's the layout I'll be using to describe various

FIGURE 4-15 The left portion of the Expense Form

```
File: Expense Form              REVIEW/ADD/CHANGE               Escape: Main Menu
========A========B========C========D========E========F========G========H=======
  1|                            HOT & COLD INC.: Expense Report
  2|
  3|Name:                                                            Week Ending:
  4|
  5|
  6|                  Mon      Tue      Wed      Thu      Fri      Sat      Sun
  7|
  8|Airfare
  9|Taxi or Limo
 10|Car Rental
 11|Lodging
 12|Breakfast
 13|Lunch
 14|Dinner
 15|Phone
 16|
 17|Daily Total
 18|
--------------------------------------------------------------------------------
A5:

Type entry or use ⌘ commands                                       ⌘-? for Help
```

FIGURE 4-16 The rest of the Expense Form

```
File: Expense Form              REVIEW/ADD/CHANGE               Escape: Main Menu
========H========I========J========K========L========M========N========O====
  1|
  2|
  3|Week Ending:
  4|
  5|                  Weekly   Daily    Daily
  6|Sat      Sun      Total    Average  Maximum
  7|
  8|
  9|
 10|
 11|
 12|
 13|
 14|
 15|
 16|
 17|
 18|
--------------------------------------------------------------------------------
H1

Type entry or use ⌘ commands                                       ⌘-? for Help
```

spreadsheet features. So I recommend that you type the same labels in the same cells that you see in the two figures. This way, when I refer to a particular cell, it will correspond exactly to the same cell in your spreadsheet. You might wonder why I didn't skip rows between Airfare, Taxi, Car Rental, etc. There are two reasons. First, I wanted to be able to show all the rows on the screen at the same time. Second, when you print the spreadsheet, you can change the line spacing in Printer Options to Double Space.

Customizing the Form

You can do several things to improve the "look" of this spreadsheet.

CENTERING COLUMN HEADINGS

Labels used for column headings, such as Mon, Tue, Weekly Total, etc., usually look better if they are centered in their cells rather than left-justified. These labels are in rows 5 and 6 in your spreadsheet. To change the label format for these two rows, move your cursor to any cell in row 5 (A5, for example) and type **L**, the Layout command. Note that you choose the Layout command, rather than the Standard Values command (V), because you only want to change the label format for *some* of the cells in your spreadsheet, not all of them. At the bottom of your screen, *AppleWorks* is asking you to choose how you want to highlight the cells whose layout you want to change. Type **R** for Rows and don't press RETURN. *AppleWorks* highlights all of row 5. Press the down-arrow key once, and both rows, 5 and 6, will be highlighted. Now press the RETURN key. You've selected which rows you want to change and *AppleWorks* is now asking which layout option you want to change. Type **L** for Label format (don't press RETURN).

You'll see a choice of four Label formats: Left-justify, Right-justify, Center, and Standard. The first three are self-explanatory, while the fourth, Standard, means to change the Label format to whatever is the Standard Value for labels. Type **C** for Center.

You may not immediately see that there has been a change in the Label format for rows 5 and 6, but look at the labels in columns K and L (Figure 4-17), and compare them to the way those columns looked before you changed their format (Figure 4-16). The effect of choosing Center format for column headings becomes even more apparent when you start filling in the form with values.

DRAWING A LINE ACROSS YOUR SPREADSHEET

Suppose you wanted to make row 7 a row of dashes. Move your cursor to cell A7 and try to type a string of dash characters. *AppleWorks* lets you type in one dash, but no more. When you typed the first dash, *AppleWorks* thought you were typing a negative *value*. And only one negative sign is allowed in a value cell.

FIGURE 4-17 Change the column headings' alignment to centered

```
File: Expense Form               REVIEW/ADD/CHANGE               Escape: Main Menu
========H========I========J========K========L========M========N========O====
  1|
  2|
  3|Week Ending:
  4|
  5|                      Weekly    Daily    Daily
  6|   Sat       Sun       Total   Average  Maximum
  7|
  8|
  9|
 10|
 11|
 12|
 13|
 14|
 15|
 16|
 17|
 18|
------------------------------------------------------------------------------
H1
Type entry or use ⌘ commands                                    ⌘-? for Help
```

Press the ESC key to erase the dash and the value designation for cell A7. (*Note:* If you try to use the DELETE key, you can erase the dash, but *AppleWorks* still thinks that A7 is a value cell. If you use the ESC key to cancel what you've been typing in a cell, the cell reverts to its former contents, if any.)

Now, before you type the first dash, type the quote symbol to tell *AppleWorks* that this cell is going to contain a label. Then type nine dashes and press RETURN.

You could do this for all the cells from A7 to L7, but there's an easier way. That's right, the Copy command. With your cursor still in cell A7, type ⌘**C**. Type **W** to select **Within worksheet**. Press the RETURN key to indicate that the only cell you want to copy is the one that the cursor is on, A7. (*Note:* The cell, or cells, you want to copy *from* are called the *Source*. The cell, or cells, you want to copy *to* are called the *Destination*.)

Press the right-arrow key once, to move the cursor to the first of the cells you want to copy to, cell B7. Press the period key, ".", to tell *AppleWorks* that you're copying cell A7 into a range of cells starting with B7. Now use your right-arrow key to move the cursor to the last cell you want to copy to, L7. This action should highlight all the cells from B7 to L7. (*Note:* If you go too far, you can use the left-arrow key to "unhighlight" one or more cells.) Once you have the correct group of cells highlighted, press RETURN. The dashed line will be drawn all the way across your spreadsheet.

For practice, do the same thing in row 16, the blank row just above Daily Total, but this time use the equals sign character, "=" (Figure 4-18). (*Note:* Don't forget to begin with a quote symbol to tell *AppleWorks* you're typing a label.)

FIGURE 4-18 Use the Copy command to draw lines

```
File: Expense Form              REVIEW/ADD/CHANGE              Escape: Main Menu
========A========B========C========D========E========F========G========H=======
  1|                            HOT & COLD INC.: Expense Report
  2|
  3|Name:                                                            Week Ending:
  4|
  5|
  6|                     Mon       Tue       Wed       Thu       Fri       Sat
  7|---------------------------------------------------------------------------
  8|Airfare
  9|Taxi or Limo
 10|Car Rental
 11|Lodging
 12|Breakfast
 13|Lunch
 14|Dinner
 15|Phone
 16|===========================================================================
 17|Daily Total
 18|
--------------------------------------------------------------------------------
A16: (Label) Repeated-=

Type entry or use ⌘ commands                                       ⌘-? for Help
```

INDICATING A RANGE OF CELLS

Many spreadsheet commands require you to indicate a range of cells for the particular command to act on. The process for indicating a cell range is always the same. You move your cursor to the first cell in the range, press the period key, move the cursor to the last cell in the range, and press RETURN.

PROTECTING THE CONTENTS OF CELLS

You can prevent accidental changes in your cells by "protecting" them. There are three types of Protection: **Labels Only**, **Values Only**, and **Nothing**. Labels Only protection means that the only data you can type in is label data. In other words, you could replace a label in a Labels Only protected cell with another label, but not with a value. Values Only protection limits cell entries to Value data only. Nothing protection means that you cannot alter the contents of protected cells at all. (*Note:* The fourth option, **Anything**, is used to cancel protection.)

At this point, you can protect the entire spreadsheet from changes. Don't worry about all the blank cells; if a cell is empty, setting Protection has no effect on it. Move your cursor to cell A1 and type **L**, the Layout command. Type **R** for Rows, and use the down-arrow key to highlight all the rows from 1 to 17. Press RETURN. Type **P** for Protection, and then **N** to allow Nothing to be typed into any nonempty cell.

While it may not look as if anything has happened, try typing something into any cell that already has a label in it. Your Apple will just beep at you. Of course, you can type anything you want, Labels or Values, into empty cells; they are unaffected by the Protection feature.

If you do want to change the contents of a protected cell, you can temporarily turn off all protection with the "Protection" option in the Standard Values command, V. If you select it, you can respond "Yes" or "No" to turn Protection on or off.

Hint: This might be a good time to save your spreadsheet (S) to disk if you haven't done so already.

Moving Your Cursor around Your Spreadsheet

Because spreadsheets tend to get rather large, there are several methods available to help you to move your cursor quickly to a different part of your spreadsheet.

THE ARROW KEYS

You already know that your cursor is controlled by the four arrow keys, but you can also use the OPEN-APPLE key along with the arrow keys. When you hold down the OPEN-APPLE key as you press an arrow key, your cursor will move one whole screen in the direction of the arrow.

1 Through 9

In the spreadsheet, 1 through 9 move your cursor in the vertical direction only. 1 moves it to row 1; 9 moves it to the last row in your spreadsheet. The other number keys move the cursor a proportional amount through the spreadsheet.

THE FIND COMMAND

The Find command, F, lets you locate a particular cell by giving either its coordinates or its Label contents. (Find can't be used to locate a cell by its Value.)

To move your cursor to location Z52, type ⌘**F**, then type **C** for Coordinates. Type the coordinates **Z52** and press RETURN. Do it again, and this time use **A1** for the coordinates of the cell you want to Find. (*Note:* You'll have to erase the old coordinates, Z52, before you can type A1. You can type CONTROL-Y to do this.)

The second option of the Find command allows you to find a cell by specifying its Label. *AppleWorks* begins searching your spreadsheet from the current position of your cursor. So, if you want to search the whole spreadsheet for a particular Label, you have to move your cursor to cell A1 before you type ⌘F. Let's try it.

With your cursor in cell A1, type ⌘ **F** and then **T** for Text. For comparison data, type **max**. *AppleWorks* moves your cursor to cell L6. Notice that the comparison is *not* case dependent. That is, *AppleWorks* doesn't pay attention to whether the letters are capitalized. The Repeat last option lets you find the same string of characters elsewhere in your spreadsheet.

Setting Up the Calculations

Up to this point, you have been concerned with the appearance of your spreadsheet. Now you need to type in the formulas or calculations that will make your spreadsheet something more than just a report generator.

SPREADSHEET FUNCTIONS

Let's tell your spreadsheet how to compute the daily total of all the expenses (Airfare, Car Rental, etc.) for Monday. You want this value to appear in cell C17, so move your cursor there. Cell C17's value is the sum of cells C8+C9+C10+C11+C12+C13+C14+C15. And you could enter that sum as the calculation for cell C17. But there is a much easier way to represent the sum of a group of cells.

AppleWorks includes 17 special functions in the spreadsheet. Table 4-2 lists these functions along with brief descriptions and examples. With the exception of two of the functions, @NA and @ERROR, all functions have the same basic format. They all begin with a "@" symbol, followed by their name (in capital or small letters). Then, depending on the function, there are one or more values or cell coordinates (or ranges of cell coordinates) enclosed in parentheses. These values (or cell coordinates that refer to values) are called *arguments*. Since all functions are numerical (except for @NA and @ERROR), all arguments must be values or refer to values. Currently, there are no functions that work with labels.

TABLE 4-2 Spreadsheet functions

Function	Argument	Example	Description/Result
@ABS	1 formula or cell	@ABS(G15-H19)	Absolute value of the argument.
@AND	2 comparisons	@AND(A1=A2, B1>B2)	Returns a value of true or false. Evaluates true only if both comparisons are true.
@AVG	cells or ranges of cells	@AVG(C6,C8,C9) @AVG(D17...D24)	Arithmetic average of cells in argument. Label and blank cells are not counted.
@CHOOSE	3 or more cells, or 1 cell and a range of cells	@CHOOSE(D3,G6 ...G9)	If D3=1, evaluates to G6. If D3=2, evaluates to G7. If D3=3, evaluates to G8. If D3=4, evaluates to G9.
@COUNT	cells or ranges of cells	@COUNT(B7...B15)	The number of Value cells in the argument.
@ERROR	none	@ERROR	Causes the word "ERROR" to appear in the cell and in all other cells that refer to it.
@IF	1 logical comparison and 2 formulas or cells	@IF(H9<Q6,C4,C7)	If H9 *is* less than Q6, evaluates to C4. If H9 *is* *not* less than Q6, evaluates to C7.
@INT	1 formula or cell	@INT(C7)	Throws away anything after the decimal point.
@LOOKUP	1 cell or formula and 1 range of cells	@LOOKUP(G5,K3 ...K8)	K3 to K8 form a Lookup table for values in L3 through L8. The values in K3 to K8 *must* be in ascending order. If the value in G5 lies between K6 and K7, this function would return the value in L6.
@MAX	2 or more cells	@MAX(M4...M23)	Maximum value in argument.

TABLE 4-2 Spreadsheet functions (continued)

Function	Argument	Example	Description/Result
@MIN	2 or more cells	@MIN(J12...Q12)	Minimum value in argument.
@OR	2 comparisons	@OR(A1=A2, B1>B2)	Returns a value of true or false. Evaluates true if either comparison is true.
@NA	none	@NA	Causes the letters "NA" to appear in the cell and all other cells that refer to it.
@NPV	1 formula and 1 range of cells	@NPV(K6,P2...W2)	Uses the value in K6 as a discount rate to compute Net Present Value for the range of cells, P2...W2.
@ROUND	2 values or cells	@ROUND(C5,D8)	Rounds the value in C5 to the number of decimal places specified in D8.
@SQRT	1 formula or cell	@SQRT(V5*S17)	Computes the square root of the argument.
@SUM	2 or more cells	@SUM(D4...D15, D17)	Computes the sum of all cells in the argument, D4 through D15 plus D17.

Some functions such as @SQRT and @ABS take only one argument. @SQRT computes the square root of the value contained in its parentheses, while @ABS displays the absolute value of the single argument in its parentheses. Other functions take more than one argument, and some functions are designed to operate on a range of cells as an argument.

THE @SUM FUNCTION

To compute the sum of a group of cells in the same row or column, the function you want is the last one on the list, @SUM. With your cursor in cell C17, type the 5 characters, **@SUM(**. You have typed the name of the function and have opened the parentheses. You now have to indicate which cells you want the @SUM function to add. This range can be entered in one of two ways: by typing in the coordinates of the first and last cells in the range (separated by three periods), or by using the cursor to point at the first and last cells in the range. Let's use the second method.

Move your cursor up to cell C8 and press the period (".") key. This action defines cell C8 as the first of a range of cells. Look at the next-to-the-last line on your screen and compare it with Figure 4-19. Press the down-arrow key seven times, so that the range of cells from C8 to C15 is highlighted, and press RETURN. Close the parentheses by typing a ")" and press RETURN again (Figure 4-20).

A zero appears in cell C17 because none of the cells from C8 to C15 have values. So let's type in a few values and watch what happens to cell C17. Before you start typing in values, change the Standard Value format to display numbers with two decimal places. Type ⌘**V**, then **V** for Value format, **F** for Fixed number of decimal places, and **2** (and RETURN) for the number of decimal places to be displayed. (Note the change in cell C17.)

Figure 4-21 shows sample data entered for Monday. Copy it into your spreadsheet and watch the effect each entry has on the Daily Total in C17.

Now fill in the rest of the entries for Tuesday, Wednesday, Thursday, and Friday from Figure 4-22. Ignore the Daily Totals for these days. I'll show you an easy way to enter those calculations in a moment.

FIGURE 4-19 The @SUM function

```
File: Expense Form                 REVIEW/ADD/CHANGE            Escape: Erase entry
========A========B========C========D========E========F========G========H====
   1|                               HOT & COLD INC.: Expense Report
   2|
   3|Name:                                                           Week Endi
   4|
   5|
   6|               Mon        Tue        Wed        Thu        Fri        Sat
   7|--------------------------------------------------------------------------
   8|Airfare
   9|Taxi or Limo
  10|Car Rental
  11|Lodging
  12|Breakfast
  13|Lunch
  14|Dinner
  15|Phone
  16|==========================================================================
  17|Daily Total
  18|
--------------------------------------------------------------------------------
C8
Value: @SUM(C8...
Use cursor moves to highlight Block, then press Return                53K Avail.
```

FIGURE 4-20 The sum is 0 because cells C8...C15 are blank

```
File: Expense Form                REVIEW/ADD/CHANGE              Escape: Main Menu
========A========B========C========D========E========F========G========H====
  1|                             HOT & COLD INC.: Expense Report
  2|
  3|Name:                                                         Week Endi
  4|
  5|
  6|                    Mon       Tue       Wed       Thu       Fri       Sat
  7|-------------------------------------------------------------------------
  8|Airfare
  9|Taxi or Limo
 10|Car Rental
 11|Lodging
 12|Breakfast
 13|Lunch
 14|Dinner
 15|Phone
 16|=========================================================================
 17|Daily Total            0
 18|
------------------------------------------------------------------------------
C17: (Value) @SUM(C8...C15)

Type entry or use ⌘ commands                                      ⌘-? for Help
```

FIGURE 4-21 Enter Monday's values

```
File: Expense Form                REVIEW/ADD/CHANGE              Escape: Main Menu
========A========B========C========D========E========F========G========H====
  1|                             HOT & COLD INC.: Expense Report
  2|
  3|Name:                                                         Week Endi
  4|
  5|
  6|                    Mon       Tue       Wed       Thu       Fri       Sat
  7|-------------------------------------------------------------------------
  8|Airfare           275.00
  9|Taxi or Limo       20.00
 10|Car Rental
 11|Lodging            85.30
 12|Breakfast
 13|Lunch               5.25
 14|Dinner             21.50
 15|Phone               6.32
 16|=========================================================================
 17|Daily Total       413.37
 18|
------------------------------------------------------------------------------
C15: (Value) 6.32

Type entry or use ⌘ commands                                      ⌘-? for Help
```

COPYING FORMULAS OR CALCULATIONS

The formula you want for cell D17 is almost the same as the one in C17. The only difference is that the range of cells for D17's @SUM function is from D8 to D15 instead of from C8 to C15.

AppleWorks lets you copy calculations with the same command you used for copying labels, the Copy command, ⌘C. You're going to copy

FIGURE 4-22 Enter values for the rest of the week

```
File: Expense Form              REVIEW/ADD/CHANGE              Escape: Main Menu
========A========B========C========D========E========F========G========H====
  1|                            HOT & COLD INC.: Expense Report
  2|
  3|Name:                                                         Week Endi
  4|
  5|
  6|                       Mon      Tue      Wed      Thu      Fri      Sat
  7|----------------------------------------------------------------------
  8|Airfare             275.00                              275.00
  9|Taxi or Limo         20.00                               20.00
 10|Car Rental                                             135.83
 11|Lodging             85.30    85.30    85.30    85.30
 12|Breakfast                     3.50     3.80     3.35     4.20
 13|Lunch                5.25    10.50     8.25     7.40     8.50
 14|Dinner              21.50    19.35    12.90    35.85
 15|Phone                6.32    15.72    14.95    11.53     9.20
 16|======================================================================
 17|Daily Total        413.37
 18|
-----------------------------------------------------------------------------
G15: (Value) 9.2

Type entry or use  commands                                     -? for Help
```

the formula from cell C17 into cells D17 through J17. This will give you totals for all seven days of the week and a grand total (in J17).

Place your cursor in cell C17 and type **C**. Press **W** to select **Within worksheet**. Press the RETURN key to indicate that C17 is the only "source" cell. Now you want to highlight the range of "destination" cells you want to copy C17 into. Move your cursor to D17, press the period key, then move the cursor to cell J17; this highlights all the cells from D17 to J17. Press RETURN.

After you press RETURN, you'll see the formula for cell C17 in the next-to-the-last line on your screen. C8 is highlighted, and on the bottom line of the screen *AppleWorks* is asking whether this cell's coordinates should be constant ("No change") or "Relative."

This is a very important question, and you'll see it every time you copy formulas from one cell to another. *AppleWorks* wants to know whether the coordinates of the first cell in @SUM's range should change as the formula moves to cell D17, E17, and so forth, or if the C8 coordinates should remain the same. Depending on the individual situation, you'll select one option or the other. In this case, you want the coordinates of the first (and the last) cell in the range to change relative to the cell that holds the formula. In other words, you want the formula in cell D17 to have the range D8 to D15, the formula in cell E17 to have the range E8 to E15, and so on. Therefore, press the "R" key to indicate Relative change (don't press RETURN).

The coordinates of the last cell in the range, C15, are then highlighted, and again you are asked if the coordinates of this cell should change or stay the same. Again press the "R" key for Relative. The formula in cell C17 is immediately copied into cells D17 through J17 (Figure 4-23).

FIGURE 4-23 Copying formulas

```
File: Expense Form              REVIEW/ADD/CHANGE              Escape: Main Menu
========A========B========C========D========E========F========G========H====
  1|                            HOT & COLD INC.: Expense Report
  2|
  3|Name:                                                          Week Endi
  4|
  5|
  6|                     Mon        Tue        Wed        Thu        Fri        Sat
  7|---------------------------------------------------------------------------
  8|Airfare             275.00                                     275.00
  9|Taxi or Limo         20.00                                      20.00
 10|Car Rental                                                    135.83
 11|Lodging              85.30      85.30      85.30      85.30
 12|Breakfast                        3.50       3.80       3.35       4.20
 13|Lunch                 5.25      10.50       8.25       7.40       8.50
 14|Dinner               21.50      19.35      12.90      35.85
 15|Phone                 6.32      15.72      14.95      11.53       9.20
 16|===========================================================================
 17|Daily Total         413.37     134.37     125.20     143.43     452.73      0.00
 18|
-----------------------------------------------------------------------------
C17: (Value) @SUM(C8...C15)

Type entry or use ⌘ commands                                        ⌘-? for Help
```

Let's practice this procedure one more time. Move your cursor to cell J8 and define J8's value as the sum of cells C8 through I8. J8's formula should be **@SUM(C8...I8)**. This time, just type the 13 characters that comprise the formula. (See Figure 4-24.)

Now let's copy the formula from cell J8 into cells J9 through J15. Leave your cursor in cell J8, type ⌘**C**, press the **W** key, then press the RETURN key. Move the cursor one cell down to J9, press the period key, move the cursor to cell J15, and press RETURN. Again, you want the cell coordinates in J8's formula to change Relative, so press the "R" key twice and compare your spreadsheet with Figure 4-25.

THE @AVG FUNCTION

Column K was set up to show the average daily expense for each category (Airfare, etc.). There are two ways of calculating the average daily expense. One way is to add up all the Airfare expenses, for example, and then divide by a constant number of days, either 5 or 7.

FIGURE 4-24 Use the @SUM function for weekly totals

```
File: Expense Form              REVIEW/ADD/CHANGE              Escape: Main Menu
========C========D========E========F========G========H========I========J====
  1|        HOT & COLD INC.: Expense Report
  2|
  3|                                              Week Ending:
  4|
  5|                                                                  Weekly
  6|   Mon      Tue      Wed      Thu      Fri      Sat      Sun     Total
  7|--------------------------------------------------------------------------
  8|  275.00                               275.00                      550.00
  9|   20.00                                20.00
 10|                                       135.83
 11|   85.30    85.30    85.30    85.30
 12|             3.50     3.80     3.35     4.20
 13|    5.25    10.50     8.25     7.40     8.50
 14|   21.50    19.35    12.90    35.85
 15|    6.32    15.72    14.95    11.53     9.20
 16|==========================================================================
 17|  413.37   134.37   125.20   143.43   452.73     0.00     0.00    550.00
 18|
--------------------------------------------------------------------------------
J8: (Value) @SUM(C8...I8)

Type entry or use  commands                                      -? for Help
```

FIGURE 4-25 Copy the Weekly Total formula into cells J9...J15

```
File: Expense Form              REVIEW/ADD/CHANGE              Escape: Main Menu
========C========D========E========F========G========H========I========J====
  1|        HOT & COLD INC.: Expense Report
  2|
  3|                                              Week Ending:
  4|
  5|                                                                  Weekly
  6|   Mon      Tue      Wed      Thu      Fri      Sat      Sun     Total
  7|--------------------------------------------------------------------------
  8|  275.00                               275.00                      550.00
  9|   20.00                                20.00                       40.00
 10|                                       135.83                      135.83
 11|   85.30    85.30    85.30    85.30                                341.20
 12|             3.50     3.80     3.35     4.20                        14.85
 13|    5.25    10.50     8.25     7.40     8.50                        39.90
 14|   21.50    19.35    12.90    35.85                                 89.60
 15|    6.32    15.72    14.95    11.53     9.20                        57.72
 16|==========================================================================
 17|  413.37   134.37   125.20   143.43   452.73     0.00     0.00   1269.10
 18|
--------------------------------------------------------------------------------
J8: (Value) @SUM(C8...I8)

Type entry or use  commands                                      -? for Help
```

The other way is to count only those days for which there was an expense in a particular category. So there would be only 2 days during which expenses were made for Airfare, 4 days for Lodging, 5 days for Lunch, etc.

The @AVG function performs this second type of calculation automatically. It adds up all the values in the declared range (or ranges) and divides by the number of cells that actually hold values.

To compute the average daily expense for each category, move your cursor to cell K8 (Daily Average for Airfare) and type in the formula, **@AVG(C8...I8)**. After you press RETURN, cell K8 should display a value of 275.00. This makes sense because the total Airfare was 550.00 and was spent over two days, Monday and Friday. *Note:* If you want the total averaged over 5 days, type zeros in cells D8, E8, and F8.

Now copy the formula from cell K8 into cells K9 through K15 (Figure 4-26). Again, this is a Relative copy.

FIGURE 4-26 The @AVG function

```
File: Expense Form              REVIEW/ADD/CHANGE                Escape: Main Menu
========D========E========F========G========H========I========J========K====
  1|HOT & COLD INC.: Expense Report
  2|
  3|                                        Week Ending:
  4|
  5|                                                          Weekly    Daily
  6|   Tue      Wed       Thu       Fri       Sat       Sun     Total   Average
  7|--------------------------------------------------------------------------
  8|                               275.00                      550.00   275.00
  9|                                20.00                       40.00    20.00
 10|                               135.83                      135.83   135.83
 11|   85.30     85.30     85.30                               341.20    85.30
 12|    3.50      3.80      3.35     4.20                       14.85     3.71
 13|   10.50      8.25      7.40     8.50                       39.90     7.98
 14|   19.35     12.90     35.85                                89.60    22.40
 15|   15.72     14.95     11.53     9.20                       57.72    11.54
 16|==========================================================================
 17|  134.37    125.20    143.43   452.73      0.00      0.00  1269.10
 18|
------------------------------------------------------------------------------
K8: (Value) @AVG(C8...I8)

Type entry or use ⌘ commands                                        ⌘-? for Help
```

THE @MAX FUNCTION

The last feature you wanted to include in your expense report form was a column that would show the maximum expense during the week for each category. In other words, it would show the greatest amount spent for dinner, the highest daily phone bill, and so forth.

The @MAX function performs this job neatly. You just specify the range of values to examine and @MAX displays the largest value in the range. Let's try it.

Move your cursor to cell L8 and type the formula **@MAX(C8...I8)**. Now, do a Relative copy of the formula in cell L8 into cells L9 through L15 and compare your spreadsheet with Figure 4-27.

If you look at row 14, the Dinner category, you can see at a glance that while the average dinner expense was 22.40, the maximum was 35.85. If you were the kind of boss who questions expense items, you might want to inquire about that dinner expense.

FIGURE 4-27 The @MAX function

```
File: Expense Form              REVIEW/ADD/CHANGE                Escape: Main Menu
========E========F========G========H========I========J========K========L====
  1|D INC.: Expense Report
  2|
  3|                              Week Ending:
  4|
  5|                                                  Weekly    Daily    Daily
  6|   Wed      Thu      Fri      Sat      Sun      Total   Average  Maximum
  7|-----------------------------------------------------------------------
  8|                    275.00                      550.00   275.00   275.00
  9|                     20.00                       40.00    20.00    20.00
 10|                    135.83                      135.83   135.83   135.83
 11|   85.30    85.30                               341.20    85.30    85.30
 12|    3.80     3.35     4.20                       14.85     3.71     4.20
 13|    8.25     7.40     8.50                       39.90     7.98    10.50
 14|   12.90    35.85                                89.60    22.40    35.85
 15|   14.95    11.53     9.20                       57.72    11.54    15.72
 16|=======================================================================
 17|  125.20   143.43   452.73     0.00     0.00  1269.10
 18|
--------------------------------------------------------------------------------
L8: (Value) @MAX(C8...I8)

Type entry or use  commands                                     -? for Help
```

By the way, the @MIN function works almost exactly like @MAX. @MIN displays the *lowest* value in a range. Blank cells and label cells that might be in the range are ignored.

Customizing the Display

You're going to print your spreadsheet in a moment, but first let's try to improve its appearance. Let's start by increasing the column width of the last three columns, J, K, and L. You adjusted the column width of a single column in the first spreadsheet example. Here, let's adjust all three columns at once.

Place your cursor anywhere in column J, and type **L**, the Layout command. Type **C** for Columns and column J will be highlighted. Before you press the RETURN key, hit the right-arrow key twice so that columns J, K, and L are all highlighted. Now press RETURN and then type **C** for Column Width. Hold down the OPEN-APPLE key and press the right-arrow key three times. This action increases the column width of each of the highlighted columns by three spaces. Press RETURN to indicate that you're through adjusting the column width.

Now let's change the value format to display all the values in those same columns in Dollars format. With your cursor still in column J, type **L**, **C** for Columns, press the right-arrow key twice, and press RETURN.

Again, columns J, K, and L should be highlighted. From the choice of Layout options select Value Format by pressing the **V** key. Type **D** for Dollars format and choose two decimal places. After you press RETURN, compare columns J, K, and L on your spreadsheet with those in Figure 4-28.

FIGURE 4-28 Change the Value format in columns J, K, and L to Dollars

```
File: Expense Form               REVIEW/ADD/CHANGE                Escape: Main Menu
========F========G========H========I=========J===========K===========L=========
  1|xpense Report
  2|
  3|                 Week Ending:
  4|
  5|                                          Weekly      Daily       Daily
  6|   Thu      Fri      Sat      Sun        Total      Average     Maximum
  7|-----------------------------------------------------------------------------
  8|           275.00                        $550.00     $275.00     $275.00
  9|            20.00                         $40.00      $20.00      $20.00
 10|           135.83                        $135.83     $135.83     $135.83
 11|   85.30                                 $341.20      $85.30      $85.30
 12|    3.35     4.20                         $14.85       $3.71       $4.20
 13|    7.40     8.50                         $39.90       $7.98      $10.50
 14|   35.85                                  $89.60      $22.40      $35.85
 15|   11.53     9.20                         $57.72      $11.54      $15.72
 16|=============================================================================
 17|  143.43   452.73     0.00      0.00   $1,269.10
 18|
--------------------------------------------------------------------------
J8: (Value, Layout-D2) @SUM(C8...I8)

Type entry or use  commands                                        -? for Help
```

Printing the Spreadsheet

Save your spreadsheet, and then type **P**, the Print command, and then **A** to select All of your spreadsheet to be printed. Before you select your printer, look at the information in the first two lines of the Print screen (Figure 4-29). These two lines tell you that your spreadsheet is 117 characters wide (at least mine is) and that your printer is only set to print 80 characters per line. If you continue to print out your spreadsheet, *AppleWorks* will have to divide it into two parts, and you will have to paste them together to see the entire spreadsheet. (*Note: AppleWorks* will not split a column when it divides your spreadsheet into sections for printing.)

Let's try to change the number of characters per line that your printer will print, so that you can print the entire spreadsheet on one page. ESC out of the Print command and type **O** to enter Printer Options (Figure 4-13).

FIGURE 4-29 Your spreadsheet won't fit on one page

```
File: Expense Form                    PRINT              Escape: Review/Add/Change
==================================================================================

                    The information that you identified
                    is 117 characters wide.

                    The Printer Options values allow
                    80 characters per line


                    Where do you want to print the report?

                    1.  My Printer
                    2.  The clipboard (for the Word Procesor)
                    3.  A text (ASCII) file on disk
                    4.  A DIF (TM) file on disk



----------------------------------------------------------------------------------

Type number, or use arrows, then press Return                          53K Avail.
```

As I mentioned earlier, of the four printer options that affect the number of characters per line, only **Characters per Inch** (CI) can be used to *increase* the characters per line. (*Note:* If you have a wide-carriage printer, you can change **Platen Width** [PW] to 13.2 inches.) Since most printers support a type size of 17 characters per inch, let's change the CI option to 17. Type **CI**, press RETURN, type **17**, and press RETURN again. Notice that the characters per line indicator increased to 136.

As long as you're in Printer Options, why don't you change the line spacing to Double Spaced? Type **DS**, and press RETURN. Finally, let's eliminate the Report Header from your printed report. Type **PH**, and press RETURN.

ESC back to Review/Add/Change, type **P**, **A**, and look again at the two information lines on the Print screen. Your spreadsheet is still 117 characters wide, but now your printer will print 136 characters per line. Select your printer from the list by typing its number and pressing RETURN. Then press RETURN again to accept the default choice of one copy to be printed (Figure 4-30).

Editing Your Spreadsheet

INSERTING AND DELETING ROWS AND COLUMNS

You can add or remove one or more rows or columns in your spreadsheet. Suppose you wanted to insert a blank row between the row of equal

FIGURE 4-30 The printed spreadsheet

HOT & COLD INC.: Expense Report

Name: Week Ending:

	Mon	Tue	Wed	Thu	Fri	Sat	Sun	Weekly Total	Daily Average	Daily Maximum
Airfare	275.00				275.00			$550.00	$275.00	$275.00
Taxi or Limo	20.00				20.00			$40.00	$20.00	$20.00
Car Rental					135.83			$135.83	$135.83	$135.83
Lodging	85.30	85.30	85.30	85.30				$341.20	$85.30	$85.30
Breakfast		3.50	3.80	3.35	4.20			$14.85	$3.71	$4.20
Lunch	5.25	10.50	8.25	7.40	8.50			$39.90	$7.98	$10.50
Dinner	21.50	19.35	12.90	35.85				$89.60	$22.40	$35.85
Phone	6.32	15.72	14.95	11.53	9.20			$57.72	$11.54	$15.72
Daily Total	413.37	134.37	125.20	143.43	452.73	0.00	0.00	$1,269.10		

signs (row 16) and the Daily Total row. You want this new blank row to be row 17, so move your cursor to any cell on the current row 17 (cell A17, for example) and type ⌘**I**, the Insert command. Press **R** to select Rows to insert. You will probably see a warning message advising you that you are about to clear or remove protected cells. Actually, you're going to move a protected row, row 17, down to row 18. Just ignore the message and press the "Y" key to reassure *AppleWorks* that you *really* want to insert the row. You are now asked how many rows (a maximum of nine) you wish to insert. Type **1** and press RETURN.

When you insert columns or rows, *AppleWorks* automatically changes the cell coordinates in your formulas to reflect the shifting of all the rows *below* the row (or all the columns to the *right* of the column) that you have inserted.

Deleting a row or a column is just as easy. Let's delete the blank row you've just inserted. Put your cursor on a cell in row 17, the blank row, and type⌘ **D**, the Delete command. Type **R** for Rows, and row 17 will be highlighted. (*Note:* If you wanted to delete more than one row, you could use the up- or down-arrow key to highlight additional rows.) Press the RETURN key and the highlighted row or rows are removed.

Columns are inserted or deleted using the same commands, ⌘I or ⌘D, but responding **C** for Columns instead of **R** for Rows.

BLANKING CELLS

AppleWorks allows you to "empty" the contents of cells, either one at a time or in groups. The Blank command,⌘ B, has four options.

The first option, **Entry**, erases the contents of the cell your cursor was on when you issued the Blank command. The second option, **Rows**, will erase the contents of all the cells in the row your cursor is on. You can use the up- or down-arrow key to select more than one row to be blanked. Selected rows appear highlighted before the RETURN key is pressed. The third option, **Columns**, blanks all of the cells in the column your cursor is in. As with the **Row** option, you can use arrow keys, left and right this time, to select more than one column to be Blanked. Option four is the **Block** option. It allows you to select part of a row or column, or parts of adjacent rows or columns. With this option, all four arrow keys may be used to highlight the group of cells you wish to blank.

With all four options, if you attempt to blank a protected cell, *AppleWorks* will warn you and ask that you verify your intention. If you decide not to blank any cells, just press ESC.

EDITING THE CONTENTS OF A SINGLE CELL

Sometimes you want to make a small change in a cell containing a long formula. Rather than type the whole formula in again, you can use the Editing Mode command, Ⓒ U. To edit the contents of a cell, place your cursor on the cell and type Ⓒ**U**. The contents of the cell appear on the next-to-the-bottom line of your screen. You can then use either the insert cursor or the overstrike cursor to make changes to the entry. You can also use the DELETE key. Pressing RETURN makes the changes permanent.

If you press ESC, you'll get out of Editing Mode and leave the cell's contents unchanged.

Editing Mode works just as well on Protected cells as it does on unprotected ones. In other words, protecting a cell does not prevent it from being changed with the Editing Mode command.

Looking at Two Parts of Your Spreadsheet at Once

There are two ways to see two separate areas of your spreadsheet on your screen at the same time: by "fixing" the titles and by "windowing."

FIXED TITLES

Your Expense Report Form is too big for you to see all of it on your screen. As you scroll your cursor to the right to look at the Weekly

Totals column, for example, the category titles in columns A and B are pushed off the screen at the left.

AppleWorks provides a way to "fix" the titles in columns A and B so that they remain on the screen as you scroll to the right. To demonstrate this feature, move your cursor to column A, so that columns A and B are visible on your screen. Then move your cursor to a cell in column C (the column to the right of the last column you want to fix). Type the Titles command, ⌘**T**. You can "fix" the top row (or rows), the leftmost column (or columns), or both. Type **L** for Left Side. Now move your cursor over to column L and watch what happens to columns A and B (Figure 4-31).

FIGURE 4-31 Fixing columns A and B

```
File: Expense Form              REVIEW/ADD/CHANGE                Escape: Main Menu
========A========B========H========I=========J===========K===========L======
  1|
  2|
  3|Name:              Week Ending:
  4|
  5|                                        Weekly       Daily        Daily
  6|                     Sat       Sun      Total       Average      Maximum
  7|----------------------------------------------------------------------------
  8|Airfare                                 $550.00      $275.00      $275.00
  9|Taxi or Limo                             $40.00       $20.00       $20.00
 10|Car Rental                              $135.83      $135.83      $135.83
 11|Lodging                                 $341.20       $85.30       $85.30
 12|Breakfast                                $14.85        $3.71        $4.20
 13|Lunch                                    $39.90        $7.98       $10.50
 14|Dinner                                   $89.60       $22.40       $35.85
 15|Phone                                    $57.72       $11.54       $15.72
 16|===========================================================================
 17|Daily Total           0.00      0.00  $1,269.10
 18|
-------------------------------------------------------------------------------
L17

Type entry or use ⌘ commands                                   ⌘-? for Help
```

Columns A and B remain fixed on your screen while the rest of your spreadsheet scrolls normally. To remove Fixed Titles, type ⌘**T** again, and press RETURN.

WINDOWS

The second method for displaying two different parts of your spreadsheet on the screen at the same time is called *windowing*. You can divide your screen, either horizontally or vertically, into two areas (or "windows") and display a different section of your spreadsheet in each window.

To see how this works, first make sure you have removed any Fixed Titles you might have set. Then move your cursor about halfway across the screen, and type **W**, the Windows command. Press **S** for Side by side windows, and look at your screen and Figure 4-32. Notice that your spreadsheet display area has been divided vertically. You now have two, smaller windows to view your spreadsheet, each with its own set of row numbers and column letters. Your cursor is in the right window.

Use the arrow keys to move the cursor around this window and see that the left window is unaffected by scrolling movement in the right window. When you want to switch your cursor over to the other window, type **J**, the Jump command.

If you use the down-arrow key to scroll up one of the windows, the other window doesn't follow it. But sometimes it's useful to have the two side-by-side windows synchronized so that they move up and down together. Type **W** again and you'll see two different choices: One and Synchronized. Type **S** for Synchronized and the two displays will be locked together in their vertical movements.

To Unsynchronize the two displays, type **W** and press the **U** key. And to go back to a single window, type **W** and press the **O** key.

Splitting your window Top and Bottom works much the same way. You move your cursor about halfway down the screen, type **W**, and press **T** for Top and bottom (Figure 4-33). Again, typing **J** jumps your cursor between the top and bottom windows. And the Synchronize option makes the two windows scroll *horizontally* together.

You can cancel Top and Bottom Windows in the same way as Side by Side Windows. Type **W** and press the **O** key for One Window.

FIGURE 4-32 Splitting the screen vertically into two windows

```
File: Expense Form             REVIEW/ADD/CHANGE               Escape: Main Menu
========A========B========C========D===========E========F========G====
  1|                           HOT & COL  1|D INC.: Expense Report
  2|                                      2|
  3|Name:                                 3|
  4|                                      4|
  5|                                      5|
  6|                    Mon        Tue    6|   Wed      Thu        Fri
  7|-----------------------------------   7|---------------------------
  8|Airfare          275.00               8|                     275.00
  9|Taxi or Limo      20.00               9|                      20.00
 10|Car Rental                           10|                     135.83
 11|Lodging           85.30      85.30   11|   85.30    85.30
 12|Breakfast                     3.50   12|    3.80     3.35      4.20
 13|Lunch              5.25      10.50   13|    8.25     7.40      8.50
 14|Dinner            21.50      19.35   14|   12.90    35.85
 15|Phone              6.32      15.72   15|   14.95    11.53      9.20
 16|===================================  16|===========================
 17|Daily Total       413.37     134.37  17|  125.20   143.43    452.73
 18|                                     18|
--------------------------------------------------------------------------------
E9

Type entry or use  commands                                          -? for Help
```

FIGURE 4-33 Splitting the screen horizontally

```
File: Expense Form              REVIEW/ADD/CHANGE              Escape: Main Menu
========A========B========C========D========E========F========G========H====
  1|                            HOT & COLD INC.: Expense Report
  2|
  3|Name:                                                             Week Endi
  4|
  5|
  6|                      Mon       Tue       Wed       Thu       Fri       Sat
  7|--------------------------------------------------------------------------
  8|Airfare            275.00                                  275.00
  9|Taxi or Limo        20.00                                   20.00
========A========B========C========D========E========F========G========H====
 10|Car Rental                                                 135.83
 11|Lodging             85.30     85.30     85.30     85.30
 12|Breakfast                      3.50      3.80      3.35      4.20
 13|Lunch                5.25     10.50      8.25      7.40      8.50
 14|Dinner              21.50     19.35     12.90     35.85
 15|Phone                6.32     15.72     14.95     11.53      9.20
 16|==========================================================================
 17|Daily Total        413.37    134.37    125.20    143.43    452.73      0.00
------------------------------------------------------------------------------
A10: (Label, Protect-N) Car Renta

Type entry or use ⌘ commands                                    ⌘-? for Help
```

Manual Recalculation

You probably haven't noticed, but by now your spreadsheet is large enough so that you can actually watch *AppleWorks* recalculating all the formulas every time you type a value into a cell. To demonstrate this, move your cursor to cell H8 (Airfare on Saturday) and enter a value of 100. Watch the screen closely as you press the RETURN key. Did you see at the bottom of your screen an indicator that said, **Calculating column**, followed by a changing column letter? While *AppleWorks* is performing this recalculation, you can't do anything with your spreadsheet. The larger your spreadsheet gets, the longer the recalculation will take. With an average-sized spreadsheet, this recalculation can take anywhere from 2 to 10 seconds or more. After awhile, it becomes tedious waiting for *AppleWorks* to recalculate every time you enter or change a value.

You can eliminate the wait by eliminating the automatic recalculation feature. The change from automatic to manual recalculation is one of the Standard Value options. Type ⌘**V** and press the **R** key for the Recalculate option. Type **F** for Frequency, and then **M** for Manual recalculation.

Now you can enter values into your spreadsheet as fast as you can type, without waiting for *AppleWorks* to recalculate after each entry.

When you do want a calculation of all the formulas in your spreadsheet, type **K**, the Calculate All Values command.

You can restore automatic recalculation to your spreadsheet by repeating the above process, starting with V, and typing **A** for the last keystroke instead of **M**. And you can remove the 100.00 value from cell H8 with the Blank command, B.

Arranging or Sorting Rows

The Arrange command, A, in the spreadsheet works in much the same way as it does in the Data Base. The command is used to organize a column (or part of a column) of entries. And it can arrange labels alphabetically or values numerically. *Note:* You cannot arrange the cells in a single column without affecting all the other cells in the rows.

Suppose you want the eight categories (Airfare, Car Rental, etc.) to appear in alphabetical order. (*Note:* You may want to save your spreadsheet before you try this command so that you can revert to the original version later.) You want to alphabetize rows 8 through 15 according to the label in column A. So, place your cursor in cell A8, the first of the cells you want to Arrange, and type **A**. You'll see the entire row 8 highlighted. Press the down-arrow key seven times so that rows 8 through 15 are all highlighted, then press RETURN (Figure 4-34). *AppleWorks* shows you four methods of arrangement, two for labels and two for values. Select option 1 (Figure 4-35).

Notice that not only were cells A8 through A15 arranged alphabetically, their entire rows (8 through 15) were arranged with them. When the rows were moved, *AppleWorks* automatically changed all the formulas that referred to any cell in any of the rows.

Moving Rows and Columns

The Move command, M, allows you to move either columns or rows from one place to another in your spreadsheet. Only entire rows or columns can be moved; you can't move individual cells with the Move command. (*Note:* You can copy individual cells. You just can't move them.)

Let's move rows 2 and 3 to the bottom of the spreadsheet. Place your cursor anywhere in row 2 (A2, for example), and type **M**. Type **W** to select **Within worksheet**, then type **R** to indicate Rows. Row 2 is highlighted, and if you press the down-arrow key once, row 3 will be

FIGURE 4-34 Arranging spreadsheet rows

```
File: Expense Form                    ARRANGE            Escape: Review/Add/Change
========A========B========C========D========E========F========G========H====




                          Rows 8 through 15 will be arranged
                          based on the contents of column A

                          Arrangement order:

                                1.  Labels from A to Z
                                2.  Labels from Z to A
                                3.  Values from 0 to 9
                                4.  Values from 9 to 0


------------------------------------------------------------------------------

Type number, or use arrows, then press Return                        53K Avail.
```

FIGURE 4-35 Rows 8 through 15 have been arranged

```
File: Expense Form                REVIEW/ADD/CHANGE              Escape: Main Menu
========A========B========C========D========E========F========G========H====
  1|                              HOT & COLD INC.: Expense Report
  2|
  3|Name:                                                               Week Endi
  4|
  5|
  6|                     Mon      Tue      Wed      Thu      Fri      Sat
  7|-------------------------------------------------------------------------
  8|Airfare            275.00                               275.00
  9|Breakfast                    3.50     3.80     3.35     4.20
 10|Car Rental                                              135.83
 11|Dinner              21.50    19.35    12.90    35.85
 12|Lodging             85.30    85.30    85.30    85.30
 13|Lunch                5.25    10.50     8.25     7.40     8.50
 14|Phone                6.32    15.72    14.95    11.53     9.20
 15|Taxi or Limo        20.00                                20.00
 16|=========================================================================
 17|Daily Total        393.37   134.37   125.20   143.43   432.73     0.00
 18|
-----------------------------------------------------------------------------
A8: (Label, Protect-N) Airfare

Type entry or use ⌘ commands                                    ⌘-? for Help
```

highlighted, too. Press RETURN and you will see a warning that you are about to clear or remove protected cells. This message appears because you protected your entire spreadsheet earlier. Ignore it, and type **Y** for Yes, you really want to do this.

You'll see a single cell highlighted and the instruction at the bottom of your screen to move your cursor to a new location. Press the down-arrow key and keep pressing it until you see the row number, 19, appear in the cell indicator. You are indicating where the *last* row of the rows you are moving will be placed. Press RETURN, and rows 2 and 3 will be moved to rows 17 and 18 (Figure 4-36). That's right. The moved rows were inserted just *above* row 19, the row your cursor was on when you pressed RETURN.

As with the Arrange command, *AppleWorks* automatically changes cell coordinates in formulas when you move rows or columns in your spreadsheet.

FIGURE 4-36 Moving spreadsheet rows

```
File: Expense Form              REVIEW/ADD/CHANGE                Escape: Main Menu
========A========B========C========D========E========F========G========H====
  1|                              HOT & COLD INC.: Expense Report
  2|
  3|
  4|                  Mon      Tue      Wed      Thu      Fri      Sat
  5|-----------------------------------------------------------------------
  6|Airfare          275.00                              275.00
  7|Breakfast                   3.50     3.80     3.35     4.20
  8|Car Rental                                           135.83
  9|Dinner            21.50    19.35    12.90    35.85
 10|Lodging           85.30    85.30    85.30    85.30
 11|Lunch              5.25    10.50     8.25     7.40     8.50
 12|Phone              6.32    15.72    14.95    11.53     9.20
 13|Taxi or Limo      20.00                               20.00
 14|=======================================================================
 15|Daily Total      393.37   134.37   125.20   143.43   432.73      0.00
 16|
 17|
 18|Name:                                                        Week Endi
---------------------------------------------------------------------------
A1

Type entry or use Ć commands                                 Ć-? for Help
```

Saving More Than One Version of a Spreadsheet

Just as with data base and word processor files, you may decide to make a small alteration to a spreadsheet and save it with a different filename. The Change Filename command, Ć N, lets you change the name of your spreadsheet so that when you save it onto your data disk, you won't erase the original version.

A Special Function: Net Present Value

Now that you've learned all about functions, I'd like to discuss a special financial function, Net Present Value. And I'd like to demonstrate it with the first spreadsheet example, Sales Proj.

If you've been following along from the beginning of this chapter, you have two spreadsheets on your *AppleWorks* Desktop. To see the Sales Proj. spreadsheet, type ⌘**Q**. This displays the Desktop Index, which shows you a list of all the files that are currently on your Desktop. (*Note: AppleWorks* allows up to 12 files on the Desktop.)

Sales Proj. is probably the first file in the index, so type **1** and press RETURN. (*Note:* If Sales Proj. isn't on your Desktop, ESC to the Main Menu. Choose option 1, **Add files**, and add the spreadsheet file to your Desktop.)

Because money depreciates in value over time (as a result of inflation and other factors), you might like to know how much money, in today's dollars, you would need in order to have the equivalent of your original $150,000 spread out over 12 months. The Net Present Value function, @NPV, will compute this for you. The function requires two arguments, a discount rate and a range of values. The general format is: @NPV(discount rate,range). (*Note:* If your value in cell D3 isn't $150,000, change it back.)

Move your cursor to cell E10 and type, **Net Present Value**. (The label will extend into cell F10.) Let's assume that money depreciates at a rate of .5 percent, .005, per month. Place your cursor in cell G10, type **@NPV(.005,C6...C17)**, and press RETURN. The @NPV function tells you that you would need only $145,013, in today's money, to equal $150,000 spread over 12 months (Figure 4-37).

FIGURE 4-37 The @NPV function

```
File: Sales Proj.                REVIEW/ADD/CHANGE              Escape: Main Menu
========A========B========C========D========E========F========G========H====
  1|         Hot & Cold Inc.
  2|
  3|Annual Sales Forecast =    $150,000
  4|
  5|
  6|  January Sales =  $14,250
  7| February Sales =  $12,750
  8|    March Sales =   $7,500
  9|    April Sales =   $8,250
 10|      May Sales =   $9,750          Net Present Value $145,013
 11|     June Sales =  $15,000
 12|     July Sales =  $17,250
 13|   August Sales =  $12,000
 14|September Sales =   $9,000
 15|  October Sales =  $12,750
 16| November Sales =  $15,750
 17| December Sales =  $15,750
 18|
--------------------------------------------------------------------------------
G10: (Value) @NPV(.005,C6...C17)

Type entry or use ⌘ commands                                    ⌘-? for Help
```

III. EXAMPLE 3: SALES COMMISSIONS AND BONUSES

You may not realize it, but if you have been doing all of the examples in this chapter, you have used every spreadsheet *command* at least once. In this third example, you'll use some different spreadsheet *functions*. But the real reason for this example is to give you more experience in creating a spreadsheet from scratch.

Designing Your Spreadsheet

You should ask yourself three questions before you type a single character into your spreadsheet:

1. What answers do I want from this spreadsheet?
2. What information do I have that will help me get the answers I want?
3. How would I go about calculating the answers I want from the information I have, if I *didn't* have a spreadsheet?

If you take the time to answer these three questions, you'll find that designing your spreadsheet is much easier. Let's try to answer these questions for the following Sales Commissions and Bonuses example.

Suppose you had four salespersons working for your company, Hot & Cold Inc. Suppose you paid them each $1,000 per month plus commissions on their sales. As an incentive to your sales force, you have set up a sliding scale of commissions. If a salesperson sells up to $5,000 of your products in one month, he or she receives a commission of 10 percent of the sales. For sales between $5,000 and $10,000, the commission rises to 12.5 percent. If sales are over $10,000 in one month, the commission will be 15 percent.

To further motivate your salespersons, you award a monthly bonus of $100 to the one who has sold the most during the month.

Answer to Question 1: You want your spreadsheet to calculate the total monthly wages (salary, commission, and bonus) for your sales staff.

Answer to Question 2: The information you have is the total monthly sales values for each salesperson. You also know the commission schedule and how bonuses are paid.

Answer to Question 3: Each salesperson's monthly wages are computed by multiplying the appropriate commission rate (which depends on how much was sold that month) times the total sales value. This is then added to the salary ($1,000). If total sales are the highest among the four salespersons, $100 is added to the wages.

Laying Out the Spreadsheet

The layout of any spreadsheet is largely a matter of personal preference. One approach is to dedicate individual rows to each salesperson, with columns labeled for the names, monthly sales, salaries, commissions, bonuses, and gross wages. Figure 4-38 shows this layout.

As you can see, I've used the Layout command, ⌘L, to change some of the column widths. Column A was expanded to 18 characters, and columns G and K were widened to 13 characters. Columns B, D, F, and H were reduced to a width of 1 character. The character in columns B, D, F, and H is a "|" symbol. These vertical lines improve the readability of the spreadsheet. Column J is 2 characters wide, and those 2 characters are "||".

All the labels in rows 3 and 4 have been centered with the Layout command. That is, their Label format has been changed to Centered.

FIGURE 4-38 Labels for the Wages spreadsheet

```
File: Wages                     REVIEW/ADD/CHANGE                Escape: Main Menu
============A=========B====C====D====E====F======G======H===I===J=======K======
  1|
  2|
  3|                  | Monthly | Monthly |   Monthly    | Sales ||    Gross
  4|    Salesperson   |  Sales  | Salary  | Commissions  | Bonus ||    Wages
  5|------------------|---------|---------|--------------|-------||-------------
  6|                  |         |         |              |       ||
  7|                  |         |         |              |       ||
  8|                  |         |         |              |       ||
  9|                  |         |         |              |       ||
 10|                  |         |         |              |       ||
 11|                  |         |         |              |       ||
 12|                  |         |         |              |       ||
 13|                  |         |         |              |       ||
 14|                  |         |         |              |       ||
 15|                  |         |         |              |       ||
 16|                  |         |         |              |       ||
 17|                  |         |         |              |       ||
 18|                  |         |         |              |       ||
-------------------------------------------------------------------------------
A6

Type entry or use ⌘ commands                                       ⌘-? for Help
```

Filling in the Spreadsheet

You now have columns for all the data you want to enter and for all the results you want the spreadsheet to compute for you. Let's put in some typical data. Figure 4-39 shows the monthly sales values and salaries for your four salespersons.

FIGURE 4-39 Enter data for the first three columns

```
File: Wages                        REVIEW/ADD/CHANGE                   Escape: Main Menu
============A=========B====C====D====E====F======G======H===I===J=======K======
 1|
 2|
 3|                    | Monthly | Monthly |   Monthly    | Sales ||     Gross
 4|    Salesperson     |  Sales  | Salary  | Commissions  | Bonus ||     Wages
 5|--------------------|---------|---------|--------------|-------||------------
 6|Kate                |     7482|     1000|              |       ||
 7|                    |         |         |              |       ||
 8|Bob                 |     5572|     1000|              |       ||
 9|                    |         |         |              |       ||
10|John                |    11003|     1000|              |       ||
11|                    |         |         |              |       ||
12|Bruce               |     3780|     1000|              |       ||
13|                    |         |         |              |       ||
14|                    |         |         |              |       ||
15|                    |         |         |              |       ||
16|                    |         |         |              |       ||
17|                    |         |         |              |       ||
18|                    |         |         |              |       ||
--------------------------------------------------------------------------------
E12: (Value) 1000

Type entry or use ⌘ commands                                      ⌘-? for Help
```

Let's change the Standard Value for Value format to Dollars with no decimal places. Type ⌘**V** (the Standard Values command), **V** (for Value format), **D** (for Dollars), and RETURN to accept zero decimal places (Figure 4-40).

Using a Lookup Table

Now you want to compute your salespersons' commissions. You want to multiply monthly sales by either 10, 12.5, or 15 percent, depending on how much was sold.

One way of selecting the correct percentage is to use a Lookup table. A Lookup table *always* consists of two columns (or two rows) of values. In the first column (or row), you put a list of values in ascending order. In this example, the first column would contain the values 0, 5000, and 10000.

FIGURE 4-40 Change the Standard Value to Dollars

```
File: Wages                        REVIEW/ADD/CHANGE                Escape: Main Menu
============A=========B====C====D====E====F======G======H===I===J=======K======
  1|
  2|
  3|                     | Monthly | Monthly |    Monthly    | Sales ||     Gross
  4|     Salesperson     |  Sales  | Salary  | Commissions   | Bonus ||     Wages
  5|---------------------|---------|---------|---------------|-------||-------------
  6|Kate                 |  $7,482 |  $1,000 |               |       ||
  7|                     |         |         |               |       ||
  8|Bob                  |  $5,572 |  $1,000 |               |       ||
  9|                     |         |         |               |       ||
 10|John                 | $11,003 |  $1,000 |               |       ||
 11|                     |         |         |               |       ||
 12|Bruce                |  $3,780 |  $1,000 |               |       ||
 13|                     |         |         |               |       ||
 14|                     |         |         |               |       ||
 15|                     |         |         |               |       ||
 16|                     |         |         |               |       ||
 17|                     |         |         |               |       ||
 18|                     |         |         |               |       ||
----------------------------------------------------------------------------------
E12: (Value) 1000

Type entry or use ⌘ commands                                       ⌘-? for Help
```

In the second column (or row), you would enter the lookup values—in this example, the three percentages expressed as decimals: .10, .125, and .15. Figure 4-41 shows this Lookup table. (*Note:* Cells N7, N8, and N9 have had their Value format changed to Percent with one decimal place. The ⌘L command was used for this.)

The purpose of this Lookup table is to allow you to use the @LOOKUP function. This function takes one value (the search value) and compares it to the list of values in the *first* column of your Lookup table. The function returns a value from the *second* column that is selected according to the following rule. @LOOKUP searches the first column for the largest value that is less than or equal to the search value. It then returns the value from the second column which is adjacent to that value in the first column.

I know this is a bit confusing, so let's try an example to see how @LOOKUP works. Suppose your search value is $7,500. The largest value in the first column that is less than or equal to $7,500 is $5,000. Therefore, the @LOOKUP function would return a value of 12.5 percent, because this value is immediately to the right of the $5,000 value. If the search value is $4,500, @LOOKUP returns 10 percent, and so forth.

The format for the function is @LOOKUP(search value, first column list). For the Lookup table in Figure 4-41, the first column list is a range of values in cells M7. . .M9. So the formula to find the amount of commission for Kate is **@LOOKUP(C6,M7...M9)*C6**. Enter this formula in cell G6 (Figure 4-42).

FIGURE 4-41 Create a Lookup table

```
File: Wages                          REVIEW/ADD/CHANGE                Escape: Main Menu
========L========M========N========O========P========Q========R========S====
  1|
  2|
  3|         Lookup Table
  4|
  5|           Sales   Percent
  6|         ----------------
  7|               $0      10.0%
  8|           $5,000      12.5%
  9|          $10,000      15.0%
 10|
 11|
 12|
 13|
 14|
 15|
 16|
 17|
 18|
--------------------------------------------------------------------------------
N9: (Value, Layout-Pl) .15

Type entry or use ⌘ commands                                       ⌘-? for Help
```

FIGURE 4-42 The @LOOKUP function

```
File: Wages                          REVIEW/ADD/CHANGE                Escape: Main Menu
========E====F======G======H===I===J=======K==========L========M========N======
  1|
  2|
  3| Monthly |    Monthly    | Sales ||    Gross              Lookup Table
  4| Salary  | Commissions   | Bonus ||    Wages
  5|---------|---------------|-------||-------------            Sales   Percent
  6|  $1,000 |          $935 |       ||                      ----------------
  7|         |               |       ||                               $0     10.0%
  8|  $1,000 |               |       ||                           $5,000     12.5%
  9|         |               |       ||                          $10,000     15.0%
 10|  $1,000 |               |       ||
 11|         |               |       ||
 12|  $1,000 |               |       ||
 13|         |               |       ||
 14|         |               |       ||
 15|         |               |       ||
 16|         |               |       ||
 17|         |               |       ||
 18|         |               |       ||
--------------------------------------------------------------------------------
G6: (Value) @LOOKUP(C6,M7...M9)*C6

Type entry or use ⌘ commands                                       ⌘-? for Help
```

The formula for Bob's commission is almost the same. The only difference is that the sales value in cell C8 is used instead of the value in cell C6. Why don't you use the Copy command to copy the formula into cells C8, C10, and C12?

With your cursor in cell C6, type ⌘ **C**. Type **W** (to select **Within worksheet)**, then press RETURN to select only cell C6 as your copy source. Move your cursor to cell C8, press the period key ("."), move your cursor down to cell C12, and press RETURN. On the next-to-the-bottom line on your screen, C6 is highlighted. *AppleWorks* wants to know whether this cell's coordinates should remain constant (No Change) or change with the cell location (Relative). Press the "R" key once. Now M7 is highlighted. You want these and M9's coordinates to be constant so press the "N" key twice. Finally, the last set of coordinates, C6, is highlighted. Press the "R" key to make these coordinates Relative.

You'll notice that you have two extra values in cells G9 and G11. Use the Blank command, B, to erase the formulas from these cells.

Now use the Layout command, L, to change the Value format in column G to Dollars with two decimal places. With your cursor in column G, type **L, C** (for Columns), and press RETURN (to select only column G). Type **V** (for Value format), **D** (for Dollars), **2** (for the number of decimal places), and press RETURN to accept. Compare your spreadsheet with Figure 4-43.

FIGURE 4-43 Copy the @LOOKUP function into cells G8...G12

```
File: Wages                        REVIEW/ADD/CHANGE               Escape: Main Menu
============A=========B====C====D====E====F======G======H===I===J=======K======
  1|
  2|
  3|                   | Monthly  | Monthly  |    Monthly    | Sales  ||     Gross
  4|    Salesperson    |  Sales   | Salary   | Commissions   | Bonus  ||     Wages
  5|-------------------|----------|----------|---------------|--------||-------------
  6|Kate               |  $7,482  |  $1,000  |       $935.25 |        ||
  7|                   |          |          |               |        ||
  8|Bob                |  $5,572  |  $1,000  |       $696.50 |        ||
  9|                   |          |          |               |        ||
 10|John               | $11,003  |  $1,000  |     $1,650.45 |        ||
 11|                   |          |          |               |        ||
 12|Bruce              |  $3,780  |  $1,000  |       $378.00 |        ||
 13|                   |          |          |               |        ||
 14|                   |          |          |               |        ||
 15|                   |          |          |               |        ||
 16|                   |          |          |               |        ||
 17|                   |          |          |               |        ||
 18|                   |          |          |               |        ||
--------------------------------------------------------------------------------
G6: (Value, Layout-D2) @LOOKUP(C6,M7...M9)*C6

Type entry or use  commands                                        -? for Help
```

Using the @IF Command

Figuring out who gets the $100 bonus is easy. All you have to do is to look at column C. The salesperson with the highest value in column C gets the bonus. The trick is to get *AppleWorks* to make the selection for you.

You want to compare a particular value in column C with the *maximum* value of all the entries in column C. If the particular value is equal to the maximum value, then $100 should be put in the appropriate cell. If they're not equal, $0 should be put in the cell.

The @IF function is just what you need to accomplish this task. @IF has three parts. The first is a logical comparison; the second and third are values. If the comparison is *true*, the function evaluates to the first value. If the comparison is *false*, the second value is used. Here is an example. Consider the statement @IF(A1=B1,100,0). This statement says that if the value in cell A1 is equal to the value in cell B1, use the value 100. If A1 does not equal B1, use the value 0.

In addition to equals (=), there are five other logical comparisons that can be made: less than (<), greater than (>), less than or equal to (<=), greater than or equal to (>=), and not equal to (<>).

The comparison you want to make for cell I6, Kate's Sales Bonus, is between Kate's Monthly Sales, cell C6, and the maximum value of the range of cells from C6 to C12. If C6 is equal to the maximum value in the range C6 through C12, you want $100 in cell I6; otherwise, you want a value of $0. You'll recall from the previous example that the function @MAX(C6. . .C12) will select the maximum value from the range of cells. So your formula for cell I6 is **@IF(C6=MAX(C6...C12),100,0)**. Place your cursor in cell I6, type the formula, and press RETURN. Cell I6 should evaluate to $0 (Figure 4-44).

Use the same formula for cells I8, I10, and I12, but change the cell coordinates on the *left* side of the "=" symbol to C8, C10, and C12, respectively (Figure 4-45). You should see a value of $100 in cell I10 and $0 in the other three cells.

CHECKING TWO COMPARISONS AT ONCE

Suppose you wanted to pay that $100 bonus to the salesperson who has the highest Monthly Sales, but only if that highest value were greater than $5,000. In other words, you want the @IF function to evaluate true if, for example, C6=@MAX(C6...C12) *and* C6>5000. The @AND function lets you make this double comparison. The expression, @AND(C6=@MAX(C6...C12),C6>5000) evaluates true only if both comparisons are true. If you use this expression in the original formula, this is how it would look:

@IF(@AND(C6=@MAX(C6...C12),C6>5000),100,0)

Now, suppose you decided to pay a $100 bonus to any salesperson who had monthly sales greater than $5,000 *or* who had the highest monthly sales. The @OR function performs this comparison neatly.

FIGURE 4–44 The @IF function

```
File: Wages                    REVIEW/ADD/CHANGE              Escape: Main Menu
============A=========B====C====D====E====F======G======H===I===J=======K======
  1|
  2|
  3|                    | Monthly | Monthly |   Monthly     | Sales ||    Gross
  4|    Salesperson     |  Sales  | Salary  | Commissions   | Bonus ||    Wages
  5|--------------------|---------|---------|---------------|-------||-----------
  6|Kate                |  $7,482 |  $1,000 |       $935.25 |    $0 ||
  7|                    |         |         |               |       ||
  8|Bob                 |  $5,572 |  $1,000 |       $696.50 |       ||
  9|                    |         |         |               |       ||
 10|John                | $11,003 |  $1,000 |     $1,650.45 |       ||
 11|                    |         |         |               |       ||
 12|Bruce               |  $3,780 |  $1,000 |       $378.00 |       ||
 13|                    |         |         |               |       ||
 14|                    |         |         |               |       ||
 15|                    |         |         |               |       ||
 16|                    |         |         |               |       ||
 17|                    |         |         |               |       ||
 18|                    |         |         |               |       ||
-------------------------------------------------------------------------------
I6: (Value) @IF(C6=@MAX(C6...C12),100,0)

Type entry or use ⌘ commands                                   ⌘-? for Help
```

FIGURE 4–45 Use the @IF function to compute the bonus

```
File: Wages                    REVIEW/ADD/CHANGE              Escape: Main Menu
============A=========B====C====D====E====F======G======H===I===J=======K======
  1|
  2|
  3|                    | Monthly | Monthly |   Monthly     | Sales ||    Gross
  4|    Salesperson     |  Sales  | Salary  | Commissions   | Bonus ||    Wages
  5|--------------------|---------|---------|---------------|-------||-----------
  6|Kate                |  $7,482 |  $1,000 |       $935.25 |    $0 ||
  7|                    |         |         |               |       ||
  8|Bob                 |  $5,572 |  $1,000 |       $696.50 |    $0 ||
  9|                    |         |         |               |       ||
 10|John                | $11,003 |  $1,000 |     $1,650.45 |  $100 ||
 11|                    |         |         |               |       ||
 12|Bruce               |  $3,780 |  $1,000 |       $378.00 |    $0 ||
 13|                    |         |         |               |       ||
 14|                    |         |         |               |       ||
 15|                    |         |         |               |       ||
 16|                    |         |         |               |       ||
 17|                    |         |         |               |       ||
 18|                    |         |         |               |       ||
-------------------------------------------------------------------------------
I12: (Value) @IF(C12=@MAX(C6...C12),100,0)

Type entry or use ⌘ commands                                   ⌘-? for Help
```

Look at the expression, @OR(C6=@MAX(C6...C12),C6>5000). This expression evaluates true if *either* of its comparisons are true. If you use the formula:

@IF(@OR(C6=@MAX(C6...C12),C6>5000),100,0)

instead of the original formula in cells I6, I8, I10, and I12, you'd pay a $100 bonus to Kate, Bob, and John.

Calculating Gross Wages

Finally, you can calculate the Gross Wages for each of your salespersons. In each case, Gross Wages are the sum of the values in columns E, G, and I. You can express this sum in one of two ways. Gross Wages for Kate can be computed as **+E6+G6+I6** or as **@SUM(E6. . .I6)**. After you have entered the four calculations in cells K6, K8, K10, and K12, use the Layout command to change column K's Value format to Dollars with two decimal places—just as you did with column G (Figure 4-46).

FIGURE 4-46 Calculate Gross Wages

```
File: Wages                  REVIEW/ADD/CHANGE                Escape: Main Menu
============A=========B====C====D====E====F======G======H===I===J=======K======
  1|
  2|
  3|                   | Monthly | Monthly |    Monthly    | Sales ||    Gross
  4|    Salesperson    |  Sales  | Salary  |  Commissions  | Bonus ||    Wages
  5|-------------------|---------|---------|---------------|-------||-------------
  6|Kate               |  $7,482 |  $1,000 |       $935.25 |    $0 ||   $1,935.25
  7|                   |         |         |               |       ||
  8|Bob                |  $5,572 |  $1,000 |       $696.50 |    $0 ||   $1,696.50
  9|                   |         |         |               |       ||
 10|John               | $11,003 |  $1,000 |     $1,650.45 |  $100 ||   $2,750.45
 11|                   |         |         |               |       ||
 12|Bruce              |  $3,780 |  $1,000 |       $378.00 |    $0 ||   $1,378.00
 13|                   |         |         |               |       ||
 14|                   |         |         |               |       ||
 15|                   |         |         |               |       ||
 16|                   |         |         |               |       ||
 17|                   |         |         |               |       ||
 18|                   |         |         |               |       ||
-------------------------------------------------------------------------------
K12: (Value, Layout-D2) +E12+G12+I12

Type entry or use ⌘ commands                                      ⌘-? for Help
```

Printing Out Part of Your Spreadsheet

You would like to print out only columns A through K of your spreadsheet so that the Lookup table is not printed. Before you start to print, go to Printer Options, ⌘O, and change the Report Header value from "Yes" to "No." ESC back to Review/Add/Change, place your cursor in column A, and type ⌘ **P**. Type **C** (for Columns) and use the right-arrow key to move your cursor so that columns A through K are highlighted. Then press RETURN. This tells *AppleWorks* to print only the section of the spreadsheet you've highlighted. Select your printer and choose one copy (Figure 4-47).

Figure 4-48 is an expanded look at columns G, I, and K. The Zoom command was used to display all the formulas in these columns.

FIGURE 4-47 The printed spreadsheet

Salesperson	Monthly Sales	Monthly Salary	Monthly Commissions	Sales Bonus	Gross Wages
Kate	$7,482	$1,000	$935.25	$0	$1,935.25
Bob	$5,572	$1,000	$696.50	$0	$1,696.50
John	$11,003	$1,000	$1,650.45	$100	$2,750.45
Bruce	$3,780	$1,000	$378.00	$0	$1,378.00

FIGURE 4-48 Formulas for columns G, I, and K

```
File: Wages                    REVIEW/ADD/CHANGE                 Escape: Main Menu
====F===========G============H==============I==============J=======K======
   1|
   2|
   3||        Monthly          |              Sales              ||    Gross
   4||      Commissions        |              Bonus              ||    Wages
   5||-------------------------|---------------------------------||-----------
   6||@LOOKUP(C6,M7...M9)*C6   |@IF(C6=@MAX(C6...C12),100,0)     ||+E6+G6+I6
   7||                         |                                 ||
   8||@LOOKUP(C8,M7...M9)*C8   |@IF(C8=@MAX(C6...C12),100,0)     ||+E8+G8+I8
   9||                         |                                 ||
  10||@LOOKUP(C10,M7...M9)*C10|@IF(C10=@MAX(C6...C12),100,0)||+E10+G10+I10
  11||                         |                                 ||
  12||@LOOKUP(C12,M7...M9)*C12|@IF(C12=@MAX(C6...C12),100,0)||+E12+G12+I12
  13||                         |                                 ||
  14||                         |                                 ||
  15||                         |                                 ||
  16||                         |                                 ||
  17||                         |                                 ||
  18||                         |                                 ||
--------------------------------------------------------------------------------
F6: (Label) |

Type entry or use ⌘ commands                                      ⌘-? for Help
```

Don't forget to save this spreadsheet. You'll need it in the next chapter.

Special Examples for Special Functions

If you've been keeping track of the functions demonstrated in the last three examples, you probably noticed that not all of them have been covered. I felt that using functions such as @SQRT and @COUNT was so straightforward that you didn't have to see specific examples of their use.

Three of the functions, @ROUND, @INT, and @CHOOSE, do require a little more explanation.

THE @ROUND FUNCTION

The @ROUND function lets you display a numerical value, rounded to a specified number of decimal places. For example, suppose you had a value of 24.8759 that you wanted to display to the nearest hundredth. The expression, @ROUND(24.8759,2) tells *AppleWorks* to display this value as 24.88. That's right, the second argument, 2, specifies the number of decimal places displayed. If you use this value in future calculations, *AppleWorks* uses the displayed number, not just the entire value.

Both arguments in the @ROUND function can be cell coordinates. You can even use a negative number for the number of decimal places. @ROUND(127.95,-1) means to display the value rounded to the nearest tens, in this case, 130. And, @ROUND(127.95,0) displays the value to the nearest whole number—128, in this example. You can round a number to a maximum of 9 decimal places.

THE @INT FUNCTION

The @INT function is similar to @ROUND. It takes the value of its argument and throws away everything to the right of the decimal. @INT doesn't round to the nearest integer; it truncates down to the next integer. In other words, @INT(3.75) evaluates to 3.

There is a way to make @INT round to the nearest integer, however. All you have to do is add .5 to the value in the argument. Suppose you wanted to round the value in cell C6 to the nearest whole number. The expression @INT(C6+.5) does just what you want it to. You can even use @INT to round a value to the nearest hundredth. @INT(100*C6+.5)/100 will round C6 to two decimal places. Notice also that @INT(100*C6+.5)/100 doesn't just display to two decimal places, it *evaluates* to two decimal places.

Now consider the following expression: @INT(C6/5000)+1. If C6 is less than 5000, @INT(C6/5000) equals 0, and, therefore, @INT(C6/5000)+1 equals 1. Similarly, if C2's value lies between 5000 and 9999, @INT(C6/5000)+1 equals 2, and so on. The purpose of this application of the @INT function is to reduce values in column C of your spreadsheet, the Monthly Sales column, to values of 1, 2, or 3. (*Note:* For the purpose of this example, we'll assume that no salesperson sells more than $14,999 in one month.)

THE @CHOOSE FUNCTION

Now let's look at @CHOOSE. This function uses an index number to choose one value from a list of values. A typical expression might be @CHOOSE(B7,10,15,75). The way this function works is that it begins by evaluating the first term (B7 in the example). If B7's value is 1, the function evaluates as 10; if B7 is 2, the function returns 15 for its value; if B7 equals 3, the function equals 75. In other words, the value of the index term determines which of the following values is used. (*Note:* If the index value is zero, or greater than the number of terms following the index, the expression evaluates as an ERROR.)

You can use the two functions, @INT and @CHOOSE, in place of @LOOKUP in column G. You'll use @INT(C6/5000)+1 as the index term, and the three commission percentages (.10, .125, and .15) as the three terms following the index. The entire expression, @CHOOSE(@INT(C6/5000)+1,.10,.125,.15), will yield the proper percent and would then be multiplied by the sales value in column C (C6 for Kate's commission).

Let's try it. Move your cursor to cell K6 and type **@CHOOSE(@INT(C6/5000)+1,.10,.125,.15)*C6** and see that the result, $935.25, remains the same (Figure 4-49). This is just a different way to calculate sales commissions in your spreadsheet. Its advantage is that it doesn't require a separate Lookup table.

FIGURE 4-49 Use @CHOOSE and @INT functions instead of a Lookup table

```
File: Wages                        REVIEW/ADD/CHANGE                 Escape: Main Menu
============A=========B====C====D====E====F======G======H===I===J=======K======
  1|
  2|
  3|                   | Monthly | Monthly |   Monthly    | Sales ||     Gross
  4|    Salesperson    |  Sales  | Salary  | Commissions  | Bonus ||     Wages
  5|-------------------|---------|---------|--------------|-------||-------------
  6|Kate               |  $7,482 |  $1,000 |      $935.25 |    $0 ||  $1,935.25
  7|                   |         |         |              |       ||
  8|Bob                |  $5,572 |  $1,000 |      $696.50 |    $0 ||  $1,696.50
  9|                   |         |         |              |       ||
 10|John               | $11,003 |  $1,000 |    $1,650.45 |  $100 ||  $2,750.45
 11|                   |         |         |              |       ||
 12|Bruce              |  $3,780 |  $1,000 |      $378.00 |    $0 ||  $1,378.00
 13|                   |         |         |              |       ||
 14|                   |         |         |              |       ||
 15|                   |         |         |              |       ||
 16|                   |         |         |              |       ||
 17|                   |         |         |              |       ||
 18|                   |         |         |              |       ||
--------------------------------------------------------------------------------
G6: (Value, Layout-D2) @CHOOSE(@INT(C6/5000)+1,.1,.125,.15)*C6

Type entry or use ⌘ commands                                       ⌘-? for Help
```

Final Comments

The spreadsheet is by far the most complex of the three *AppleWorks* applications. But, as with the other two, the more you use it, the easier it is to use. Think up your own spreadsheet applications and use the three-step process outlined above. Being able to use a spreadsheet to answer "what if?" type questions places an incredibly powerful analytical tool at your fingertips.

CHAPTER

5 CUTTING AND PASTING

Up to this point, you have been using the Copy and Move commands to shift data around within the file you were currently working with. The real power of an integrated set of applications, such as *AppleWorks*, is that you can move sections (or even all) of one file into another file. Not only can you take part of one spreadsheet and put it into another spreadsheet, but you can also move your spreadsheet into a word processor document, or your data base into your spreadsheet.

In this chapter, you'll see how to do both types of cutting and pasting—between files of the same application, and between files of different applications. As a special cut-and-paste example, you'll merge a data base file with a word processor document to create a personalized form letter.

You'll need your data disk, which should have the seven files you created in Chapters 2, 3, and 4. Start up *AppleWorks*, choose option 1 from the Main Menu, and then select option 1 from the Add Files Menu. If you have been creating and saving the files from the examples of the last three chapters, your AppleWorks Files folder will look like Figure 5-1.

I. CUTTING AND PASTING IN THE SAME APPLICATION

In this section, you'll see how to copy or move sections of one *Apple-Works* file into another file of the same type. Let's start with the word processor application.

Using the Clipboard with Word Processor Files

Load the document Formatted Memo onto your Desktop. (*Note:* If you don't have the document Formatted Memo, which was created in Chapter 2, you can use any word processor document for this exercise.)

Now, suppose you wanted to create another memo that contained only the eight items from your Formatted Memo and a title line: Hot & Cold's Pricing Policy. First, you need to create a *new* word processor document.

ESC to the Main Menu, choose option 1 (**Add files to the Desktop**), select option 3 (**Make a new file for the: Word Processor**), and create it from scratch. Name this new document "Pricing Policy." You now have

FIGURE 5-1 ***AppleWorks* files on your data disk**

```
Disk: Disk 2 (Slot 6)          APPLEWORKS FILES          Escape: Add Files

    Main Menu
       Add Files
          AppleWorks files
          Disk volume /DATA has 121K available
              Name            Type of file    Size     Date      Time
          =========================================================
          Formatted Memo      Word Processor   3K    2/12/85   11:07 pm
          Office Memo         Word Processor   3K    2/12/85    4:54 pm
          Customer List       Data Base        2K    2/12/85    4:53 pm
          Repair Calls        Data Base        1K    2/12/85    4:53 pm
          Expense Form        Spreadsheet      2K    2/12/85    4:53 pm
          Sales Proj.         Spreadsheet      1K    2/12/85    4:53 pm
          Wages               Spreadsheet      2K    2/12/85    4:53 pm

Use Right Arrow to choose files, Left Arrow to undo              56K Avail.
```

two word processor documents on your Desktop, Formatted Memo and the newly created Pricing Policy.

Before you type in the title line on Pricing Policy, go to the Printer Options page, ⌘O, type **CN**, and press RETURN. (*Note:* You do this so your title will be centered when you type it.) ESC out of Printer Options and type **Hot & Cold's Pricing Policy**. Press RETURN. Go back to Printer Options and reset the alignment to Unjustified by typing **UJ** and pressing RETURN. ESC out of Printer Options.

SELECTING A DOCUMENT FROM THE DESKTOP

You want to go back to your Formatted Memo so that you can copy the eight numbered items from that memo into the Pricing Policy document. Type ⌘**Q**, and *AppleWorks* will display the Desktop Index—a list of all the files currently on the Desktop (Figure 5-2). You can have a maximum of 12 files on your Desktop at the same time. You can select any one of them by using the up- or down-arrow key to highlight the file you want to see, or by typing the number (1 through 12) of the document. Pressing the RETURN key completes the selection. (*Note:* Figure 5-2 is shown "Zoomed in" so that the two Printer Options are displayed.)

FIGURE 5-2 The Desktop Index

```
File: Pricing Policy            REVIEW/ADD/CHANGE            Escape: Main Menu
=====|====|====|====|====|====|====|====|====|====|====|====|====|====|====|===
--------Centered
             HOT & COLD'S PRICING POLICY
--------Unjustified



                        Desktop Index
                   --------------------------
                   1.  Formatted Memo    WP
                   2.  Pricing Policy    WP




-------------------------------------------------------------------------------
Type number, or use arrows, then press Return                        52K Avail.
```

COPYING TEXT TO THE CLIPBOARD

Select Formatted Memo from the Desktop Index and type ⌘**Z** so that you can see the Printer Options imbedded in the text. You would like to copy not only the eight items from the memo, but the **Indent: 5 chars** Printer Option as well. Move your cursor to the **Indent: 5 chars** line and type ⌘**C**, the Copy command (Figure 5-3). Type **T** to select: **To Clipboard**. You're going to copy a portion of your memo into *AppleWorks'* Clipboard.

Use the down-arrow key to highlight all the text up to the end of the eighth item. Then press the RETURN key. Those eight items, including the **Indent 5 chars** option, are now on the Clipboard.

COPYING TEXT FROM THE CLIPBOARD

Type ⌘**Q** and select Pricing Policy from the Desktop Index. Move your cursor so that it is a couple of lines below the title and type ⌘**C**. This time, type **F** to select: **From Clipboard**, and the contents of the Clipboard will be copied into your document (Figure 5-4).

The Clipboard still has the text from Formatted Memo in it. If you wanted to, you could copy the same text into several documents. The text will stay on the Clipboard until you either exit *AppleWorks* or put something else on the Clipboard.

Save the Pricing Policy document, ⌘S, and then ESC to the Main Menu. Use option 4, **Remove files from the Desktop**, to remove the two word processor files from your Desktop.

FIGURE 5-3 Copying text to the Clipboard

```
File: Formatted Memo              COPY TEXT          Escape: Review/Add/Change
=====|====|====|====|====|====|====|====|====|====|====|====|====|====|====|===
by all H & C employees so we can avoid customer
misunderstandings. Here are some guidelines which should
help you answer any service charge questions your on site
customer might have.

--------Left Margin:  1.5 inches
--------Right Margin:  1.5 inches
--------Indent: 5 chars
     1.   Labor is billed at $45.00 per hour. Time
          starts when the service technician arrives at
          the customer's location.

     2.   There is a minimum one hour labor charge. If
          the job takes more than one hour, then time
          is billed by the quarter hour, rounded up to
          the nearest quarter hour. In other words, if
          the job takes one hour and twenty minutes,
          the customer is charged for an hour and a
          half.

------------------------------------------------------------------------------
Copy Text? Within document  To clipboard   From clipboard
```

FIGURE 5-4 Copying text from the Clipboard

```
File: Pricing Policy          REVIEW/ADD/CHANGE              Escape: Main Menu
=====|====|====|====|====|====|====|====|====|====|====|====|====|====|====|===
--------Centered
                HOT & COLD'S PRICING POLICY
--------Unjustified

--------Indent: 5 chars
1.   Labor is billed at $45.00 per hour. Time starts when
     the service technician arrives at the customer's
     location.

2.   There is a minimum one hour labor charge. If the job
     takes more than one hour, then time is billed by the
     quarter hour, rounded up to the nearest quarter hour.
     In other words, if the job takes one hour and twenty
     minutes, the customer is charged for an hour and a
     half.

3.   If the job requires two men, the labor charge per hour
     will double.

4.   We will not use customer purchased parts in our repairs
------------------------------------------------------------------------------
Type entry or use 🍎 commands          Line 5  Column  1         🍎-? for Help
```

Using the Clipboard with Data Base Files

Suppose you wanted to divide the customers you have in the Customer List data base file into several groups, so that each group would have its own file. You might want to do this if your customer file got so large that *AppleWorks* wouldn't let you add any more records to the file. You would have to decide how you wanted to divide your customers—perhaps alphabetically, perhaps by zip code, or maybe by the year in which each became a customer of Hot & Cold Inc. You'll remember (from Chapter 3) that the first two digits of the Acct. No. represented the year the customer first opened an account with your company. So, let's use that factor to divide the original Customer List file into three separate files—one for '83 customers, one for '84 customers, and one for '85 customers.

First, you'll have to create three new data base files. The categories for these files will be exactly the same as those for your original Customer List file. Figure 5-5 shows the list of category names from Customer List. From the Main Menu, add a new data base file to your Desktop. Call it "Customers.83," and enter the seven category names from Figure 5-5.

FIGURE 5-5 Categories for the Customers.83 file

```
File: Customer List          CHANGE NAME/CATEGORY     Escape: Review/Add/Change


Category names
================================================================================
Customer Name                                  |
Address                                        | Options:
City                                           |
State                                          | Change category name
Zip                                            | Up arrow   Go to filename
Phone                                          | Down arrow Go to next category
Acct. No.                                      | ⌘-I        Insert new category
                                               | ⌘-D        Delete this category
                                               |
                                               |
                                               |
                                               |
                                               |
                                               |
--------------------------------------------------------------------------------
Type entry or use ⌘ commands                                          53K Avail.
```

After you finish typing the last category name, and have pressed the RETURN key, press ESC three times to go back to the Main Menu. Add a second new data base file to your Desktop. Call this one "Customers.84," and enter the same seven category names. Repeat the process one more time, creating a data base file called "Customers.85."

You should now have three data base files on your Desktop, each with the same seven category names. Again ESC to the Main Menu. This time you want to add a data base file from your data disk. Load the file called "Customer List." (*Note:* If you don't have this file, and you want to continue with this exercise, refer back to Chapter 3 and create the Customer List file.)

When the Customer List file is loaded, you should be looking at the multiple record format screen of Review/Add/Change (Figure 5-6). (If you're looking at the single record format screen, type ⌘**Z.**)

FIGURE 5-6 The original Customer List file

```
File: Customer List           REVIEW/ADD/CHANGE             Escape: Main Menu

Selection: All records


Acct.  Customer Name               Address                 City        Phone
================================================================================
84-220 Ms. D. McMullen             1615 Ninth Ave.         Bayshore    555-0593
85-103 Ms. Gail Dooley             512 E. Main St.         East Meadow 555-8211
84-109 Mr. & Mrs. Terry Dethloff   R.R. 1                  Farmtown    555-3961
84-104 Mr. & Mrs. Rob Smith        1423 First Ave.         Meadowbrook 555-3562
83-282 Mr. Steve Miller            573 W. Elm St.          Meadowbrook 555-6342








--------------------------------------------------------------------------------
Type entry or use ⌘ commands                                        ⌘-? for Help
```

Use the Record Selection command, ⌘R, to display only those records whose Account Numbers begin with 83. Type ⌘**R**, choose the seventh category (Acct. No.), then choose option 8, **begins with**. Type **83** for the comparison information, press RETURN, and then ESC back to Review/Add/Change. This selects only those records with account numbers beginning with 83, and if you have entered only the five records listed in Chapter 3, only one record will be selected (Figure 5-7).

Now let's use the Copy command, ⌘C, to copy the record out of the Customer List file and paste it into the Customer.83 file. Type ⌘**C** and press the **T** key to select: **To Clipboard**. Your one record is highlighted. If there had been several records listed, you would have used the down-arrow key to highlight them all. Press the RETURN key and the highlighted record is copied to the Clipboard.

Type ⌘**Q** to see the Desktop Index. Select Customers.83 and press RETURN. Because this file hasn't any records in it, you'll see a screen advising you that the file is empty. Press the Space Bar, and you'll see

FIGURE 5-7 Select records whose Acct. No. begins with 83

```
File: Customer List            REVIEW/ADD/CHANGE              Escape: Main Menu

Selection: Acct. No. begins with 83

Acct.  Customer Name                 Address                  City        Phone
================================================================================
83-282 Mr. Steve Miller              573 W. Elm St.           Meadowbrook 555-6342








--------------------------------------------------------------------------------
Type entry or use ⌘ commands                                        ⌘-? for Help
```

the standard Insert New Records screen. Instead of typing in records, you're going to paste them in from the Clipboard. So press the ESC key to get to the Review/Add/Change screen, and then type ⌘**Z** to Zoom out to the multiple record format screen. You can only paste into the multiple record format Review/Add/Change screen. Type ⌘**C**, **F** (Figure 5-8). You'll notice that you have an empty record, indicated by dashes in each category. You can use the Delete command, ⌘D, to remove this record.

Go back to the Customer List file (with the ⌘Q command) and use Record Selection to select those records with account numbers beginning with 84 (Figure 5-9). Again use ⌘C to copy all three of these records to the Clipboard. Then use ⌘Q to select the Customers.84 file. Again press the Space Bar, ESC, and ⌘Z to get to the multiple record format Review/Add/Change screen. Type ⌘**C**, **F**, and the three records you copied from the Customer List file will be pasted into the Customers.84 file (Figure 5-10).

For practice, repeat the process one more time, selecting the record from the Customer List file whose account number begins with 85, copying it to the Clipboard, and pasting it into the Customers.85 file.

Save the three new files onto your data disk. ESC to the Main Menu and select option 3, **Save Desktop files to disk**. Use the right- and down-

FIGURE 5-8 Paste the record into the new file

```
File: Customers.83            REVIEW/ADD/CHANGE             Escape: Main Menu

Selection: All records

Customer Name   Address          City            State           Zip
===============================================================================
Mr. Steve Mille 573 W. Elm St.   Meadowbrook     IL              60099
-               -                -               -               -









-------------------------------------------------------------------------------
Type entry or use ⌘ commands                                      ⌘-? for Help
```

FIGURE 5-9 Select records whose Acct. No. begins with 84

```
File: Customer List           REVIEW/ADD/CHANGE             Escape: Main Menu

Selection: Acct. No. begins with 84

Acct.  Customer Name            Address                  City        Phone
===============================================================================
84-220 Ms. D. McMullen          1615 Ninth Ave.          Bayshore    555-0593
84-109 Mr. & Mrs. Terry Dethloff R.R. 1                  Farmtown    555-3961
84-104 Mr. & Mrs. Rob Smith     1423 First Ave.          Meadowbrook 555-3562









-------------------------------------------------------------------------------
Type entry or use ⌘ commands                                      ⌘-? for Help
```

arrow keys to indicate that you want to save the first three files (Figure 5-11). Then press RETURN. For each of the three files, you will be asked whether you want to save this file to the current data disk or change to a different data disk. Press the RETURN key to indicate you want to use the same data disk.

FIGURE 5-10 Paste copied records into the new file

```
File: Customers.84              REVIEW/ADD/CHANGE              Escape: Main Menu

Selection: All records


Customer Name   Address         City            State           Zip
===============================================================================
Ms. D. McMullen 1615 Ninth Ave. Bayshore        IL              60990
Mr. & Mrs. Terr R.R. 1          Farmtown        IL              60095
Mr. & Mrs. Rob  1423 First Ave. Meadowbrook     IL              60099
-               -               -               -               -

-------------------------------------------------------------------------------
Type entry or use ⌘ commands                                        ⌘-? for Help
```

FIGURE 5-11 Save all three new files

```
Disk: Disk 2 (Slot 6)                SAVE FILES               Escape: Main Menu
```

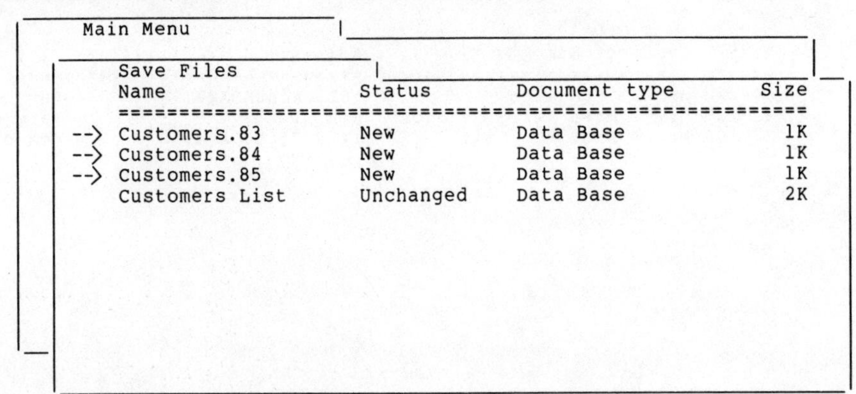

```
    Main Menu
       Save Files
       Name                Status       Document type        Size
       ==========================================================
   --> Customers.83        New          Data Base              1K
   --> Customers.84        New          Data Base              1K
   --> Customers.85        New          Data Base              1K
       Customers List      Unchanged    Data Base              2K
```

```
Use Right Arrow to choose files, Left Arrow to undo                  51K Avail.
```

Using the Clipboard with Spreadsheet Files

Now that you've saved the three new data base files, remove all four files from your Desktop and load in the Expense Form spreadsheet. Suppose you wanted to create a weekly summary report of the expenses from all your employees' expense forms. If you could move the bottom line, the Daily Total line, from each individual expense form to a summary spreadsheet, you could then easily add up the values in the Total column to get the total expenses for the week.

Before you can move anything from your Expense Form spreadsheet into the Weekly Summary spreadsheet, you have to create the Weekly Summary spreadsheet. ESC to the Main Menu, and add a new spreadsheet called "Weekly Summary." After you add this new spreadsheet to your Desktop, type **HOT & COLD INC: Weekly Expense Report** in cells C1 through G1 (don't forget to press the RETURN key when you're through typing the label). Now go back to your Expense Form spreadsheet by using the Q command (Figure 5-12).

FIGURE 5-12 Use the Desktop Index to move between files

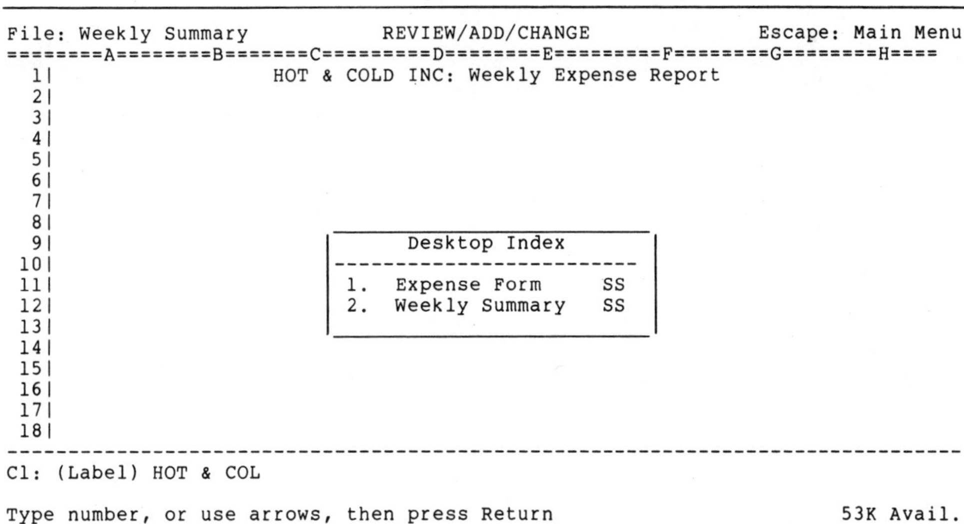

Because you'll be moving sections of your Expense Form spreadsheet to the Weekly Summary spreadsheet, you should disable the protection feature from Expense Form spreadsheet. This will prevent your seeing warning messages every time you Move or Copy a portion of the spreadsheet. Type **V** (the Standard Values command), **P** (for Protection), and **N** (for No).

To make it easier to identify which column contains the Total expenses, let's move the row with the column headings and the row below it (rows 6 and 7) to the Weekly Summary spreadsheet. Place your cursor in cell A6 and type **M**, the Move command. Type **T** to select: **To Clipboard**, and row 6 is highlighted. Notice that you can only cut and

and paste whole rows from one spreadsheet to another. You cannot cut columns, a single cell, or a group of cells. Press the down-arrow key once, so that rows 6 and 7 are both highlighted. Then press RETURN to move these rows to the Clipboard.

Now you see the difference between using Copy and using Move to place a section of your document in the Clipboard (Figure 5-13). The Move command deletes the section from your document; the Copy command leaves the document unaltered.

FIGURE 5-13 Moving data to the Clipboard

```
File: Expense Form             REVIEW/ADD/CHANGE              Escape: Main Menu
========A========B========C========D========E=======F========G========H====
  1|                           HOT & COLD INC: Expense Report
  2|
  3|Name:                                                         Week Endi
  4|
  5|
  6|Airfare             275.00                            275.00
  7|Taxi or Limo         20.00                             20.00
  8|Car Rental                                            135.83
  9|Lodging             85.30    85.30    85.30    85.30
 10|Breakfast                     3.50     3.80     3.35    4.20
 11|Lunch                5.25    10.50     8.25     7.40    8.50
 12|Dinner              21.50    19.35    12.90    35.85
 13|Phone                6.32    15.72    14.95    11.53    9.20
 14|=================================================================
 15|Daily Total        413.37   134.37   125.20   143.43   452.73     0.00
 16|
 17|
 18|
--------------------------------------------------------------------------------
A6: (Label, Protect-N) Airfare

Type entry or use  commands                                  -? for Help
```

Don't worry about messing up the Expense Form spreadsheet. The original, untouched version is still on your data disk. As long as you *don't* save the current version of this spreadsheet, the disk copy will remain unchanged.

Use the Q command to go to the Weekly Summary spreadsheet. Move your cursor to cell A4 (you want the column headings to be pasted into row 4). Type **M** and **F**. The two rows from your Expense Form spreadsheet have been pasted into your Weekly Summary spreadsheet (Figure 5-14).

Go back to Expense Form spreadsheet (Q). You want to copy the Daily Total row from the Expense Form spreadsheet and paste it into the Weekly Summary spreadsheet. (You would do this for all of your Expense Forms for the week so that you could add them together. That's the whole point of this exercise.) The problem is that you *can't* just cut and paste cells with formulas in them. Let's try it, and you'll see what I mean.

FIGURE 5-14 Pasting data into the new spreadsheet

```
File: Weekly Summary            REVIEW/ADD/CHANGE              Escape: Main Menu
========A========B========C========D========E=======F=========G========H====
  1|                  HOT & COLD INC: Weekly Expense Report
  2|
  3|
  4|                   Mon        Tue        Wed        Thu        Fri        Sat
  5|-----------------------------------------------------------------------
  6|
  7|
  8|
  9|
 10|
 11|
 12|
 13|
 14|
 15|
 16|
 17|
 18|
--------------------------------------------------------------------------------
A4

Type entry or use ⌘ commands                                       ⌘-? for Help
```

Move your cursor to A15 and type ⌘**C**, **T**, and RETURN. (Press the "Y" key if you see a caution message.) This places row 15 in the Clipboard. Now go to the Weekly Summary spreadsheet. Place your cursor in A6 and type ⌘**C** and **F** (Figure 5-15).

What happened? Those ERROR markers tell you that *AppleWorks* couldn't figure out what you wanted it to do. Move your cursor to the first ERROR marker in cell C6, and you'll see what went wrong. *AppleWorks* tried to paste cells containing *formulas* (for example, SUM(C6...C13)) from one spreadsheet to another. When the formula arrived at the second spreadsheet, your Weekly Summary spreadsheet, the cells referred to in the formula weren't there.

Somehow you need to transfer only the values from row 15 in your Expense Form spreadsheet—*not* the formulas. There is a way to do this, but it's a bit more complex than just cutting and pasting. What you'll do is create a special file on your data disk containing only row 15 (the Daily Total row) from your Expense Form spreadsheet. This row of data will be recorded in what is called DIF (Data Interchange Format). The DIF file will be read back in as a new spreadsheet file and can then be cut and pasted into your Weekly Summary spreadsheet. I know this sounds complicated, but follow along step-by-step, and you'll see it's not as difficult as it looks.

First, delete row 6 from your Weekly Summary spreadsheet. (Type ⌘**D** and press the RETURN key twice.) Return to the Expense Form spreadsheet with the Desktop Index command, ⌘Q.

FIGURE 5-15 You can't cut and paste formulas between different spreadsheets

```
File: Weekly Summary            REVIEW/ADD/CHANGE               Escape: Main Menu
========A========B=========C========D=======E=======F=========G========H====
  1|                  HOT & COLD INC: Weekly Expense Report
  2|
  3|
  4|                     Mon        Tue        Wed        Thu        Fri        Sat
  5|----------------------------------------------------------------------------
  6|Daily Total           ERROR      ERROR      ERROR      ERROR      ERROR      ERROR
  7|
  8|
  9|
 10|
 11|
 12|
 13|
 14|
 15|
 16|
 17|
 18|
--------------------------------------------------------------------------------
A6: (Label, Protect-N) Daily Tot

Type entry or use ⌘ commands                                          ⌘-? for Help
```

Move your cursor to a cell in row 15. You're going to print that row to your data disk in DIF. Type ⌘**P** and press the "R" key to indicate that you want to print selected rows. Row 15 is highlighted, and since this is the only row you want to print, press RETURN. You should see at least four choices for where you want to print (Figure 5-16). One of them, probably number 4, will be **A DIF (TM) file on disk**. Select this option. At the bottom of your screen, you will be asked for: **DIF order**. Type **C**, for Columns.

You'll be asked to type a pathname for the file. A pathname consists of the disk's *volume* name and the file's *filename*. Assuming you named your data disk *DATA* when you formatted it, type **/DATA/DIF** for the pathname. (*Note:* If your computer system has two disk drives, the data disk named DATA should be in drive 2. If you have a single-drive system, you will be prompted to replace your *AppleWorks* program disk with your data disk.)

After your spreadsheet row has been "printed" to your data disk, ESC to the Main Menu and choose: **Add files to the Desktop**. From the Add Files Menu, select option 5, **Make a new file for the: Spreadsheet**.

At this point, you usually choose option 1, **From scratch**. This time, choose option 2, **From a DIF (TM) file**. In response to the pathname prompt, type the same pathname you used when you created the DIF file, **/DATA/DIF**. And when you're asked to type a name for this spreadsheet, type **DIF** and press RETURN. Figure 5-17 shows the new DIF spreadsheet.

FIGURE 5-16 Save the spreadsheet as a DIF file

```
File: Expense Form                    PRINT            Escape: Review/Add/Change
================================================================================

                    The information that you identified
                    is 117 characters wide.

                    The Printer Options values allow
                    120 characters per line.


                    Where do you want to print the report?

                    1.  My Printer
                    2.  The clipboard (for the Word Processor)
                    3.  A text (ASCII) file on disk
                    4.  A DIF (TM) file on disk



--------------------------------------------------------------------------------

Type number, or use arrows, then press Return                         52K Avail.
```

FIGURE 5-17 Load the DIF file into a separate spreadsheet

```
File: DIF                        REVIEW/ADD/CHANGE                Escape: Main Menu
=======A=========B========C========D========E=========F========G========H====
  1|Daily Total            413.37   134.37    125.2    143.43   452.73        0
  2|
  3|
  4|
  5|
  6|
  7|
  8|
  9|
 10|
 11|
 12|
 13|
 14|
 15|
 16|
 17|
 18|
--------------------------------------------------------------------------------
C1: (Value) 413.37
```

This is the row of data that you can cut and paste into your Weekly Summary spreadsheet. With your cursor on a cell in row 1, type ⌘**M** and **T**, and press RETURN. Use ⌘Q to go to the Weekly Summary spreadsheet. Now, with your cursor on a cell in row 6, type ⌘**M** and **F**. Success, at last! (*Note:* Of course, you would have to repeat the process for each of the Expense Forms for the week, and then total up columns C-G to get the weekly totals.)

Summarizing

Cutting and Pasting between two word processor files, two data base files, or two spreadsheet files can really save you time and effort when you are producing reports. The above three examples were chosen simply to illustrate the method of Cutting and Pasting, using the files you had already created in earlier chapters. Here is a typical situation where Cutting and Pasting between documents of the same type would be very useful.

Suppose you regularly sent out form letters to clients. A typical form letter might contain four or five paragraphs selected from 20 or so standard paragraphs—the choice of paragraphs depending on the client. You could keep the 20 standard paragraphs in one document on your Desktop, create a new word processor document for the form letter to a particular client, and Cut and Paste appropriate paragraphs to create a "personalized" form letter.

II. CUTTING AND PASTING IN DIFFERENT APPLICATIONS

Many *AppleWorks* users (and I am one of them) feel that the real power of *AppleWorks* lies in its ability to move documents easily from the data base or the spreadsheet to the word processor. Not only can you incorporate the data base report or spreadsheet into your word processor files, but you can add "special effects" to your reports, such as underlining and boldface printing, which are available only in the word processor.

From the Data Base to the Word Processor

Load the file Repair Calls from your data disk into the *AppleWorks* Desktop. (*Note:* If you don't have the Repair Calls data base file, you can either go back to Chapter 3 and create it or use one of your own data base files.) Figure 5-18 is the report you created for this file. (It's actually a copy of Figure 3-47.)

One of the limitations of the standard Tables report format is that you can either choose to have the entire, four-line report heading printed, or you can set the Print Heading (PH) Printer Option to "No" and have no headings printed at all. But suppose you wanted your

FIGURE 5-18 The final report from the Repair Calls data base

```
File:    Repair Calls
Report:  Weekly Report
Date     Technician  Acct. No.  Hours Billed  Labor Cost  Parts Cost   Total Cost
-------  ----------  ---------  ------------  ----------  ----------  ------------

Jun 24   Bill        83-115             2.00       90.00       55.20        145.20

Jun 25   Bill        84-200             1.00       45.00         .85         45.85

Jun 25   Bill        84-138             1.50       67.50       67.35        134.85

                                        4.50                  123.40        325.90

Jun 24   Chuck       83-211             1.50       67.50      120.75        188.25

Jun 24   Chuck       85-114             1.00       45.00                     45.00

Jun 25   Chuck       83-121             2.50      112.50      248.75        361.25

Jun 25   Chuck       85-147             1.25       56.25       45.30        101.55

                                        6.25                  414.80        696.05

Jun 24   Penney      85-109             1.00       45.00                     45.00

Jun 24   Penney      84-142             1.75       78.75       79.40        158.15

Jun 25   Penney      83-101             1.50       67.50      110.95        178.45

                                        4.25                  190.35        381.60

                                       15.00*                 728.55*      1403.55*
```

report to have column headings (Date, Technician, etc.) but not the top two lines that contain the name of the file, the name of the report, page number, etc. With the data base report generator, you can't choose to print just some of the heading. You either get all of the heading or none of it.

What you *can* do is to print the entire data base report to the Clipboard, and then paste it into a word processor document. Then you can use all of the text editing features of the word processor to customize your report before you print it.

PRINTING TO THE CLIPBOARD

The first step is to print the report to the Clipboard. You have already loaded the Repair Calls file and you should be looking at the Review/Add/Change screen (Figure 5-19). Type **P** to get to the Report Menu (Figure 5-20). Select option 1, **Get a report format**, and press RETURN to accept the Weekly Report format. (*Note:* If your data base file doesn't have a Weekly Report format already created, you'll have to create one first, before you can continue with this example. Refer to Chapter 3 if you need help creating a report format.)

FIGURE 5-19 The Repair Calls data base

```
File: Repair Calls              REVIEW/ADD/CHANGE            Escape: Main Menu

Selection: All records

Technician     Acct. No.      Date           Hours Billed    Parts Cost
===========================================================================
Bill           83-115         Jun 24         2               55.20
Bill           84-200         Jun 25         1               .85
Bill           84-138         Jun 25         1.5             67.35
Chuck          83-211         Jun 24         1.5             120.75
Chuck          85-114         Jun 24         1               0
Chuck          83-121         Jun 25         2.5             248.75
Chuck          85-147         Jun 25         1.25            45.30
Penney         85-109         Jun 24         1               0
Penney         84-142         Jun 24         1.75            79.40
Penney         83-101         Jun 25         1.5             110.95

---------------------------------------------------------------------------
Type entry or use ⌘ commands                                   ⌘-? for Help
```

FIGURE 5-20 Get the Weekly Report format

```
File: Repair Calls                 REPORT MENU         Escape: Review/Add/Change
Report: None

===========================================================================

                         1.  Get a report format
                         2.  Create a new "tables" format
                         3.  Create a new "labels" format
                         4.  Duplicate an existing format
                         5.  Erase a format

---------------------------------------------------------------------------
Type number, or use arrows, then press Return                      54K Avail.
```

From the Report Format screen (Figure 5-21), type⌘**P** to print your report (Figure 5-22). But instead of selecting your printer as the destination for the report, choose option 3, **The clipboard (for the Word Processor)**. You'll be asked to type a report date for your report; just press RETURN. *AppleWorks* will then tell you that your report is now

FIGURE 5-21 The Weekly Report

```
File: Repair Calls                    REPORT FORMAT                 Escape: Report Menu
Report: Weekly Report
Selection: All records


Group Totals on: Technician
================================================================================
--> or <--  Move cursor                            -J  Right justify this category
 >    <    Switch category positions              -K  Define a calculated category
--> <--   Change column width                    -N  Change report name and/or title
-A  Arrange (sort) on this category               -O  Printer options
-D  Delete this category                          -P  Print the report
-G  Add/remove group totals                       -R  Change record selection rules
-I  Insert a prev. deleted category               -T  Add/remove category totals
--------------------------------------------------------------------------------

Date     Technician  Acct. No.  Hours Billed  Labor Cost  Parts Cost  Total Cost
-A----- -B--------- -C-------- -D---------- -E--------- -F--------- -G---------
Jun 24  Bill        83-115     999999999.99 9999999.99  9999999.99   99999999.
Jun 25  Bill        84-200     999999999.99 9999999.99  9999999.99   99999999.
Jun 25  Bill        84-138     999999999.99 9999999.99  9999999.99   99999999.
                               ============             ==========  ==========
---------------------------------------------------------------------- More --->
Use options shown above to change report format                      54K Avail.
```

FIGURE 5-22 Print the Weekly Report to the clipboard (for the Word Processor)

```
File: Repair Calls                  PRINT THE REPORT               Escape: Erase entry
Report: Weekly Report
Selection: All records

Group totals on: Technician
================================================================================

                       Where do you want to print the report?

                       1.  My Printer
                       2.  The screen
                       3.  The clipboard (for the Word Processor)
                       4.  The clipboard (for Mail Merge)
                       5.  A text (ASCII) file on disk
                       6.  A DIF (TM) file on disk




--------------------------------------------------------------------------------
Type number, or use arrows, then press Return  3                     54K Avail.
```

on the Clipboard and can be moved or copied into word processor documents.

Press the Space Bar to return to the Report Format screen, and then press the ESC key three times to go *AppleWorks*' Main Menu.

PASTING THE REPORT INTO THE WORD PROCESSOR

Choose **Add files to the Desktop** and make a new file for the word processor, from scratch, called "WP Report." Before you paste the report into this document, you'll want to change some of the printer options. So, type ⌘**O**. Change the Left and Right Margins to 0". And set Characters per Inch to 12 (Figure 5-23). (*Note:* If your printer doesn't support 12 characters per inch, try 17.) The reason you want to increase the number of characters per inch is that your original data base report was wider than 80 characters per line. Choosing zero Left and Right margins and 12 Characters per Inch will give you 96 characters per line when you print your report from the word processor. ESC back to Review/Add/Change.

FIGURE 5-23 Change the printer options for the new document

```
File: WP Report                    PRINTER OPTIONS        Escape: Review/Add/Change
=====|====|====|====|====|====|====|====|====|====|====|====|====|====|====|===
--------Left Margin:  0.0 inches
--------Right Margin:  0.0 inches
--------Chars per Inch: 12 chars




   PW=8.0  LM=0.0  RM=0.0  CI=12  UJ  PL=11.0  TM=0.0  BM=2.0  LI=6  SS
Option:                 UJ: Unjustified     GB: Group Begin     BE: Boldface End
                        CN: Centered        GE: Group End       +B: Superscript Beg
PW: Platen Width        PL: Paper Length    HE: Page Header     +E: Superscript End
LM: Left Margin         TM: Top Margin      FO: Page Footer     -B: Subscript Begin
RM: Right Margin        BM: Bottom Margin   SK: Skip Lines      -E: Subscript End
CI: Chars per Inch      LI: Lines per Inch  PN: Page Number     UB: Underline Begin
P1: Proportional-1      SS: Single Space    PE: Pause Each page UE: Underline End
P2: Proportional-2      DS: Double Space    PH: Pause Here      PP: Print Page No.
IN: Indent              TS: Triple Space    SM: Set a Marker    EK: Enter Keyboard
JU: Justified           NP: New Page        BB: Boldface Begin  MM: Mail Merge
```

Now type ⌘**M** (or ⌘**C**) and press the **F** key to select **From Clipboard** and compare your screen with Figure 5-24. You'll notice that your data base report seems "folded" as it is displayed in the word processor; that is, each line of the report takes up two lines on your screen. Don't worry about it. When you print out the document, it will have the proper format. That's why you changed the values for the Left and Right Margins and Characters per Inch.

EDITING THE REPORT

Now let's delete the top "two" lines from the report. (Remember, that's why you were doing this example in the first place.) Type ⌘**1** to move

FIGURE 5-24 Paste the data base report into the document

```
File: WP Report                  REVIEW/ADD/CHANGE                 Escape: Main Menu
=====|====|====|====|====|====|====|====|====|====|====|====|====|====|====|===
File:    Repair Calls
             Page  1
Report: Weekly Report
Date     Technician   Acct. No.   Hours Bi'lled  Labor Cost  Parts Cost    Total
Cost
------- ----------- ---------- ------------  ----------  ----------
------------

Jun 24  Bill         83-115              2.00       90.00       55.20
145.20

Jun 25  Bill         84-200              1.00       45.00         .85
45.85

Jun 25  Bill         84-138              1.50       67.50       67.35
134.85

                                         4.50                  123.40
325.90

--------------------------------------------------------------------------------
Type entry or use ⌘ commands              Line 4  Column  1        ⌘-? for Help
```

your cursor to the beginning of your document. Now type ⌘**D**. Press the down-arrow key three times and the left-arrow key once, so that all the text above the column headings is highlighted. (*Note:* The printer options should not be highlighted.) Then press RETURN (Figure 5-25).

That accomplishes the one bit of editing you wanted to do, but as long as you have the report in front of you, let's take advantage of at least one other word processor feature: underlining. Let's underline each of the Group Total values. You'll remember that your report printed Group Totals on Hours Billed, Parts Cost, and Total Cost, every time the Technician name changed. The first Group Total line occurs when the Technician name changes from Bill to Chuck. The three Group Total values on this line are: 4.50, 123.40, and 325.90. Move your cursor to the first digit in 4.50 and type **CONTROL-L** (hold down the CONTROL key while you type the letter "L"). You'll remember from Chapter 2 that this begins underlining, and a caret symbol (ˆ) appears to the left of 4.50 to indicate this. Now move your cursor just to the right of the zero in 4.50 and type **CONTROL-L** again. Another caret appears to indicate the ending of underlining.

In a similar manner, set up underlining for the other two values on the Group Total line, 123.40 and 325.90 (Figure 5-26) Notice that as each caret is typed, the remaining text on the line is shifted to the right. Don't worry about lining up the numbers. When the report is printed, everything will line up properly in columns.

FIGURE 5-25 Delete the top two lines of the Report Header

```
File: WP Report                    REVIEW/ADD/CHANGE                 Escape: Main Menu
=====|====|====|====|====|====|====|====|====|====|====|====|====|====|====|===
Date     Technician  Acct. No.  Hours Billed  Labor Cost  Parts Cost    Total
Cost
------- ----------- ---------- ------------  ----------  ----------
------------

Jun 24   Bill         83-115              2.00        90.00       55.20
145.20

Jun 25   Bill         84-200              1.00        45.00         .85
45.85

Jun 25   Bill         84-138              1.50        67.50       67.35
134.85

                                          4.50                   123.40
325.90

Jun 24   Chuck        83-211              1.50        67.50      120.75
188.25

--------------------------------------------------------------------------------
Type entry or use ⌘ commands               Line 4  Column  1          ⌘-? for Help
```

FIGURE 5-26 Add underlining

```
File: WP Report                    REVIEW/ADD/CHANGE                 Escape: Main Menu
=====|====|====|====|====|====|====|====|====|====|====|====|====|====|====|===
Date     Technician  Acct. No.  Hours Billed  Labor Cost  Parts Cost    Total
Cost
------- ----------- ---------- ------------  ----------  ----------
------------

Jun 24   Bill         83-115              2.00        90.00       55.20
145.20

Jun 25   Bill         84-200              1.00        45.00         .85
45.85

Jun 25   Bill         84-138              1.50        67.50       67.35
134.85

                                         ^4.50^                 ^123.40^
^325.90^

Jun 24   Chuck        83-211              1.50        67.50      120.75
188.25

--------------------------------------------------------------------------------
Type entry or use ⌘ commands               Line 19  Column  9         ⌘-? for Help
```

Now move down to the two other Group Total lines (the line between Chuck and Penney, and the line between Penney and the Grand Total line). Add underlining to the three values in the two lines.

As a final touch, you can add dollar signs to the last two values in the bottom line, the Grand Total line (Figure 5-27). Change to the

FIGURE 5-27 Add dollar signs

```
File: WP Report                  REVIEW/ADD/CHANGE              Escape: Main Menu
=====|====|====|====|====|====|====|====|====|====|====|====|====|====|====|===
Jun 25   Chuck        85-147              1.25        56.25        45.30
101.55

                                        ^6.25^                   ^414.80^
^696.05^

Jun 24   Penney       85-109              1.00        45.00
45.00

Jun 24   Penney       84-142              1.75        78.75        79.40
158.15

Jun 25   Penney       83-101              1.50        67.50       110.95
178.45

                                        ^4.25^                   ^190.35^
^381.60^

                                       15.00*                  $728.55*
$1403.55*
------------------------------------------------------------------------------
Type entry or use ⌘ commands              Line 49  Column  1       ⌘-? for Help
```

overstrike cursor (⌘E) to add the dollar signs in front of 728.55 and 1403.55. To place a $ in front of the 1403.55 value, place the overstrike cursor on the first character of the value, the number "1," press the left-arrow key once, and type a $.

Print out the report and compare it with Figure 5-28.

Save WP Report and then remove it and the Repair Calls file from the Desktop with option 4 from the Main Menu. Remember to change your cursor back to insert type, if this is the cursor you normally use.

From the Spreadsheet to the Word Processor

Now let's try cutting and pasting part of a spreadsheet into a word processor document. Suppose you wanted to send a memo to your four salespersons (from Hot & Cold Inc.) listing the total sales each salesperson was responsible for during the past month. You have the data in your Wages spreadsheet, so what you'll do is to start the memo in the word processor and then paste in part of your Wages spreadsheet.

Make a new file for the word processor, from scratch, called "Monthly Sales." Start the memo as shown in Figure 5-29. When you're through typing the last line, press the RETURN key a couple of times so that your cursor is a line or two below the last line of your document.

ESC back to the Main Menu and load the Wages spreadsheet from your data disk. (*Note:* If you haven't created the Wages spreadsheet, you

FIGURE 5-28 The enhanced report

Date	Technician	Acct. No.	Hours Billed	Labor Cost	Parts Cost	Total Cost
Jun 24	Bill	83-115	2.00	90.00	55.20	145.20
Jun 25	Bill	84-200	1.00	45.00	.85	45.85
Jun 25	Bill	84-138	1.50	67.50	67.35	134.85
			4.50		123.40	325.90
Jun 24	Chuck	83-211	1.50	67.50	120.75	188.25
Jun 24	Chuck	85-114	1.00	45.00		45.00
Jun 25	Chuck	83-121	2.50	112.50	248.75	361.25
Jun 25	Chuck	85-147	1.25	56.25	45.30	101.55
			6.25		414.80	696.05
Jun 24	Penney	85-109	1.00	45.00		45.00
Jun 24	Penney	84-142	1.75	78.75	79.40	158.15
Jun 25	Penney	83-101	1.50	67.50	110.95	178.45
			4.25		190.35	381.60
			15.00*		$728.55*	$1403.55*

FIGURE 5-29 Create a Monthly Sales memo

```
File: Monthly Sales           REVIEW/ADD/CHANGE              Escape: Main Menu
=====|====|====|====|====|====|====|====|====|====|====|====|====|====|====|===
To:        All Salespersons

From:      (your name)

Date:      (today's date)

Subject:   Last Month's Sales Figures

The table below shows the sales figures for last month.






-------------------------------------------------------------------------------
Type entry or use ⌘ commands            Line 10  Column 56           ⌘-? for Help
```

can use one of your own spreadsheets or follow the instructions in Chapter 4 and make the Wages spreadsheet now.)

You're going to print the Salesperson and Monthly Sales columns to the Clipboard so that you can paste them into your word processor document. Before you do this, type ⌘ **O** to enter Printer Options and set the value of PH (Print Header) to "No." (Type **PH** and press RETURN.) The header in a spreadsheet contains the name of the file, the page number of the report, and the report date. You won't need this information in your word processor document. ESC back to Review/Add/Change.

Place your cursor in cell A3 and type **P**. You are asked what part of your spreadsheet you want to print. Type **B**, for Block. Use a combination of right- and down-arrow keys to highlight all the cells from A3 to C12 (Figure 5-30), then press RETURN (Figure 5-31).

As in the previous example, select option 2, **The clipboard (for the Word Processor)**, as your print destination and press RETURN.

You'll see a message telling you that your report has been printed to the Clipboard. Press the Space Bar to return to the Review/Add/Change screen.

Type **Q** to display the Desktop Index and select the Monthly Sales document.

Your cursor should still be at the bottom of your document (type **9** if it isn't). All you have to do now is paste in the table from the Clipboard. Type **C** (or **M**) and press the **F** key.

Leave your cursor where it is and go into Printer Options (O). Change the Left Margin to 2″ and ESC out.

You can move your cursor down to the top salesperson of the month, John, and use boldface to emphasize this line of the table. Place your cursor on the first letter of "John" and type **CONTROL-B** (Figure 5-32). Because both underlining and boldface printing are turned off

FIGURE 5-30 Highlight the block of cells from A3...C12

```
File: Wages                                PRINT             Escape: Review/Add/Change
============A=========B====C====D====E====F======G======H===I===J=======K======
  1|
  2|
  3|                          | Monthly | Monthly |   Monthly    | Sales ||    Gross
  4|       Salesperson        |  Sales  | Salary  | Commissions  | Bonus ||    Wages
  5|--------------------------|---------|---------|--------------|-------||------------
  6|Kate                      |  $7,482 | $1.000  |      $935.25 |    $0 ||  $1,935.25
  7|                          |         |         |              |       ||
  8|Bob                       |  $5,572 | $1,000  |      $696.50 |    $0 ||  $1,696.50
  9|                          |         |         |              |       ||
 10|John                      | $11,003 | $1,000  |    $1,650.45 |  $100 ||  $2,750.45
 11|                          |         |         |              |       ||
 12|Bruce                     |  $3,780 | $1,000  |      $378.00 |    $0 ||  $1,378.00
 13|                          |         |         |              |       ||
 14|                          |         |         |              |       ||
 15|                          |         |         |              |       ||
 16|                          |         |         |              |       ||
 17|                          |         |         |              |       ||
 18|                          |         |         |              |       ||
-------------------------------------------------------------------------------------
C12: (Value) 3780

Use cursor moves to highlight Block, then press Return                 54K Avail.
```

FIGURE 5-31 Print selected cells to the Clipboard

```
File: Wages                          PRINT              Escape: Review/Add/Change
=================================================================================

                    The information that you identified
                    is 28 characters wide.

                    The Printer Options values allow
                    80 characters per line.

                    Where do you want to print the report?

                    1.  My Printer
                    2.  The clipboard (for the Word Processor)
                    3.  A text (ASCII) file on disk
                    4.  A DIF (TM) file on disk

---------------------------------------------------------------------------------

Type number, or use arrows, then press Return                          54K Avail.
```

FIGURE 5-32 Paste the spreadsheet data into your document

```
File: Monthly Sales            REVIEW/ADD/CHANGE                  Escape: Main Menu
=====|====|====|====|====|====|====|====|====|====|====|====|====|====|====|===
To:      All Salespersons

From:    (your name)

Date:    (today's date)

Subject: Last Month's Sales Figures

The table below shows the sales figures for last month.

                             | Monthly
             Salesperson     |  Sales
         --------------------|---------
         Kate                |  $7,482
                             |
         Bob                 |  $5,572
                             |
         ^John               | $11,003
                             |
---------------------------------------------------------------------------------
Type entry or use ⌘ commands             Line 20  Column 12         ⌘-? for Help
```

after a carriage return, you don't have to turn off boldface yourself. *AppleWorks* will do it for you.

Print out your memo, and compare it with Figure 5-33.

Save the Monthly Sales memo and then remove it and the Wages spreadsheet from your Desktop.

FIGURE 5-33 The printed memo

```
To:        All Salespersons

From:      (your name)

Date:      (today's date)

Subject:   Last Month's Sales Figures


The table below shows the sales figures for last month.

                            | Monthly
               Salesperson  |  Sales
          ------------------|---------
          Kate              |  $7,482
                            |
          Bob               |  $5,572
                            |
          John              | $11,003
                            |
          Bruce             |  $3,780
```

From the Data Base to the Spreadsheet

Transferring data from a data base file to a spreadsheet (or from a spreadsheet to a data base file) requires the use of a DIF file. In this example, you will copy the data from your Repair Calls data base file into a spreadsheet.

You might wonder why anyone would want to do this. One reason is that there are far more calculation functions in the spreadsheet than in the data base. But it is usually easier to enter data in the data base.

Load the Repair Calls data base onto your Desktop and type ⌘**P** to go to the Report Menu. Choose option 1, **Get a report format**, and then press RETURN to select the Weekly Report format. Type ⌘**P** to print your report and choose option 6, **A DIF (TM) file on disk**, as the destination for your report. (*Note:* If you have more than one printer installed on your copy of *AppleWorks*, the DIF file option will be numbered 7 or 8.)

You will be prompted for a pathname. Type: **/DATA/REPAIRS** and press RETURN. That's all you have to do in your data base file, so press

ESC three times to go back to the Main Menu and choose **Add files to the Desktop**.

You want to make a new file for the spreadsheet, so take option 5. You're going to make this new spreadsheet file **From a DIF (TM) file**. Select option 2 and type the same pathname you used to save the original DIF file: **/DATA/REPAIRS**. Name this new file "SS Repairs." Your new spreadsheet should look like Figure 5-34.

FIGURE 5-34 Load the data base DIF file into a spreadsheet

```
File: SS Repairs              REVIEW/ADD/CHANGE              Escape: Main Menu
========A========B========C========D========E========F========G========H====
  1|Jun 24    Bill        83115          2      55.2
  2|Jun 25    Bill        84200          1       .85
  3|Jun 25    Bill        84138        1.5     67.35
  4|Jun 24    Chuck       83211        1.5    120.75
  5|Jun 24    Chuck       85114          1         0
  6|Jun 25    Chuck       83121        2.5    248.75
  7|Jun 25    Chuck       85147       1.25      45.3
  8|Jun 24    Penney      85109          1         0
  9|Jun 24    Penney      84142       1.75      79.4
 10|Jun 25    Penney      83101        1.5    110.95
 11|
 12|
 13|
 14|
 15|
 16|
 17|
 18|
------------------------------------------------------------------------------
A1: (Label) Jun 24

Type entry or use ♂ commands                                      ♂-? for Help
```

Note that only the original data was recorded to the DIF file. Headings were not recorded, nor were calculated categories nor any totals. That's the way DIF files work.

You can, of course, modify the spreadsheet in any number of ways, including adding extra rows and columns, to create the kind of report you want. Figure 5-35 shows a typical report.

Four extra rows were inserted at the top of the report so that the actual data begins in row 5. Column F is computed as $45 times the value in column D; column G is column E plus column F. The totals at the bottom use the @SUM function. Columns E, F, and G were widened and appropriate Label and Value formats were chosen to improve the "look" of the report.

Try duplicating these features so that you can use this spreadsheet in the next exercise. Save the SS Repairs spreadsheet.

FIGURE 5-35 Add Labor and Total columns

```
File: SS Repairs                 REVIEW/ADD/CHANGE                Escape: Main Menu
========A========B========C========D=========E==========F==========G======
  1|                             Repair Calls Weekly Report
  2|
  3| Date       Tech       Acct. #      Hours    Parts       Labor       Total
  4|======================================================================
  5|Jun 24     Bill           83115       2.00    $55.20      $90.00     $145.20
  6|Jun 25     Bill           84200       1.00      $.85      $45.00      $45.85
  7|Jun 25     Bill           84138       1.50    $67.35      $67.50     $134.85
  8|Jun 24     Chuck          83211       1.50   $120.75      $67.50     $188.25
  9|Jun 24     Chuck          85114       1.00     $0.00      $45.00      $45.00
 10|Jun 25     Chuck          83121       2.50   $248.75     $112.50     $361.25
 11|Jun 25     Chuck          85147       1.25    $45.30      $56.25     $101.55
 12|Jun 24     Penney         85109       1.00     $0.00      $45.00      $45.00
 13|Jun 24     Penney         84142       1.75    $79.40      $78.75     $158.15
 14|Jun 25     Penney         83101       1.50   $110.95      $67.50     $178.45
 15|
 16|______________________________________________________________________
 17|Totals                               15.00   $728.55     $675.00   $1,403.55
 18|
------------------------------------------------------------------------------
G17: (Value, Layout-D2) @SUM(G5...G14)

Type entry or use ⌘ commands                                      ⌘-? for Help
```

From the Spreadsheet to the Data Base

Suppose you now wanted to transfer rows 5 through 14 (Figure 5-35) back into a data base file. You might want to do this in order to have the two "calculated" columns, Labor and Total, as part of the actual data base file. That way, if you wanted to Arrange the file in the order of greatest to least total repair cost, you could. (Remember that when Total Cost was a calculated category in your original Repair Calls data base file, you couldn't use the Arrange function on a calculated category.)

Place your cursor on cell A5 and type ⌘**P**. Then type **B**, for Block. Use the right-arrow key to highlight the cells from A5 through G5. Use the down-arrow key to highlight rows 5 through 14. Then press RETURN. Again, you're going to select **A DIF (TM) file on disk** as the destination for your report. The DIF order you want is Columns, so type the letter "C." And use **/DATA/CALLS** for the pathname.

ESC back to the Main Menu. You're going to add a new data base file to your Desktop. The source for this new file will be a DIF file named "/DATA/CALLS." Name this new file "Complete Repair" (Figure 5-36).

Notice that *AppleWorks* didn't know what you wanted to name the categories, so it chose "Category 1," "Category 2," etc. You can change these default names to something more descriptive with the ⌘N com-

FIGURE 5-36 Load the spreadsheet DIF file into a new data base

```
File: Complete Repair          REVIEW/ADD/CHANGE              Escape: Main Menu

Selection: All records

Category  1       Category  2       Category  3       Category  4       Category  5
====================================================================================
Jun 24            Bill              83115             2                 55.2
Jun 25            Bill              84200             1                 .85
Jun 25            Bill              84138             1.5               67.35
Jun 24            Chuck             83211             1.5               120.75
Jun 24            Chuck             85114             1                 0
Jun 25            Chuck             83121             2.5               248.75
Jun 25            Chuck             85147             1.25              45.3
Jun 24            Penney            85109             1                 0
Jun 24            Penney            84142             1.75              79.4
Jun 25            Penney            83101             1.5               110.95



------------------------------------------------------------------------------------
Type entry or use ⌘ commands                                          ⌘-? for Help
```

mand. Type ⌘N and press RETURN to accept the name of the file, as is. For each category name, type **CONTROL-Y** to erase the default name, then type the new category name (Date, Tech, Acct. #, Hours, Parts, Labor, or Total), and press RETURN (Figure 5-37).

When you've finished changing the last category name, ESC back to the Review/Add/Change screen (Figure 5-38). I've used the Layout command to adjust the column widths of the categories in the multiple record format display so that all seven categories are displayed.

Now if you want to arrange your data according to the values in the Total column, you're free to do so. Just press the TAB key until your cursor is in the Total column, type ⌘**A** (the Arrange command), and choose the fourth Arrange option: **From 9 to 0**.

When you're ready to go on to the next example of cutting and pasting, save Complete Repair to your data disk and then remove all the files from your Desktop.

From the Word Processor to the Data Base

A special situation may arise when you are preparing a word processor document. The document might contain a list of items, perhaps names. After you are through typing the list, you decide that you want the list to be in alphabetical order. What can you do?

FIGURE 5-37 Change the category names

```
File: Complete Repair         CHANGE NAME/CATEGORY     Escape: Review/Add/Change



Category names
================================================================================
Date                                              |
Tech                                              | Options:
Acct. #                                           |
Hours                                             | Type category name
Parts                                             | Up arrow   Go to previous category
Labor                                             |
Total                                             |
                                                  |
                                                  |
                                                  |
                                                  |
                                                  |
                                                  |
                                                  |
--------------------------------------------------------------------------------
Type entry or use ⌘ commands                                          51K Avail.
```

FIGURE 5-38 Adjust the column widths so you can see all categories

```
File: Complete Repair         REVIEW/ADD/CHANGE                 Escape: Main Menu

Selection: All records


Date      Tech        Acct. #    Hours     Parts        Labor        Total
================================================================================
Jun 24    Bill        83115      2         55.2         90           145.2
Jun 25    Bill        84200      1         .85          45           45.85
Jun 25    Bill        84138      1.5       67.35        67.5         134.85
Jun 24    Chuck       83211      1.5       120.75       67.5         188.25
Jun 24    Chuck       85114      1         0            45           45
Jun 25    Chuck       83121      2.5       248.75       112.5        361.25
Jun 25    Chuck       85147      1.25      45.3         56.25        101.55
Jun 24    Penney      85109      1         0            45           45
Jun 24    Penney      85142      1.75      79.4         78.75        158.15
Jun 25    Penney      83101      1.5       110.95       67.5         178.45



--------------------------------------------------------------------------------
Type entry or use ⌘ commands                                         ⌘-? for Help
```

You can transfer the list to a data base file and use the Arrange command. Then you can copy the alphabetized list back to the word processor document. Let's try it.

Figure 5-39 shows the original memo with a list of five names. Type the memo into a new word processor document called "Profit Sharing."

FIGURE 5-39 Type this Profit Sharing memo

```
File: Profit Sharing              REVIEW/ADD/CHANGE                Escape: Main Menu
=====|====|====|====|====|====|====|====|====|====|====|====|====|====|====|===
To:        All Employees
From:      Bookkeeping Dept.
Date:      December 21
Subject:   Profit Sharing


The following persons have been employed by Hot & Cold Inc.
for at least one year.  They are therefore eligible to
participate in this company's Profit Sharing Plan.

Employee                  Date of Hire
------------------------------------
Losik, Dennis             3/5/83
Crail, Steve              4/25/83
Drury, Tom                10/2/83
Sumner, Elizabeth         5/14/84
Rose, Ellen               9/3/84


-------------------------------------------------------------------------------
Type entry or use  commands             Line 1  Column  1          -? for Help
```

In order to copy the list of names to a data base file, you have to print the list to your data disk as an ASCII text file. (*Note:* The term ASCII is an acronym for American Standard Code for Information Interchange.) You might wonder why you don't print out the list in DIF format as you did in previous examples. The reason is that DIF files aren't supported in the word processor. You can either print on paper with your printer or print an ASCII file to your data disk.

You don't want to print the entire memo to the ASCII file, just the list of names. To do this, place your cursor on the first character of the first name, the "L" in "Losik," and type **P**. You want to print from the cursor position to the end of your memo so type **C**, for Cursor. Select option 2, **A text (ASCII) file on disk**, type **/DATA/ASCII** for the pathname, and press RETURN.

After the file has been recorded on your data disk, ESC to the Main Menu and select option 1. You're going to make a new data base file **From a text (ASCII) file**. You'll be asked: **How many categories per record?** Since each record will contain just the name of the employee (along with the date of hire), respond with **1** and press RETURN (Figure 5-40). The ProDOS pathname for the ASCII file is "/DATA/ASCII." Call your new data base file "Names."

Your screen should look like Figure 5-41. I know it looks as if only the names of the employees were transferred to the data base, but the dates of hire are there, too. In the multiple record format screen, which you are looking at now, only the first 16 characters of a category are

FIGURE 5-40 Load the word processor ASCII file into a new data base

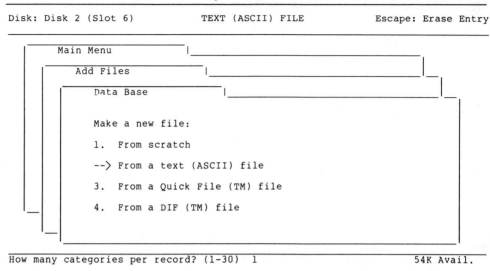

```
Disk: Disk 2 (Slot 6)          TEXT (ASCII) FILE          Escape: Erase Entry

    Main Menu
      Add Files
        Data Base

          Make a new file:

          1.  From scratch

          --> From a text (ASCII) file

          3.  From a Quick File (TM) file

          4.  From a DIF (TM) file

How many categories per record? (1-30)  1                   54K Avail.
```

FIGURE 5-41 Only the first 16 characters are displayed

```
File: Names                    REVIEW/ADD/CHANGE              Escape: Main Menu

Selection: All records

Category 01
===============================================================================
Losik, Dennis
Crail, Steve
Drury, Tom
Sumner, Elizabe
Rose, Ellen

-------------------------------------------------------------------------------
Type entry or use ⌘ commands                                       ⌘-? for Help
```

displayed. Type ⌘**L**, the Layout command. Then hold down the OPEN-APPLE key and press the right-arrow key about 18 times until the dates appear.

ESC back to Review/Add/Change. The point of this example was to alphabetize the list of names, so type ⌘**A** and press RETURN to accept the first Arrangement order: **From A to Z** (Figure 5-42).

FIGURE 5-42 Arrange the names in alphabetic order

```
File: Names                    REVIEW/ADD/CHANGE                Escape: Main Menu

Selection: All records


Category 01
================================================================================
Crail, Steve               4/25/83
Drury, Tom                 10/2/83
Losik, Dennis              3/5/83
Rose, Ellen                9/3/84
Sumner, Elizabeth          5/14/84













--------------------------------------------------------------------------------
Type entry or use ⌘ commands                                         ⌘-? for Help
```

Now that the list is alphabetized, you want to paste it back into your Profit Sharing memo. To do this, you'll have to print the data base file to the Clipboard. Then you can paste from the Clipboard into your memo.

Type ⌘**P** to get to the Report Format screen. Choose option 2 and name the new Tables report "Clipboard." Hold down the OPEN-APPLE key and press the right-arrow key until the Length Indicator shows a value of 35 (Figure 5-43).

You don't want a Report Header to be printed with your list of names, so type ⌘**O** to get to Printer Options. Type **PH** and press RETURN to change the value of the Print Report Header option to "No." Then ESC back to the Report Format screen.

Now type ⌘**P** and send your report to **The clipboard (for the Word Processor)**. This should be option 4 on the Print the Report screen. (*Note:* If you see a message to type in a report date, then you didn't set the PH option to "No." ESC out and try again.)

After you see the message telling you that your report is on the Clipboard, press the Space Bar. Type ⌘**Q** and select the Profit Sharing document from the Desktop Index. Your cursor should still be on the "L" in "Losik" (move it there if it isn't). Now delete the list of names from your memo with the Delete command. Type ⌘**D**, press the down-arrow key five times, and press RETURN. To paste in the alphabetized list from the Clipboard, type ⌘**M** and **F** (Figure 5-44).

FIGURE 5-43 Create a new Tables report

```
File: Names                          REPORT FORMAT                  Escape: Report Menu
Report: Clipboard
Selection: All records


================================================================================
--> or <--   Move cursor                      -J  Right justify this category
 >    <     Switch category positions        -K  Define a calculated category
-->  <--   Switch column width              -N  Change report name and/or title
-A  Arrange (sort) on this category          -O  Printer options
-D  Delete this category                     -P  Print the report
-G  Add/remove group totals                  -R  Change record selection rules
-I  Insert a prev. deleted category          -T  Add/remove category totals
--------------------------------------------------------------------------------

Category 01                        L
-A-------------------------------- e
Crail, Steve             4/25/83   n
Drury, Tom               10/2/83   3
Losik, Dennis            3/5/83    5

--------------------------------------------------------------------------------
Use options shown above to change report format                     54K Avail.
```

FIGURE 5-44 Paste the Clipboard report into your memo

```
File: Profit Sharing           REVIEW/ADD/CHANGE                 Escape: Main Menu
=====|====|====|====|====|====|====|====|====|====|====|====|====|====|====|===
To:        All Employees
From:      Bookkeeping Dept.
Date:      December 21
Subject:   Profit Sharing


The following persons have been employed by Hot & Cold Inc.
for at least one year. They are therefore eligible to
participate in this company's Profit Sharing Plan.

Employee                 Date of Hire
-------------------------------------
Crail, Steve             4/25/83
Drury, Tom               10/2/83
Losik, Dennis            3/5/83
Rose, Ellen              9/3/84
Sumner, Elizabeth        5/14/84



--------------------------------------------------------------------------------
Type entry or use  commands            Line 13  Column  1          -? for Help
```

There is, theoretically, one more way of using Cut and Paste, from the word processor to the spreadsheet. Practically, however, this exchange of data can't be done. The only type of data file that can be written from the word processor is an ASCII text file, but *AppleWorks* spreadsheets can't accept ASCII files, only DIF files or *VisiCalc* files. (You'll learn about *VisiCalc* files in the next chapter.)

III. SPECIAL APPLICATION: MAIL MERGE

The major feature added to version 2.0 of *AppleWorks* is the mail merge utility. This feature lets you create personalized form letters using data from a data base to supply names and addresses for a word processor document.

Here's a practical example. Imagine that you wanted to send a notice to each of your customers, advising them that your company, Hot & Cold Inc., had opened a second store. You want each letter to be "personalized" with the customer's name and address as well as an appropriate salutation.

Producing personalized form letters is a three-step process. First, you write the letter, complete except for the inside address and salutation. Second, you create a data base (or use an existing one) with the data you'll need (e.g., first name, last name, address, city, etc.). And third, you merge the letter and the data base to produce form letters.

CREATING THE FORM LETTER

Figure 5-45 shows the letter you intend to send to your customers. Add a new word processor document to your *AppleWorks* desktop named "Form Letter."

Type the letter you see in Figure 5-45, and save it. You can, of course, type your own form letter, but notice that there are 6 blank lines between the date and the salutation. This is where you'll eventually place the inside address for each of your customers.

CREATING THE DATA BASE

After you've typed in and saved the form letter, ESC to the Main Menu and add a new data base to your desktop. Name it "Customers."

This data base is similar to one you created in Chapter 3. Instead of placing the customer's entire name in one category, I've used three categories: one for the title (Mr., Ms., Dr., etc.), one for the first name, and one for the last name. As the mail merge project develops, you'll see why this is necessary. I've also combined the City, State, and Zip categories into a single category. (*Note:* If you would like to be able to arrange the records of your Customer data base by zip code, then you'd have to keep the zip code entries in their own separate category.)

Figure 5-46 shows the list of six category names for the Customer data base. Type them in (don't forget to press RETURN after each name,

FIGURE 5-45 The body of the form letter

```
October 12




Dear

For the past four years, we at Hot & Cold Inc. have been
serving our customers from our original location in downtown
Rolling Meadows. Your continued patronage and good
references to your friends and neighbors have resulted in a
very gratifying increase in our business.

I want to thank you personally for thinking of us when you
had a heating or air conditioning problem. I know we have
satisfied you in the past and I pledge that we'll continue
to satisfy you in the future.

In order to better serve our customers, especially those in
nearby Elk Grove, we have opened a second facility there.
Our new store is:

          Hot & Cold Inc.
          326 S. Main St.
          Elk Grove

          (312) 555-7540

We invite you to stop by and see our new store. We're really
proud of it.


Sincerely,

Mike Sloan
President
```

including the last one). When you're through entering the category names, press ESC and then the Space Bar to get to Insert New Records.

Enter the three records you see in Figure 5-47 (and any others you like). Notice that the third record has no entry for the company. I did this so that you could see one of the special options in the mail merge utility. When you've finished entering the last record, press ESC and Ⓒ Z to go to the multiple record Review/Add/Change display.

FIGURE 5-46 Create a new data base with these categories

```
File: Customers          CHANGE NAME/CATEGORY          Escape: Review/Add/Change



Category names
================================================================================
Title                                       |
FirstName                                   | Options:
LastName                                    |
Company                                     | Type category name
Address                                     | Up arrow   Go to previous category
City, State, Zip                            |
                                            |
                                            |
                                            |
                                            |
                                            |
                                            |
                                            |
--------------------------------------------------------------------------------
Type entry or use ⌘ commands                                         54K Avail.
```

FIGURE 5-47 Enter these three records

```
File: Customers               REVIEW/ADD/CHANGE                Escape: Main Menu

Selection: All records


Title FirstName LastName Company        Address           City, State, Zip
================================================================================
Mr.   Harry     Glass    Paint Plus     1232 Carpenter    Northbrook, IL  60189
Ms.   Joan      Adams    Ace Computers  561 Montclair     Elk Grove, IL  60029
Dr.   Horace    Greene   -              62 Federal Ct.    Arlington, IL  60001







--------------------------------------------------------------------------------
Type entry or use ⌘ commands                                       ⌘-? for Help
```

MERGING THE DATA BASE WITH THE FORM LETTER

Before you can add data from this data base to your form letter, you have to place the data on the Clipboard. Type ⌘**P** to enter the report generator, and then select option 2 to create a new Tables format. Name the new format "Mail Merge."

From the Report Format screen, type ⌘**P** and choose option 4, **The clipboard (for Mail Merge)**. *AppleWorks* tells you that the mail merge data is now on the Clipboard. Press the Space Bar. Then use the Desktop Index (⌘**Q**) to switch to your Form Letter.

Now you can add the data base categories for title, first name, and so forth, to your letter. Move your cursor to the beginning of the second blank line under the date in your letter. On this line you'll place data for the title, first name, and last name of your customers.

Type ⌘**O** to display Printer Options. The last printer option on the list is MM, Mail Merge. Type **MM**, and press RETURN. Figure 5-48 shows the Mail Merge screen with its list of categories from your Customer data base. (*Note:* If you see a message saying there is no mail merge data on the Clipboard, you didn't make the correct Print choice from your Customer data base. Go back to the report format of your data base, type ⌘**P**, and be sure to choose the option **The clipboard (for Mail Merge)**. Also, be careful not to place anything else on the Clipboard while you're performing the mail merge. If you do, you'll wipe out the mail merge data on the Clipboard.)

FIGURE 5-48 The Mail Merge list of data base categories

```
File: Form Letter                MAIL MERGE              Escape: Printer Options
|====|====|====|====|====|====|====|====|====|====|====|====|====|====|===|====|

Select a data base category

 1.  Title
 2.  FirstName
 3.  LastName
 4.  Company
 5.  Address
 6.  City, State, Zip








--------------------------------------------------------------------------------
Type number, or use arrows, then press Return                        53K Avail.
```

The first category you want to insert is Title. Since it's already highlighted, just press RETURN to select it. At the bottom of your screen, *AppleWorks* asks if you want to omit the line when all entries on the line are blank. I'll discuss this option in a moment, but for now, accept the default choice of "No" by pressing RETURN.

AppleWorks inserts the Title mail merge category into your letter (Figure 5-49).

FIGURE 5-49 The Title category is inserted into the form letter

```
File: Form Letter          PRINTER OPTIONS          Escape: Review/Add/Change
====|====|====|====|====|====|====|====|====|====|====|====|====|====|====|===
October 12

^<Title>



Dear

For the past four years, we at Hot & Cold Inc. have been
serving our customers from our original location in downtown
  PW=8.0  LM=1.0  RM=1.0  CI=10  UJ  PL=11.0  TM=0.0  BM=2.0  LI=6  SS
Option:                UJ: Unjustified      GB: Group Begin      BE: Boldface End
                       CN: Centered         GE: Group End        +B: Superscript Beg
PW: Platen Width       PL: Paper Length     HE: Page Header      +E: Superscript End
LM: Left Margin        TM: Top Margin       FO: Page Footer      -B: Subscript Begin
RM: Right Margin       BM: Bottom Margin    SK: Skip Lines       -E: Subscript End
CI: Chars per Inch     LI: Lines per Inch   PN: Page Number      UB: Underline Begin
P1: Proportional-1     SS: Single Space     PE: Pause Each page  UE: Underline End
P2: Proportional-2     DS: Double Space     PH: Pause Here       PP: Print Page No.
IN: Indent             TS: Triple Space     SM: Set a Marker     EK: Enter Keyboard
JU: Justified          NP: New Page         BB: Boldface Begin   MM: Mail Merge
```

Let's insert two more mail merge categories on the same line. Type **MM** again, and press RETURN. This time choose the second category, FirstName (type **2** and press RETURN). Press RETURN again to accept the "No" choice for the "omit line" option.

AppleWorks inserts the FirstName category next to the Title category and automatically separates them by a space. Now add the LastName category to your letter. Type **MM**, press RETURN, select the third category, LastName, from the list, and press RETURN twice.

Now all three categories are on the first line of the letter's inside address. ESC back to the Review/Add/Change screen, and use the arrow keys to move your cursor to the beginning of the next line (don't press RETURN). This line will contain one category, the company name.

Type ⌘**O**, and choose the MM print option. Select the fourth category, Company. But this time, instead of accepting the default choice of "No," for omit line, press the "Y" key for "Yes." ESC out of Printer Options, and look at the inserted category in your letter (Figure 5-50).

Notice that *AppleWorks* has enclosed the Company category in square brackets rather than angle brackets. It does this to indicate that if a data base record has no entry for Company, it not only won't print anything but it will also eliminate the empty line from your document. If you had said "No" to the omit line option instead of "Yes," then records with no Company entry would show a blank line in their letters where the Company name would normally be inserted.

FIGURE 5-50 The Company category is enclosed in square brackets

```
File: Form Letter              REVIEW/ADD/CHANGE              Escape: Main Menu
====|====|====|====|====|====|====|====|====|====|====|====|====|====|====|===
October 12

^<Title> ^<FirstName> ^<LastName>
^[Company]


Dear

For the past four years, we at Hot & Cold Inc. have been
serving our customers from our original location in downtown
Rolling Meadows. Your continued patronage and good
references to your friends and neighbors have resulted in a
very gratifying increase in our business.

We want to thank you personally for thinking of us when you
had a heating or air conditioning problem. I know we have
satisifed you in the past and I pledge that we'll continue
to satisfy you in the future.

--------------------------------------------------------------------------------
Type entry or use ⌘ commands            Line 4  Column 12       ⌘-? for Help
```

Use the arrow keys to move your cursor to the beginning of the next line. Type ⌘ **O**, choose the MM option, and select the fifth category, Address. Since all records will have addresses, accept the "No" choice for omit line by pressing RETURN.

ESC out of Printer Options, and use the arrow keys to move your cursor to the beginning of the next line. Go back to Printer Options, choose Mail Merge (MM), and insert the last category, City, State, Zip. Again accept the "No" choice for omit line, and ESC to Review/Add/Change.

That completes the letter's inside address; now for the salutation. Use the arrow keys to move your cursor one space to the right of the word "Dear." You want the salutation to read "Dear Mr. Glass" or "Dear Dr. Greene." In other words, you want it to read "Dear <Title> <LastName>."

Enter Printer Options and choose MM. Select the Title category, and say "No" to omit line. Choose MM again, and select the LastName category. Accept the "No" choice for omit line, ESC back to your letter, and compare it with Figure 5-51.

It's *almost* the same. It needs a colon after the LastName category on the salutation line. Press the left-arrow key once to back the cursor up one space. Then type a colon (:).

Save this letter again.

FIGURE 5-51 All the mail merge categories have been inserted

```
File: Form Letter                 REVIEW/ADD/CHANGE              Escape: Main Menu
====|====|====|====|====|====|====|====|====|====|====|====|====|====|====|===
October 12

^<Title> ^<FirstName> ^<LastName>
^[Company]
^<Address>
^<City, State, Zip>

Dear ^<Title> ^<LastName>:

For the past four years, we at Hot & Cold Inc. have been
serving our customers from our original location in downtown
Rolling Meadows. Your continued patronage and good
references to your friends and neighbors have resulted in a
very gratifying increase in our business.

We want to thank you personally for thinking of us when you
had a heating or air conditioning problem. I know we have
satisfied you in the past and I pledge that we'll continue
to satisfy you in the future.

--------------------------------------------------------------------------------
Type entry or use ⌘ commands            Line 8  Column 27        ⌘-? for Help
```

PRINTING MAIL MERGE LETTERS

OK, let's print the letters and see what they look like. Make sure your printer is turned on and has paper. Then type ⌘**P**. Choose your printer from the list and press RETURN.

AppleWorks knows your letter is a mail merge document. It's asking you (Figure 5-52) whether you want to print the actual form letters with merged data (choice 1), or just a copy of the letter with the category names showing (choice 2).

Accept choice 1 by pressing RETURN. Then press RETURN again to select one copy of each form letter. *AppleWorks* will print a copy of the form letter for each record in your Customer data base.

Look at the third form letter. Notice that the inside address is only three lines long instead of four. This customer's record had no entry for Company.

Two comments about printing form letters: First, when you want to print form letters, you have to have both the data base and the letter on your *AppleWorks* Desktop. Remember, you must print the data base report to the Clipboard (for Mail Merge) before the mail merge utility can use the data.

Second, *AppleWorks* prints the form letters in the order of the records in the data base. In other words, if you want the letters printed

FIGURE 5-52 Choose option 1 to print your form letters

```
File: Form Letter              PRINT MENU              Escape: Review/Add/Change
====|====|====|====|====|====|====|====|====|====|====|====|====|====|====|====|===



                    1.  Merge data base items with this document

                    2.  Print document without merging





--------------------------------------------------------------------------------
Type number, or use arrows, then press RETURN                        53K Avail.
```

in alphabetical order by company name, for example, you must sort (Arrange) the data base file by Company *before* you print the file to the Clipboard.

Final Comments

The ease with which you can Cut and Paste between *AppleWorks* documents is one of the major advantages of this integrated software package. Practice each of the above examples, especially the mail merge example, until you are comfortable doing them. This will be time well spent.

CHAPTER

6 APPLEWORKS AND THE OUTSIDE WORLD

One way of judging the overall usefulness of a computer program such as *AppleWorks* is to see how (or if) it can be used with other existing computer programs. In this chapter, you'll see how to use *AppleWorks* with different programs and hardware products.

The first section of the chapter discusses how to convert files between ProDOS and DOS 3.3. This is a skill you'll have to master in order to use *AppleWorks* in conjunction with other programs such as *Business Graphics* and *VisiCalc*.

Section two shows you how to use *AppleWorks* with nine different, popular programs. Three of them, *Apple Writer*, *VisiCalc*, and *Business Graphics*, have been around for several years. A fourth, *Access //*, is a typical data communications package. *The Graphics Department* is a full-featured graphics arts program. *Quick File* was written by the same author who wrote *AppleWorks* and is similar to its data base section. *The Sensible Speller* is a program that checks for correct spelling in word processor documents.

Section three describes a variety of software products that were written especially for use with *AppleWorks*. Programs such as *Mega-Works*, *Spellworks*, and *HabaMerge* provide mail merge capability to those of you who have early versions of *AppleWorks* (earlier than version 2.0). Another program, *ReportWorks*, enhances *AppleWorks*' report generating features. There's also an entire group of programs from Pinpoint Publishing that add a number of new features to your *AppleWorks* program.

The last section of the chapter describes several pieces of computer hardware that can increase the usefulness of *AppleWorks*.

I. CONVERTING FILES BETWEEN DOS 3.3 AND PRODOS

Before you try to use *AppleWorks* files with other programs (or other programs' files with *AppleWorks*), you need to understand a bit about your Apple's disk operating system. The disk operating system of a computer controls the way data is stored on, and retrieved from, your disk. You may remember, back in Chapter 1, that you formatted a data disk for *AppleWorks*. It was the disk operating system that told your Apple computer how to format the disk. When you type S to save a file, it's the disk operating system that knows how to record your file onto your data disk.

The reason for this discussion is that there is more than one disk operating system for your Apple computer. *AppleWorks* was written under the *ProDOS* operating system, while programs such as *VisiCalc* were written under an older operating system called *DOS 3.3*. If you want to exchange data between *AppleWorks* and programs such as *VisiCalc*, you'll have to learn how to convert your data files from one operating system to the other.

Fortunately, you have a program that will perform this conversion for you. It's the same System Utilities program you used to copy the *AppleWorks* disks back in Chapter 1.

One of the first things to remember, when you want to convert files from one operating system to the other, is that only standard text files can be converted. Since *AppleWorks* files are *not* standard text files, they cannot be converted from ProDOS to DOS 3.3. But you *can* convert an *AppleWorks* ASCII text file from ProDOS to DOS 3.3 (and back), and all three *AppleWorks* applications allow you to print their files to disk as ASCII text files. These files, and DIF files produced from the data base and spreadsheet sections of *AppleWorks*, can be converted from ProDOS format to DOS 3.3. (*Note:* ASCII and DIF formats are discussed in Chapter 5.)

When you convert the other way, from DOS 3.3 to ProDOS, you'll be able to convert virtually any type of file—ASCII, DIF, or even *VisiCalc* files. In DOS 3.3, these files are all saved as text files, so converting isn't a problem. Converting *Quick File* files for use with the data base section of *AppleWorks* is even easier—you don't convert them at all. *AppleWorks* will use *Quick File* files exactly as they are.

Before you begin converting files between DOS 3.3 and ProDOS, take two blank disks and label one of them "ProDOS Files (converted from DOS 3.3)." Label the other disk "DOS 3.3 Files (converted from ProDOS)."

Start up your Apple computer with the System Utilities disk. (*Note:* If you're still in *AppleWorks*, quit the program with option 6 from the Main Menu, and restart your Apple with the System Utilities disk.) Apple IIe and IIGS owners press the "Y" key when the program asks if you prefer 80-column display.

The process of converting files between DOS 3.3 and ProDOS is the same for all Apple computers—IIe, IIc, or IIGS. The only difference is the names given to the disk drives. On an Apple IIe or IIGS, disk drives are referred to as "Slot 6, Drive 1" or "Slot 6, Drive 2," while on an Apple IIc, they're referred to as "Built-in Drive" or "External Disk IIc."

In the following discussion, I'll assume you have an Apple IIe (or IIGS), but if you own an Apple IIc, don't worry. Every time you see a reference to "Slot 6, Drive 1," just substitute "Built-in Drive." Similarly, "Slot 6, Drive 2" really means "External Disk //c" for Apple IIc owners.

Formatting ProDOS and DOS 3.3 Disks

From the Main Menu of System Utilities (Figure 6-1), choose option 6, **Format a Disk**, by typing **6**, and pressing RETURN.

Remove the System Utilities disk and insert the blank disk you labeled "ProDOS Files." Apple IIe and IIGS owners press RETURN three times to select the Slot 6, Drive 1 disk drive. (Apple IIc owners press RETURN just once to select the Built-in Drive.)

FIGURE 6-1 System Utilities Main Menu

```
System Utilities                                                   Main Menu
Version 2.1          Copyright Apple Computer, Inc. 1984, 1985
--------------------------------------------------------------------------------
                     Work on Individual Files

                     1.  Copy Files
                     2.  Delete Files
                     3.  Rename Files
                     4.  Lock/Unlock Files

                         Work on Entire Disks

                     5.  Duplicate a Disk
                     6.  Format a Disk
                     7.  Identify and Catalog a Disk
                     8.  Advanced Operations

                     9.  Exit System Utilities

Type a number or press ↓ or ↑ to select
an option.  Then press RETURN.
--------------------------------------------------------------------------------
For Help: Press -? or -?
--------------------------------------------------------------------------------
```

The program wants to know which operating system to use to format your disk (Figure 6-2). Since you inserted the blank disk labeled "ProDOS Files," select the ProDOS operating system by pressing RETURN.

Every ProDOS disk is given a name (called its *volume name*) when it's formatted. All Volume names begin with a slash character (/). The program makes up a name for you, using the word "BLANK" followed

FIGURE 6-2 Format the first disk using ProDOS

```
System Utilities                                          Format a Di
Version 2.1                                               ESC: Main Me

                    Using Slot: 6, Drive 1

                    Select the Operating System

                    1.  <PRODOS>

                    2.  DOS 3.3

                    3.  Pascal

                    4.  I don't know which one to use


Type a number or press ↓ or ↑ to select
an option.  Then press RETURN.

For Help: Press -? or ⌘-?
```

by a two-digit number (e.g., /BLANK27), but I'd like you to name your ProDOS disk, /PRODOS. Type the 7 characters **/PRODOS** and press RETURN.

Press RETURN once more, and the disk will be formatted. (*Note:* If your "ProDOS Files" disk has been formatted previously, you'll see a message asking you if it's OK to erase the disk. Press RETURN to indicate "Yes.") After about 20 seconds, you'll see the message Formatting ... Done! (Figure 6-3).

Remove the ProDOS Files disk and insert the DOS 3.3 Files disk. Press the RETURN key, and again select Slot 6, Drive 1 (Built-in Drive for Apple IIc owners). This time, choose the second listed operating system (see Figure 6-2), DOS 3.3, by pressing the **2** key and then RETURN.

With the disk you labeled DOS3.3 Files in your disk drive, press RETURN again, and this disk will be formatted for DOS 3.3. (*Note:* The program names all DOS 3.3 disks "Vol 254" so you don't have to name them. The DOS 3.3 operating system doesn't really use the disk name for anything.)

Saving a File as an ASCII Text File

Before you can transfer a file from ProDOS to DOS 3.3, you must have a file to transfer. So let's quit the utilities program, and use

FIGURE 6-3 Formatting was successful

```
System Utilities                                    Format a Disk
Version 2.1                                        ESC: Main Menu

                  Using Slot: 6, Drive: 1

                  Operating System : ProDOS

                  New Volume Name : /PRODOS

                  Formatting ... Done!

Format complete; Press RETURN to continue; ESC to return to the Main Menu
```

AppleWorks to save an ASCII file to your ProDOS Files disk. Press the ESC key to return to the System Utilities Main Menu. Choose option 9, **Exit System Utilities**, and press RETURN when the program asks if you really want to quit.

Start up *AppleWorks*, and load the file Office Memo (or any other word processor document). Type ⌘**P** and press RETURN to print the document from the beginning.

You want to print this document to your ProDOS Files disk as an ASCII file, so choose option 2, **A text (ASCII) file on disk**. At the bottom of your screen, *AppleWorks* wants to know the pathname for the ASCII file.

A pathname tells the operating system where to look for a particular file. The name consists of the volume name of the disk (/PRODOS) and the name you give to the file. Suppose you name the file, "MEMO." Then the pathname would be /PRODOS/MEMO. All ProDOS pathnames begin with a slash (/) and use another slash to separate the volume name from the filename. Type the 12 characters /PRODOS/MEMO (Figure 6-4), and press RETURN.

AppleWorks will try to save your memo as an ASCII file and will not succeed. In fact, you'll see a message saying **Unable to begin /PRODOS/MEMO**. *AppleWorks* looked for a ProDOS disk with the volume name /PRODOS and couldn't find it. Now it's asking you if you want it to try again.

Let's help *AppleWorks* out. Remove the *AppleWorks* Program disk, and insert the ProDOS Files disk. Press the "Y" key so that *AppleWorks*

FIGURE 6-4 Save Office Memo to your data disk as an ASCII file

```
File: Office Memo                  PRINT MENU                Escape: Erase entry
====|====|====|====|====|====|====|====|====|====|====|====|====|====|====|===



                    While the disk is running
                    you can use these keys:

                    Escape        to stop printing and
                                  return to Review/Add/Change

                    Space Bar     to pause
                                  to continue printing


--------------------------------------------------------------------------------
Pathname?  /PRODOS/MEMO                                              54K Avail.
```

will try once more, and this time your ASCII file will be successfully saved.

Feel free to use the same process to save any of your other *AppleWorks* files (data bases and spreadsheets, too) as ASCII files. With data base files, create a Tables report, then print the file as either an ASCII file or a DIF file. For spreadsheets, you also have the choice of ASCII or DIF. If you choose DIF, *AppleWorks* will ask if you want the file saved in "Row" or Column" order. Choose "Row" order. Give each ASCII or DIF file a different file name, but remember that each pathname must begin with the same volume name, /PRODOS. Remember also that ProDOS names cannot include spaces. If you want to use the name "Expense Form," for example, substitute a period (.) for the space between the two words. When you're through saving documents as ASCII (or DIF) files, quit *AppleWorks*.

Converting the Files

Start up the System Utilities program again, and choose option 1, **Copy Files**, from the Main Menu. Then remove the Utilities disk, and insert the ProDOS Files disk. If you have a two-drive system, place the disk labeled DOS 3.3 Files in drive 2 (the external drive for IIc owners).

Select Slot 6, Drive 1 (Built-in Drive for IIc owners) as your source drive for copying files. If your computer system is a two-drive system, select Slot 6, Drive 2 as the destination drive (External Disk //c). If yours is a single-drive system, select Slot 6, Drive 1 as your destination drive.

Press the RETURN key to copy "Some" of the files instead of "All" the files. The program will show you a list of the files on your disk. Near the top of your screen, just under the solid line, you'll see the volume name of your disk, /PRODOS. Utilities selects the first file on the list by placing brackets around the name. To choose this file to be copied to your DOS 3.3 disk, press the right-arrow key. A check appears next to the name. If you change your mind and decide not to copy the file, press the left-arrow key to remove the checkmark. The up- and down-arrow keys move the brackets from one filename to the next, so that you can indicate whether you want to copy each file in the list. (*Note:* If you had chosen to copy "All" the files, you wouldn't see this list of files.)

Press the RETURN key when you've finished selecting the files you want to copy. If you have a two-drive system, that's all you have to do. The Utilities program will copy the files you selected from the ProDOS Files disk to the DOS 3.3 Files disk. If you have a one-drive system, Utilities will prompt you to swap the "source" disk with the "destination" disk (Figure 6-5). Remember, for this example, the source disk is your ProDOS Files disk; the destination disk is your DOS 3.3 Files disk.

FIGURE 6-5 Swap the source and destination disks

```
System Utilities                                         Copy Files
Version 2.1                                          ESC: Main Menu
-------------------------------------------------------------------
Copying MEMO ...



   ----------------------------------------------------------
   | Place the destination disk in the Slot: 6, Drive: 1.  Be sure to
   | use the correct disk.
   |
   |
   | Press RETURN to continue; ESC to return to the Main Menu.
   |
   ----------------------------------------------------------
```

As each file is copied, you'll see a listing of the file's name, and the word "Done" when Utilities has finished copying it. After all the files you selected have been copied, press the ESC key to return to the Main Menu. Let's examine the DOS 3.3 Files disk to see that the ProDOS files you chose were indeed copied. From the Main Menu, select option 7,

Identify and Catalog a Disk. Your DOS 3.3 Files disk will be in either drive 1 or drive 2. Choose the drive that contains the DOS 3.3 disk, then press RETURN again to list the files on your screen (Display) instead of to your printer. Figure 6-6 shows a typical list. The actual filenames you'll see depend on your original choice of which files to copy.

FIGURE 6-6 Looking at the DOS 3.3 Files disk

```
System Utilities                                  Identify and Catalog a Disk
Version 2.1                                                  ESC: Main Menu

Disk Name : Vol 254                               Disk Format : DOS 3.3
Filename                      Type                        Size
 MEMO                         Text                          9
 EXPENSE.FORM                 Text                          9

2 Files Listed, 18 Sectors Listed, 478 Available


Listing complete; Press RETURN to continue; ESC to return to the Main Menu.
```

If you try to copy a ProDOS file that is not a text file, you'll see a warning message (Figure 6-7). Utilities will ignore this file (after you press the RETURN key) and attempt to convert the remaining files you've selected.

When you want to copy DOS 3.3 files to ProDOS, use the DOS 3.3 Files disk as the source disk, and the ProDOS Files disk as the destination disk. Otherwise, the conversion process is unchanged.

II. USING *APPLEWORKS* WITH OTHER PROGRAMS

In this section, you'll learn how to use your *AppleWorks* program with other software programs. The programs discussed here fall into three categories. With the first group of programs (e.g., *Apple Writer*, *Quick File*, *VisiCalc*), you'll be transferring data files from the application to *AppleWorks*. It'll be just the reverse with programs such as *Business Graphics*, *The Graphics Department*, and *Access //*—you'll be converting *AppleWorks* files to use with these programs. The last group of programs are packages that were created solely to enhance *AppleWorks*.

FIGURE 6-7 Don't try to copy standard *AppleWorks* files to DOS 3.3 disks

```
System Utilities                                             Copy Files
Version 2.1                                              ESC: Main Menu
Copying OFFICE.MEMO ...



     Incompatible File Type

     Only files that have a corresponding file type on the destination
     disk can be copied.  For example, DOS 3.3 Text and Binary files can
     be copied to ProDOS disks, since ProDOS supports Text and Binary
     files.

     Press RETURN to continue.
```

Word Processor: *Apple Writer*

Apple Computer has brought out several versions of this popular word processor program. The earliest version (*Apple Writer* 1.0) dates back to 1979 and was written under the DOS 3.2 operating system. This program was revised twice—once as *Apple Writer* 1.1, still in DOS 3.2, the second time as *Apple Writer* 1.1 but in DOS 3.3 format. However, files created with any of these early versions of *Apple Writer* are incompatible with *AppleWorks*. These versions of *Apple Writer* did not produce standard ASCII text files.

In 1981, the program was completely rewritten by Paul Lutus and was titled *Apple Writer*][. This version and all succeeding versions did use ASCII text files for their document file format. In 1982, Apple introduced another version of *Apple Writer*, still in DOS 3.3, called *Apple Writer* //. This version sported new features and could be run only on an Apple IIe. Two years later, a ProDOS version of this program, called *Apple Writer* 2.0, appeared for the Apple IIe and IIc, and a year later, version 2.1 was released to correct an error in version 2.0.

Starting with the 1981 release of *Apple Writer*][, all versions up to the present create files that can be used by *AppleWorks*. Files from the DOS 3.3 versions of *Apple Writer* require converting to ProDOS format, but files from versions 2.0 and 2.1 can be read directly by *AppleWorks*. If your copy of *Apple Writer* (or any other word processor that produces ASCII text files) is in DOS 3.3, refer to the discussion in the first part of this chapter and convert the file from DOS 3.3 to ProDOS.

Here's how to get *AppleWorks* to read a standard ASCII text file from a ProDOS disk. (*Note:* In the following examples, I'm going to assume that the ProDOS disk with files from your *Apple Writer* or *VisiCalc* programs has been given the volume name /PRODOS. If you are using a disk with a different volume name, substitute your disk's volume name any time you see /PRODOS used.)

Start up *AppleWorks* and select option 1 from the Main Menu. From the Add Files Menu, choose option 3, **Make a new file for the Word Processor**. From the Word Processor Menu (Figure 6-8), tell *AppleWorks* that you want to make a new file: **From a text (ASCII) file**.

FIGURE 6-8 Creating a word processor document from an ASCII file

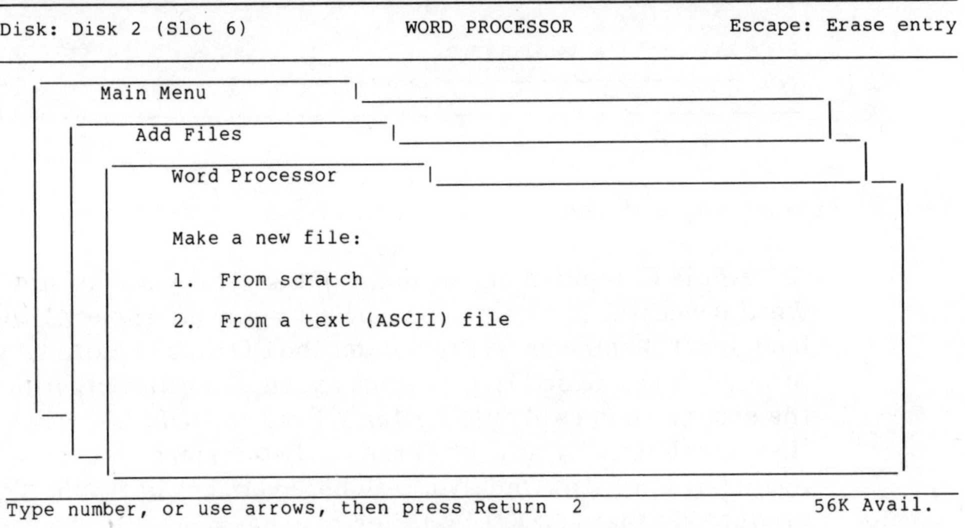

Insert the PRODOS data disk in the drive indicated at the top left of your screen. At the bottom of the screen, *AppleWorks* will ask you for the pathname of the ASCII file. Remember that a pathname consists of the volume name of the disk plus the name of the file. If the file's name was MY.RESUME, the pathname would be: /PRODOS/MY.RESUME. Be sure you have the PRODOS disk in one of your disk drives. After you press the RETURN key, *AppleWorks* will read the text file and then ask you to name the word processor file. You can give it any legitimate *AppleWorks* name. And that's all there is to it.

Here's a point to remember. Most word processors, including *Apple Writer*, allow you to insert control characters into the text. These control characters are used to send special commands to your printer. When you save the original word processor file to disk, the control characters are saved along with the rest of the text. But, when you read the file into *AppleWorks*, all imbedded control characters are changed into number (#) symbols. You can use the Replace command, ⌘R, to remove them.

Getting a word processor to read *AppleWorks* word processor files is almost as easy as going the other way. The only snag is to remember that ordinary *AppleWorks* files are *not* standard ASCII files. Other word processors can't read them. The solution is to print your *AppleWorks* word processor file to disk, using the option from the Print Menu (usually option 2) that says: **A text (ASCII) file on disk**. You'll be asked to supply a pathname for the ASCII file (/PRODOS/SAMPLE, for example).

Once the file has been printed to disk as an ASCII file, you can convert it to DOS 3.3 (if your word processor is in that format) and then have your word processor read the file, just as if it had originally created it.

Data Base: *Quick File*

If you bought an Apple IIe before *AppleWorks* was released and you needed a data base program, you probably purchased *Quick File //e*. This program, written by Rupert Lissner, the author of *AppleWorks*, was the forerunner of the data base section of *AppleWorks*. Several features are available to *AppleWorks* users that were not available to owners of *Quick File*. In addition to having a much-improved report-generating section, *AppleWorks* allows you to combine two or more data base files into one large file (up to the limit of your Apple's memory) by using the "Cut and Paste" feature. With *Quick File*, there was no way to merge separate files.

Transferring files from *Quick File* to *AppleWorks* is fairly simple. Start up *AppleWorks* and select option 1, **Add Files**, from the Main Menu. Tell *AppleWorks* you want to create a new data base file by choosing option 4 from the Add Files Menu. Now, from the Data Base Menu (Figure 6-9), select option 3, **From a Quick File (TM) file**. After you select this option, place your *Quick File* data disk in the drive indicated at the upper left corner of your screen, and press the Space Bar.

AppleWorks will show you a list of the *Quick File* files on that disk (Figure 6-10). Type the number of the file you want, and press RETURN. Then type a name for your *AppleWorks* data base file. (*Note:* The *AppleWorks* name can be the same as the *Quick File* name, but

FIGURE 6-9 ***Quick File* files are read directly by *AppleWorks***

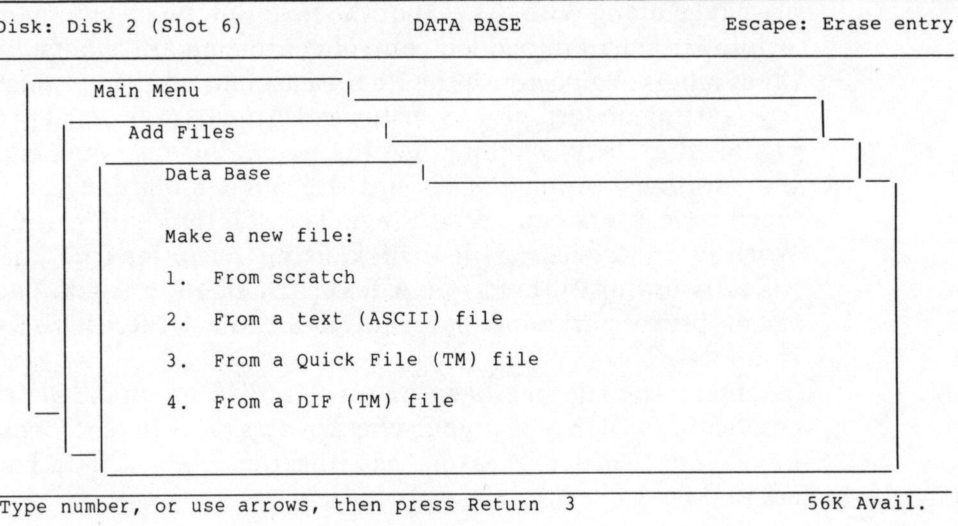

FIGURE 6-10 **A listing of *Quick File* files**

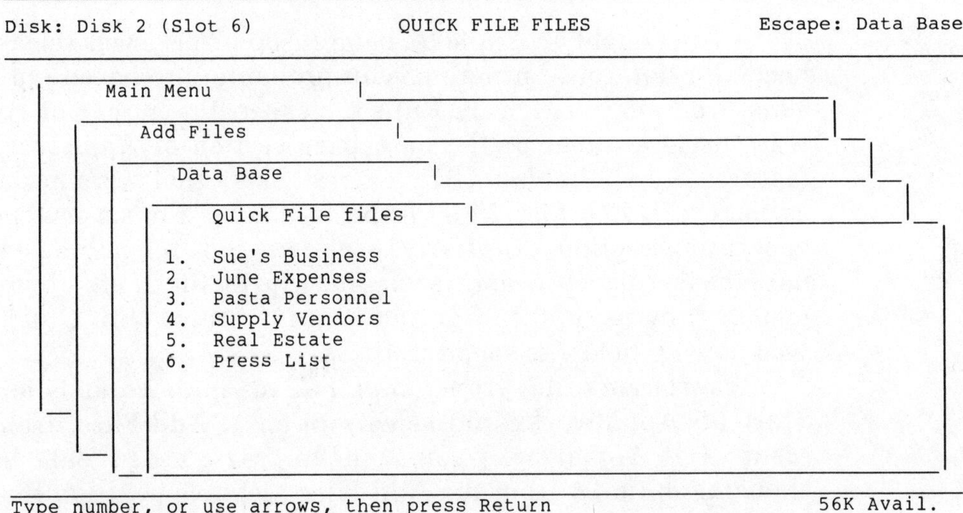

remember that an *AppleWorks* filename is made up of letters, numbers, periods, and spaces, only.) That's all there is to it.

If you want to transfer more than one *Quick File* file, you'll need to repeat the entire process for each file. This means that each *Quick File* file will be a separate *AppleWorks* data base file. If you want to combine two or more of them into a single file, you can use the "Cut and Paste" feature to Move or Copy the data from one file into the Clipboard, switch to another file, then paste the Clipboard into this file.

Report formats are also transferred, even though *Quick File* measures vertical spacing values (Top Margin, Page Length, etc.) in lines, while *AppleWorks* measures these parameters in inches. The transfer process does the conversion automatically by assuming that your printer moves paper vertically at the rate of 6 lines per inch.

By the way, this process of transferring data files from *Quick File* to *AppleWorks* works just as well (and uses exactly the same steps) with *Quick File ///* (written for the Apple III computer) as it does with *Quick File //*. Bear in mind, though, that you can't convert data base files the other way—from *AppleWorks* to either *Quick File //* or *Quick File ///*. That utility hasn't been written.

Spreadsheet: *VisiCalc*

In 1979, a company named Software Arts, Inc. developed a computer program that allowed personal computers to perform a completely new and different type of function—that of an electronic spreadsheet. They called their program *VisiCalc*, and it soon became the hottest selling piece of computer software in the industry. The first version of *VisiCalc* was written for the Apple II under DOS 3.2. Later versions were released under DOS 3.3, and when Apple brought out the Apple IIe, there was a version of *VisiCalc* written to take advantage of the IIe's special features. In 1984, a ProDOS version of *VisiCalc*, called *FlashCalc*, was released. All versions of *VisiCalc*, beginning with the first version written under DOS 3.3, produce files that can be read by the spreadsheet section of *AppleWorks*.

If your version of *VisiCalc* is a DOS 3.3 version, you'll have to transfer the file to a ProDOS disk (the disk you named /PRODOS) as explained earlier in this chapter. If you're using *FlashCalc*, you can use the data file, just as it is, from your *FlashCalc* data disk. (It's written under ProDOS.) Once you have the *VisiCalc* file on a ProDOS disk, it's easy to read the file into *AppleWorks*.

From *AppleWorks'* Main Menu, choose option 1. Then, from the Add Files Menu, select option 5, **Make a new file for the: Spreadsheet**. From the Spreadsheet Menu (Figure 6-11), select option 3, **From a VisiCalc (R) file**. At the bottom of the screen, you'll be asked for the pathname of the *VisiCalc* file. Type it in (see the above discussion on pathnames) and press RETURN. Then type a name for the new *AppleWorks* spreadsheet. That's it.

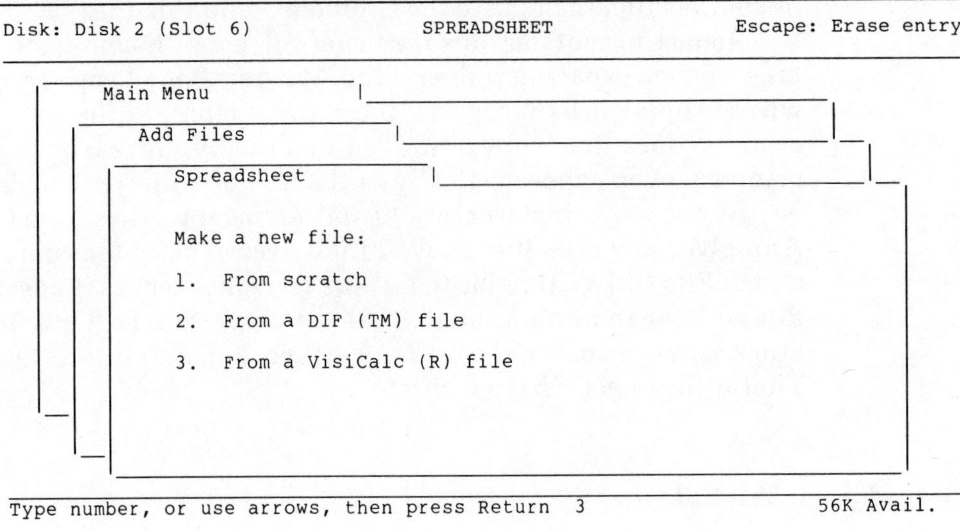

FIGURE 6-11 *VisiCalc* files are read with formulas

Your spreadsheet will look exactly the same in *AppleWorks* as it did in *VisiCalc*. Labels, values, *and* formulas are transferred.

You may wonder what the difference is between reading a *VisiCalc* file into *AppleWorks* and reading a DIF file (written by *VisiCalc* or another spreadsheet program) into *AppleWorks*. Both procedures work, but DIF files contain only labels and values—not formulas.

Unfortunately, if you want to read a spreadsheet file from *AppleWorks* into *VisiCalc*, the only way is to use DIF files. Print all or part of your *AppleWorks* spreadsheet to disk as a DIF file (use Row order). Convert the file from ProDOS to DOS 3.3 if necessary, and then load the file into *VisiCalc* by typing **/S#L (filename) R**.

If you are unfamiliar with commands in *VisiCalc*, here is an explanation of the above command, character by character. The slash (/) tells *VisiCalc* that what follows is to be treated as a command, as opposed to a label or a value. The "S" indicates a disk command (saving, loading, etc.). The "#" tells *VisiCalc* to expect a DIF file instead of a standard *VisiCalc* file. The "L" selects "Load" from the choice of "Load" or "Save." The filename is the name of the DIF file. If you can't remember the name, type **,D1** or **,D2** (depending on the location of your data disk) and press RETURN. *Visicalc* will show you the name of the first file on the disk. If this is the file you want, press the RETURN key. If not, press the right-arrow key, and the name of the next file on the disk will be displayed. After you have selected the DIF file you want

VisiCalc to read, type **R**, to indicate that the DIF file was saved in Row order.

Remember that DIF files contain only labels and values. Any formulas in your original spreadsheet are evaluated, and their values placed in their respective cells.

Graphics: *Business Graphics, The Graphics Department,* and *GraphWorks*

I've selected three graphics programs to discuss here: *Business Graphics* from Apple Computer, *The Graphics Department* from Sensible Software, and *GraphWorks* from PBI Software, Inc. All three programs can create graphs with data from an *AppleWorks* spreadsheet. *Business Graphics* has been available since 1981 and is a general-purpose graph plotter.

The Graphics Department is a newer program whose latest version was released in 1985. Its features include multicolor three-dimensional graphs, custom lettering (with a large choice of type styles and sizes), the overlaying of two or more graphs, painting, free-hand drawing, and many others. It will even use the Apple mouse.

GraphWorks was written specifically for use with *AppleWorks* spreadsheet data. It is by far the easiest graphics program to use. In fact, it operates just like *AppleWorks*.

To plot any graph, you need two sets of data, one for the horizontal axis, the other for the vertical axis. Usually, the data for the horizontal axis consists of labels, while the vertical axis data are values.

Normally, you would type in the sets of labels or values from the keyboard and then have your graphics program draw the graph for you.

There are times, such as when you're working with a spreadsheet, that a graph of the data would be really useful. You could write down or print out the data and then retype it into your graphics program. But there's an easier way. You can save the data from your *AppleWorks* spreadsheet, and use it in one of the three graphics programs.

BUSINESS GRAPHICS AND *THE GRAPHICS DEPARTMENT*

Both *Business Graphics* and *The Graphics Department* require that you save the *AppleWorks* spreadsheet containing the data you wish to plot as a DIF file. Let's review this process briefly, using the Sales Proj. spreadsheet as an example. Start up *AppleWorks* (if you're not currently using it), and load the Sales Proj. spreadsheet from your data disk. Figure 6-12 shows this spreadsheet. (*Note:* If you haven't created this

FIGURE 6-12 The Sales Proj. spreadsheet

```
File: Sales Proj.                  REVIEW/ADD/CHANGE                 Escape: Main Menu
========A========B========C========D========E========F========G========H====
  1|          Hot & Cold Inc.
  2|
  3|Annual Sales Forecast =      $150,000
  4|
  5|
  6|       Jan Sales =  $14,250
  7|       Feb Sales =  $12,750
  8|       Mar Sales =   $7,500
  9|       Apr Sales =   $8,250
 10|       May Sales =   $9,750             Net Present Value $145,013
 11|       Jun Sales =  $15,000
 12|       Jul Sales =  $17,250
 13|       Aug Sales =  $12,000
 14|       Sep Sales =   $9,000
 15|       Oct Sales =  $12,750
 16|       Nov Sales =  $15,750
 17|       Dec Sales =  $15,750
 18|
--------------------------------------------------------------------------------
A1

Type entry or use  commands                                         -? for Help
```

spreadsheet, you can turn to Chapter 4 and create it now, or use one of your own spreadsheets.)

I have made one small change in the spreadsheet. I've used only the first three letters of the names of the months in column A. I've done this because there wouldn't be room on the horizontal axis of the graph for the complete names of all 12 months.

To save the spreadsheet as a DIF file, type **P**, the Print command, and press RETURN to select printing All of it. Now choose the option to print the spreadsheet to **A DIF (TM) file on disk** (Figure 6-13). Press RETURN again to print the DIF file in Rows order, and when you're prompted for a pathname for your DIF file, make sure your data disk is in your disk drive, and type the pathname **/DATA/SALES.DIF**. *Apple-Works* will save your spreadsheet onto your data disk in DIF format.

Business Graphics requires that you convert the DIF file from ProDOS format to DOS 3.3. *The Graphics Department* exists in both DOS 3.3 and ProDOS versions. If you have the earlier, DOS 3.3 version, you'd have to convert the DIF file.

The DIF file is then read into *Business Graphics* or *The Graphics Department*, and a graph is drawn of the data. Figure 6-14 shows a bar graph of the spreadsheet data drawn with *Business Graphics*. The program automatically scales the vertical axis and lets you title the graph and label the axis.

Figure 6-15 shows the same data plotted as a three-dimensional pie chart with *The Graphics Department*. As you can see, *The Graphics*

FIGURE 6-13 Print the spreadsheet to your data disk as a DIF file

```
File: Sales Proj.                    PRINT                     Escape: Erase entry
==================================================================================

                    The information that you identified
                    is 63 characters wide.

                    The Printer Options values allow
                    80 characters per line.


                    Where do you want to print the report?

                    1.  My Printer
                    2.  The clipboard (for the Word Processor)
                    3.  A text (ASCII) file on disk
                    4.  A DIF (TM) file on disk


----------------------------------------------------------------------------------

Type number, or use arrows, then press Return  4                       55K Avail.
```

FIGURE 6-14 A bar chart from *Business Graphics*

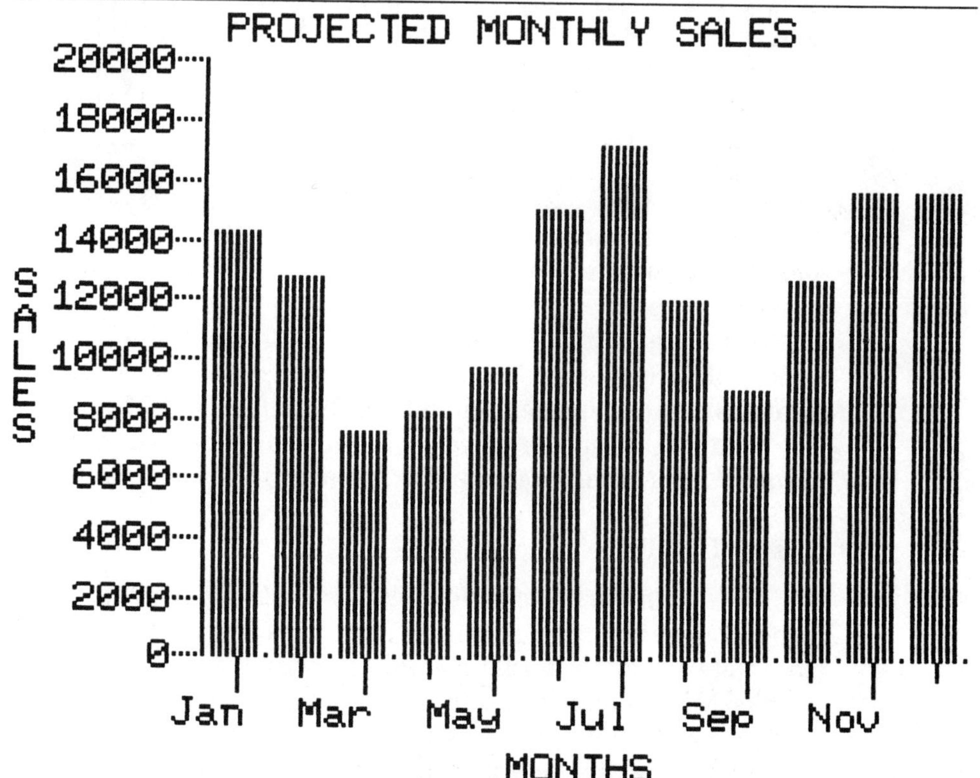

FIGURE 6-15 A pie chart from *The Graphics Department*

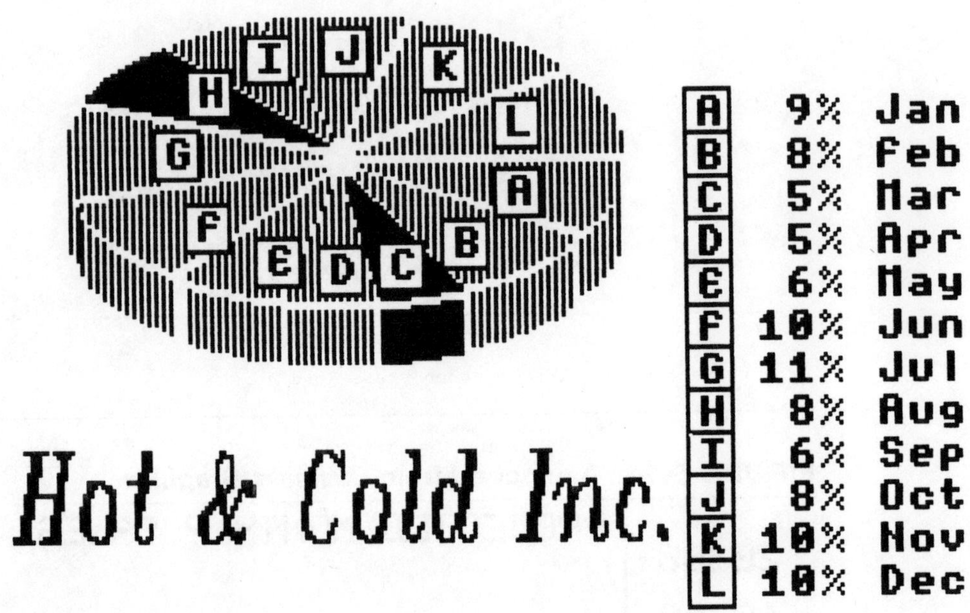

Department is more than just a graph plotter. It provides you with a variety of customizing tools, including adding your own drawings to existing graphs.

You might wonder whether this procedure of transferring data using DIF files actually saves time, compared with retyping the data. The answer, of course, depends on how fast and accurate a typist you are and how large the data set is. But as you'll see in a moment, using *GraphWorks* eliminates the data conversion process altogether.

GRAPHWORKS

Using *GraphWorks* is a lot like using *AppleWorks*. Not only is the program menu driven, but it also uses the same desktop metaphor complete with file folders. Look at Figure 6-16, which shows *Graph-Works'* Main Menu, and you'll see what I mean.

You load your *AppleWorks* spreadsheets into *GraphWorks* using option 1, **Add AppleWorks files to the Desktop**, from the Main Menu (Figure 6-17). After loading the spreadsheet, you use the second Main

FIGURE 6-16 Main Menu for *GraphWorks*

```
Disk: Drive 1                          GraphWorks 1.3

    Main Menu

    1.    Add AppleWorks files to the Desktop

    2.    Work with one of the files on the Desktop

    3.    Remove files from the Desktop

    4.    Other activities

    5.    Print a spreadsheet file sideways

    6.    Quit

Type number, or use arrows, then press Return
```

FIGURE 6-17 Loading an *AppleWorks* spreadsheet into *GraphWorks*

```
Disk: Drive 2                       GraphWorks 1.3                  Escape: Main Menu
```

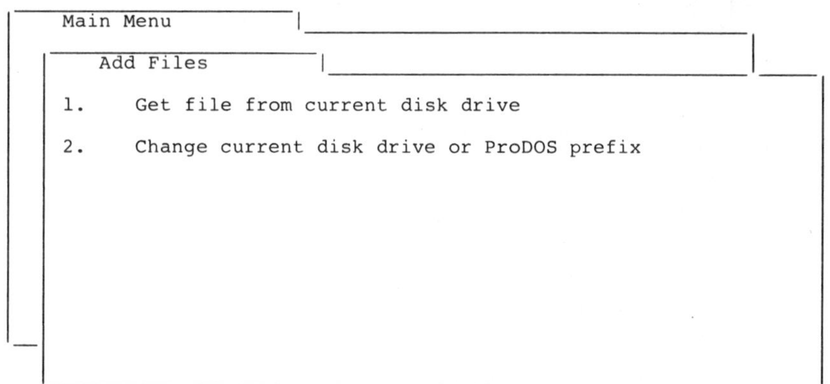

Main Menu
Add Files
1. Get file from current disk drive
2. Change current disk drive or ProDOS prefix


```
Type number, or use arrows, then press RETURN
```

Menu option, **Work with one of the files on the Desktop**, to create the graph.

GraphWorks doesn't allow you to alter the contents of your spreadsheet, so any changes you wish to make have to be made in *AppleWorks*. The "work" you do with the spreadsheet in *GraphWorks* consists of indicating which cells you intend to use in your graph. *GraphWorks* draws four kinds of graphs: pie charts, line charts, bar, and stacked bar graphs.

Indicating value and label ranges is easy. You simply move your cursor to the start of the range, type a letter (A, B, C, D, E, or F), extend the range horizontally or vertically with arrow keys, and press RETURN. You can specify up to six data ranges; each range corresponds to a letter, A-F, and represents a separate graph. Labels are specified the same way, and the program lets you review the choices you've made (Figure 6-18).

FIGURE 6-18 Setting data and label ranges in *GraphWorks*

```
File:SALES.PROJ.                       Review/Graph              Escape : Main Menu
========A========B========C========D========E========F========G========H========
    |         Hot & Cold Inc.                                 ________________
    |                                                        |  Data Ranges    |
    |Annual Sales Forecast =       150000                    | A: (C6..C17)    |
    |                                                        | B:              |
    |                                                        | C:              |
    |January   Sales=      14250                             | D:              |
    |February  Sales=      12750                             | E:              |
    |March     Sales=       7500                             | F:              |
    |April     Sales=       8250                             |   Legends       |
  0 |May       Sales=       9750        Net Present Value    | A:              |
  1 |June      Sales=      15000                             | B:              |
  2 |July      Sales=      17250                             | C:              |
  3 |August    Sales=      12000                             | D:              |
  4 |September Sales=       9000                             | E:              |
  5 |October   Sales=      12750                             | F:              |
  6 |November  Sales=      15750                             |                 |
  7 |December  Sales=      15750                             | L: (A6..A17)    |
  8 |                                                        |_________________|
--------------------------------------------------------------------------------
16

Press Return to continue.                                          ? for help
```

Titles, additional legends, and axis labels can be added by just typing onto the graph. The completed graph can be printed in two sizes: 3″ × 5″ and 6″ × 10″. Figure 6-19 shows a pie chart drawn from the Sales Proj. spreadsheet using *GraphWorks*.

Data Communications: *Access //*

Access // is a data communications program written specifically for the Apple IIe, IIc, and IIGS computers. It's a ProDOS-based program, which means that you won't have to convert your *AppleWorks* files in order to use them with *Access //*.

FIGURE 6-19 A pie chart from *GraphWorks*

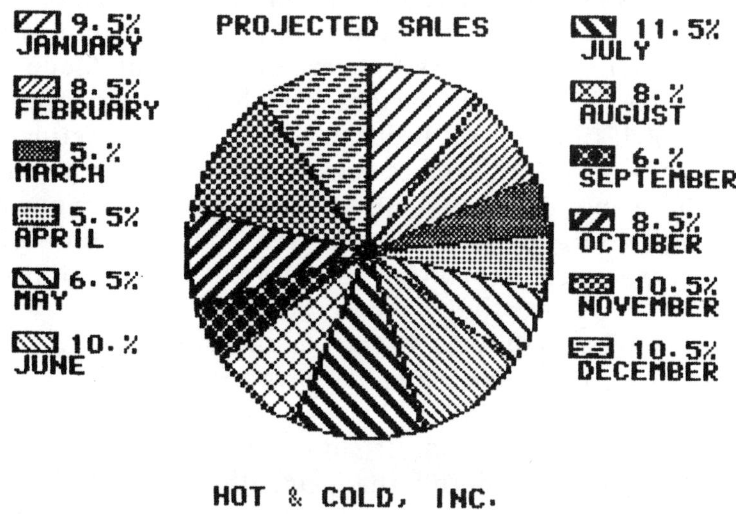

You might buy a program such as *Access //* to make it easier for you to communicate with other computers, usually over the telephone. You might use your Apple to tie into large data bases available from GEnie, CompuServe, The Source, and others. Another increasingly important use is electronic mail. Here, you can send a message to a specific person using a modem (a piece of equipment that lets your computer send data over the phone) and have it held electronically until your person requests it. Data communications programs allow you to transmit previously prepared documents with a single command. This is where *AppleWorks* comes in.

You already know how easy it is to edit a document with a word processor. Features such as global search/replacement and "Cut and Paste" allow you to create exactly the kind of document you want. These features are rarely, if ever, available from dial-up data bases and electronic mail networks. So, it makes sense to prepare in advance any documents you wish to transmit by computer. Preparing documents in advance can also save you money. Most major data bases charge you a fixed rate per "connect minute." And it takes a lot less time to transmit a document from a text file than it does to type it in by hand while you're connected to the electronic mail service.

The process of preparing a document for use by *Access //*, or another data communications program, seems straightforward, but, regrettably, it isn't. As noted above, *AppleWorks* files are not standard text files. Therefore, other programs, like *Access //*, can't read them.

One obvious solution is to print the *AppleWorks* file as an ASCII text file, one of the options in the Print Menu. Unfortunately, this procedure has one serious drawback. When *AppleWorks* prints to an ASCII file on disk, it doesn't issue carriage returns at the end of every line—only at the end of every paragraph. The problem is that most data base and electronic mail systems require carriage returns at the end of each line and usually restrict the length of a line of text to fewer than 80 characters. So, printing your *AppleWorks* word processor document as an ASCII text file won't work.

What will work is setting up a special kind of "printer" that prints to your data disk instead of printing on paper. Some of you will be able to add this special printer directly to your *AppleWorks* disk. Others will need to make a separate copy of the *AppleWorks* Program disk. So that everybody is doing the same thing, let's all make a copy of the *AppleWorks* Program disk to use with this example. You can refer to Chapter 1 for instructions on how to copy your *AppleWorks* disks. After you have made the copy, label the disk "AppleWorks Program Disk—for data communications" so that you can distinguish it from the regular *AppleWorks* Program disk you use for normal printing.

Start *AppleWorks*, and use the new copy of the Program disk when you are instructed to swap disks. (*Note:* If you're running *AppleWorks* from a 3.5" disk, just copy the entire disk, label it "AppleWorks—for data communications" and start it.)

Since this is the first time you're using this disk, you're going to have to set up this special printer I've been talking about.

Select option 5, **Other Activities**, from the Main Menu and then choose option 7, **Specify information about your printer**, from the Other Activities Menu. You should have only three options showing. If you have any printers showing up as options 4, 5, or 6, use option 3, **Remove a printer**, to delete them. Now select option 2, **Add a printer** (Figure 6-20).

You should now be looking at a list of printers. Select number 12, Custom printer. (*Note:* If you are using an older version of *AppleWorks*, version 1.0 or 1.1, the Custom printer will be choice 11.) Name this printer *Access II*. *AppleWorks* will ask you how the printer is to be accessed; in other words, which slot or port is the printer connected to. If you have an Apple IIe or IIGS, respond with choice 7, **Print onto disk or on another Apple** (Figure 6-21). If you have an Apple IIc, select the same option by choosing number 3 (Figure 6-22). After the choice has been made, escape back to the Main Menu.

FIGURE 6-20 Select Custom printer from the list

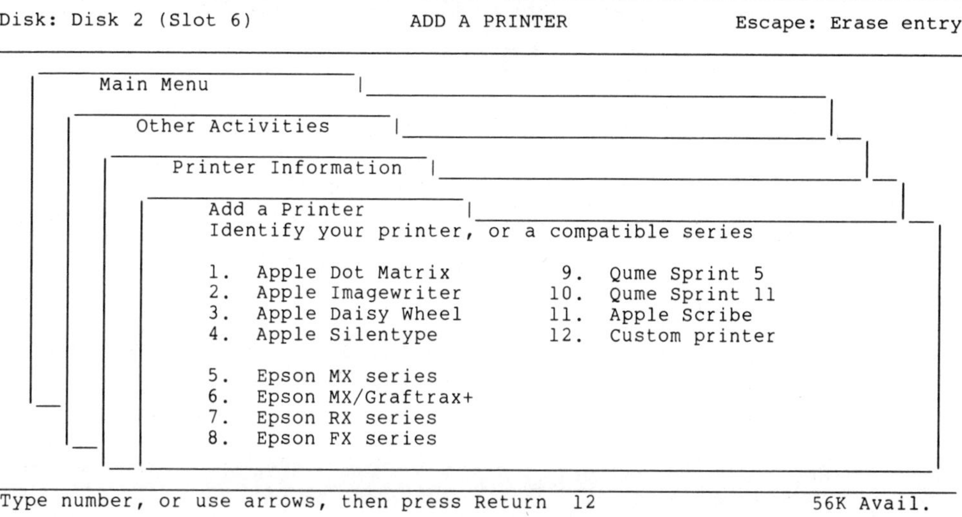

FIGURE 6-21 Apple IIe and IIGS owners select option 7

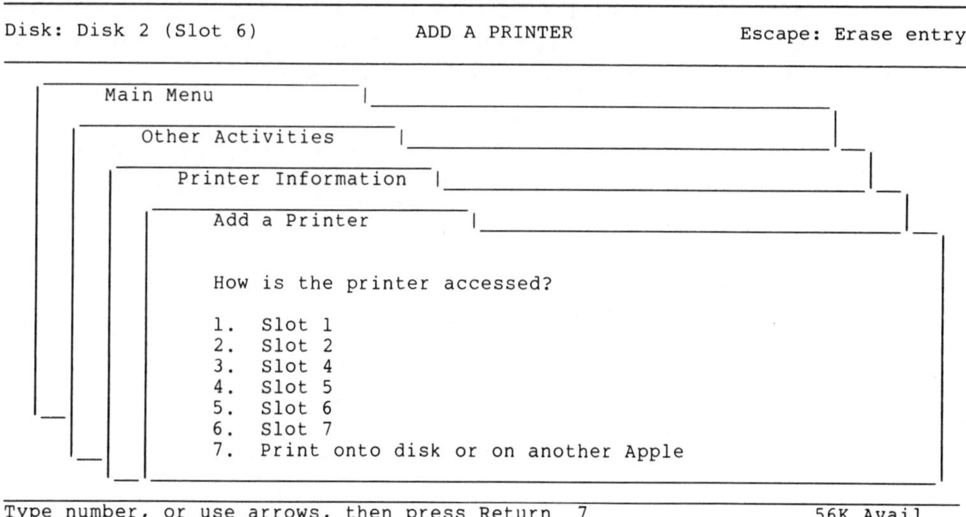

Now you can create documents for *Access //*. For this example, you can load in any word processor document from your *AppleWorks* data disk. You can set Left, Right, Top, and Bottom Margins to any values you want. If you don't change the default values, your document will have Left and Right Margins of 1" (10 characters), no Top Margin, and a

FIGURE 6-22 Apple IIc owners select option 3

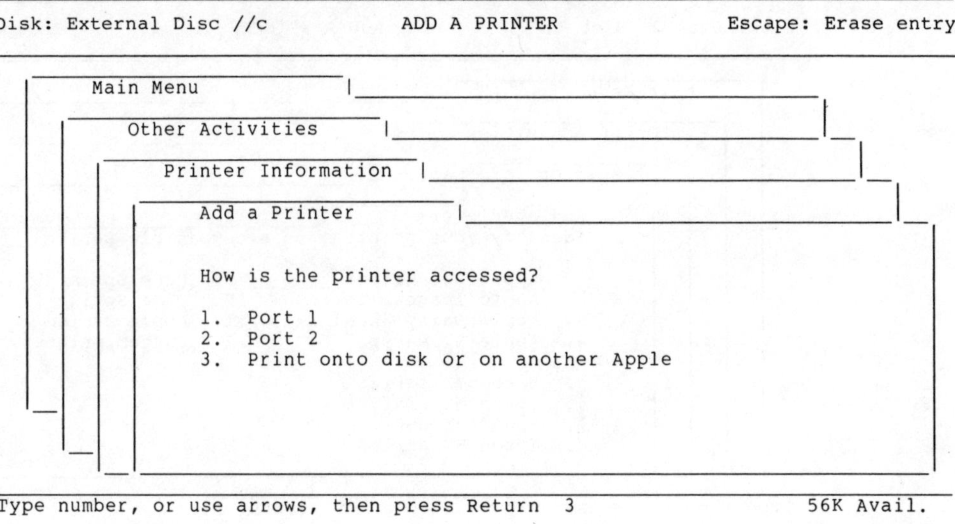

Bottom Margin of 2″. I usually set the Left Margin to zero, the Right Margin to 0.5″, leave the Top Margin at zero, and make the Bottom Margin zero, too. Don't change the default character size, 10 characters per inch.

Avoid the use of boldfacing and underlining in documents sent to other computer systems. When *AppleWorks* saves your document to disk, it translates those caret symbols, "^", to control characters that have special meaning for your printer. These control characters can be very confusing to other computers.

When you're ready to save your document to a file for later use by *Access //*, type **P**. Press RETURN to print All of the document. Then select option 1, **Access // (disk)**, from the Print Menu. With your *AppleWorks* data disk in your disk drive, type **/DATA/EMAIL** for the pathname, and press RETURN. (*Note:* I'm assuming that DATA is the name of your *AppleWorks* data disk. You can substitute any ProDOS filename in place of EMAIL.)

If you have a DOS 3.3-based data communications program instead of *Access //*, refer to the discussion at the beginning of this chapter and copy the *AppleWorks* ProDOS file to a DOS 3.3 disk.

Your data communications program will be able to use this file, as it would any ASCII text file. With *Access //*, you would establish communications with the particular electronic mail or data base service you are using. Then, when you're ready to send the document, type **ESC** to get back to the Main Menu of *Access //*, and take option 4, **Transmit a file**. When you're asked for the filename, type the same pathname you used to print the file to disk, /DATA/EMAIL in this example. (*Note:* Make sure your data disk is in one of your disk drives so that *Access //* can find it.)

Spelling Checker: *The Sensible Speller*

I had been using *AppleWorks* for several months before I "discovered" *The Sensible Speller*. The program was originally released in a DOS 3.3 version in 1983, but a ProDOS version has been available since 1984.

The Sensible Speller checks a word processor document against one or more dictionaries and "flags" each word it can't match. The program comes with the 81,000-word Random House dictionary divided into two sections. The main dictionary contains 44,000 of the most often-used words. The remaining 37,000 words are in a separate, supplemental dictionary. There are utilities for adding your own words to the Random House dictionary files or creating your own dictionary from scratch.

Since *The Sensible Speller* can check documents from other ProDOS-based word processors, besides *AppleWorks* (*Apple Writer* and *Word Juggler*), there are utilities for customizing the program for *AppleWorks*.

The program comes with a 64-page manual and a good index. It is "menu driven" (as is *AppleWorks*) and is very easy to use. To use it with *AppleWorks* word processor files requires no additional work at all. Just save your document in the usual way, quit *AppleWorks*, and start up *The Sensible Speller*.

After you have customized *The Sensible Speller* to work with *AppleWorks* files (something you'll have to do only once), you'll see the Main Menu screen (Figure 6-23). Type **C**, Check spelling of a document, and press RETURN. You'll see a message to insert your document disk (your *AppleWorks* data disk) and press RETURN. At this point, you can remove *The Sensible Speller* Program disk from drive 1 (the built-in drive on a IIc) and insert your data disk.

You will then be shown a list of the files on your data disk. When you see the one you want, type in its name and the file will be examined by *The Sensible Speller*. The program looks at all the words in your document and tells you both the total number of words and the number of unique words, excluding duplications. (*Note:* You can, at this point, get a list of these unique words, and how many times you used each word, either displayed on your screen or printed out on your printer.)

FIGURE 6-23 ***The Sensible Speller* Main Menu**

```
          The SENSIBLE SPELLER for ProDOS

     Copyright 1984, Sensible Software, Inc.
     ---------------------------------------


          C - Check spelling of a document

          L - List dictionary words

          A - Add words to dictionary

          D - Delete words from dictionary

          Q - Quit speller program


     ---------------------------------------
     Which would you like to do? [ ]
```

If your computer system has two disk drives, a copy of the main Random House dictionary should be in drive 2 (the external drive on a IIc). (*Note:* I strongly recommend that you make copies of both sides of the dictionary disk. Use them, and save the original disk for backup.) If your system has only one drive, remove your *AppleWorks* data disk and insert the dictionary disk.

The program will compare the list of unique words from your document with the dictionary; this will take about a minute. If it can't find one or more words in the dictionary, you can use another dictionary or go on to the correcting section of the program. (*Note:* If you have a single-drive system, you'll be instructed to remove the dictionary disk and replace your data disk.)

One at a time, each word that wasn't found in the dictionary will be displayed, highlighted in context, at the top of your screen. You can then choose one of several options for dealing with each instance. If you know the word is spelled correctly, you can either add the word to the dictionary, so that *The Sensible Speller* will recognize the word the next time it sees it, or you can tell the program to ignore the word entirely. If you see your mistake, you can type in the correct word yourself. If, however, you think the word may be spelled wrong, but you're not sure, you can have *The Sensible Speller* suggest proper spellings. If you select this option, the program will search the dictionary looking for words close to your spelling and will display on the screen its eight best guesses. If one of these is the word you had in mind, you can make the replacement with a single keystroke.

Anytime you replace a word in your document, *The Sensible Speller* asks you whether you want to replace all the occurrences of the original word (global replacement). Normally, you would respond, "Yes."

There are things *The Sensible Speller* can't do. It can't correct your grammar or your punctuation. And it can't correct the misuse of words. If you write "I have *to* Apples" instead of "I have *two* Apples," the program won't spot the error because "to" is a legitimate word. But, for those of us whose spelling accuracy leaves something to be desired, this program is very welcome.

Mail Merge: *HabaMerge, MegaWorks,* and *Spellworks*

Those of you who have an earlier version of *AppleWorks* (1.1, 1.2, or 1.3) don't have the mail merge feature that was added to version 2.0. Three programs, *HabaMerge*, *MegaWorks*, and *Spellworks*, provide this missing mail merge feature. All three programs were written specifically for use with *AppleWorks* files, and all contain an extra feature, in addition to mail merge. *HabaMerge* allows you to print mailing labels two or three across, for 2-up or 3-up label forms (*AppleWorks* prints labels in a single column only). *MegaWorks* and *Spellworks* provide a spelling checker, similar to *The Sensible Speller*, for *AppleWorks* word processor files. All three programs will work with single disk drive systems, but all of them recommend the addition of a second drive. *HabaMerge* and *Spellworks* require a minimum of 128K of computer memory (as does version 2.0 of *AppleWorks*).

As you saw in Chapter 5, mail merge is the ability to combine a data base file of information with a word processor document to produce form letters.

The three programs differ somewhat in the way they merge data, but the basic concept is the same. Figure 6-24 shows the body of a typical mail merge letter. Notice the blank area where the inside address would normally be, and the missing name after the word "Dear." This is where data from a data base would be inserted.

After creating the form letter, you would next prepare a data base containing the data you want to merge into your form letter. Figure 6-25 shows the category names for such a data base. Notice that each name would use three separate categories, Title, FirstName, and LastName. This is done so that the salutation line can combine the Title (Mr., Ms., etc.) with the last name, as in "Dear Ms. Smith."

FIGURE 6-24 A typical form letter

```
October 12



Dear

For the past four years, we at Hot & Cold Inc. have been
serving our customers from our original location in downtown
Rolling Meadows. Your continued patronage and good
references to your friends and neighbors have resulted in a
very gratifying increase in our business.

I want to thank you personally for thinking of us when you
had a heating or air conditioning problem. I know we have
satisfied you in the past and I pledge that we'll continue
to satisfy you in the future.

In order to better serve our customers, especially those in
nearby Elk Grove, we have opened a second facility there.
Our new store is:

          Hot & Cold Inc.
          326 S. Main Street
          Elk Grove

          (312) 555-7540

We invite you to stop by and see our new store.  We're really
proud of it.


Sincerely,

Mike Sloan
President
```

Finally, you'd go back to the form letter and add special symbols that tell the mail merge program where to insert the appropriate data from the data base.

Figure 6-26 shows these symbols added for the *HabaMerge* program. The numbers (^1, ^2, and so forth) refer to the category names in the data base. For example, category 1 is the Title, so anywhere in the document that "^1" is found, *HabaMerge* will insert data from the Title category. It's the same for the remaining 6 categories.

FIGURE 6-25 Categories for a mail merge data base

```
File: Customers               CHANGE NAME/CATEGORY     Escape: Review/Add/Change



Category names
================================================================================
Title                                            |
FirstName                                        | Options:
LastName                                         |
Address                                          | Change filename
City                                             | Return      Go to first category
State                                            |
Zip                                              |
                                                 |
                                                 |
                                                 |
                                                 |
                                                 |
                                                 |
                                                 |
--------------------------------------------------------------------------------
Type filename:  Customers                                            40K Avail.
```

FIGURE 6-26 Data category markers for *HabaMerge*

```
File: Merge Letter               REVIEW/ADD/CHANGE                Escape: Main Menu
=====|====|====|====|====|====|====|====|====|====|====|====|====|====|====|====|===
October 12

^1 ^2 ^3
^4
^5, ^6 ^7

Dear ^1 ^3,

For the past four years, we at Hot & Cold Inc. have been
serving our customers from our original location in downtown
Rolling Meadows. Your continued patronage and good
references to your friends and neighbors have resulted in a
very gratifying increase in our business.

I want to thank you personally for thinking of us when you
had a heating or air conditioning problem. I know we have
satisfied you in the past and I pledge that we'll continue
to satisfy you in the future.

In order to better serve our customers, especially those in
--------------------------------------------------------------------------------
Type entry or use ⌘ commands           Line 7  Column 12          ⌘-? for Help
```

MegaWorks and *Spellworks* operate a little differently; instead of using numbers to indicate data base categories, they use the category names themselves, preceded by two dollar symbols ($$). Look at Figure 6-27 and you'll see what I mean.

Once the data base and the form letter have been set up, each program uses its own technique for merging them. The result is the

FIGURE 6-27 Data category markers for *MegaWorks* and *SpellWorks*

```
File: MegaLetter                 REVIEW/ADD/CHANGE              Escape: Main Menu
=====|====|====|====|====|====|====|====|====|====|====|====|====|====|====|===
October 12

$$Title $$FirstName $$LastName
$$Address
$$City, $$State $$Zip

Dear $$Title $$LastName,

For the past four years, we at Hot & Cold Inc. have been
serving our customers from our original location in downtown
Rolling Meadows. Your continued patronage and good
references to your friends and neighbors have resulted in a
very gratifying increase in our business.

I want to thank you personally for thinking of us when you
had a heating or air conditioning problem. I know we have
satisfied you in the past and I pledge that we'll continue
to satisfy you in the future.

In order to better serve our customers, especially those in
--------------------------------------------------------------------------------
Type entry or use ⌘ commands             Line 7  Column 25          ⌘-? for Help
```

same. You get one personalized letter for each record in the data base. If you wanted the letters printed in a particular order, perhaps by zip code, you would first arrange (sort) the data base records before you merged them with the form letter.

Enhancing Data Base Reports: *ReportWorks*

One of the limiting factors to the data base section of *AppleWorks* is its restriction to two types of reports, Labels and Tables. While these two report formats may be adequate for many (or even most) applications, several *AppleWorks* users felt the need for a more flexible data base report generator. *ReportWorks* from Megahaus provides just about all of the reporting features you could ask for.

ReportWorks lets you design your own report form, using up to a full page for each record (*AppleWorks* Label reports are limited to 15 lines). Reports consist of three sections: a title page, the main body of the report, and a summary page. The title and summary pages are optional, but using them tends to improve the look of your reports.

The program abounds with useful features. Headers and footers can be as many lines as you wish and can contain category data as well as text. Headers and footers print on every page in the report's main body, but not on the title or summary pages.

ReportWorks will not only automatically number the pages of your report, but it will also consecutively number a field in the report. For example, if you were using *ReportWorks* to generate invoices, the program could increment an invoice number for each invoice.

But the real power of *ReportWorks* lies in its ability to produce reports using data from more than one data base. Here's an example. Suppose you kept a master file of all your Hot & Cold, Inc. customers. The file might contain the customer's account number, name, address, city, state, zip, and phone number. Suppose you kept a second file of repairs performed on customer's equipment. This file might contain the customer's account number, a description of the damaged equipment, the date purchased, the date repaired, the cost of the repair, and the repair technician's name.

ReportWorks lets you design a report that would pull customer data from the customer master file, and repairs records for that customer from the repair file. This data would be combined into a single report. And you could do this for one single customer or all of your customers. The report could also total the repair cost for each customer.

ReportWorks can even extract data from *AppleWorks* spreadsheets.

The program sports several spreadsheet-type mathematical functions including absolute value, rounding to a specified number of decimal places, square root, average, count, maximum and minimum values, and sum.

The program can add the current date to your reports and even do date arithmetic. It can compute the difference between two dates, or add a constant number of days to a date entry. For example, it can add 30 days to an invoice date and print the result in a "date due" area on the report.

Text functions include conversions of numbers, dates, and times to expanded text. For example, dates from an *AppleWorks* date category in the format "4/10/88" can be expanded automatically to "April 10, 1988." Numbers can be printed with your choice of decimal places. Text entries can be converted to all upper-case, all lower-case, or what's called "firstcaps" (every word begins with a capital letter).

Logical functions such as IF, CHOOSE, and MATCH are available to give your reports added flexibility. And the CHR function lets you use the special features of your printer (boldface, underline, etc.) anywhere in the report.

ReportWorks requires a 128K Apple IIe, IIc, or IIGS, with one disk drive (two recommended).

The Pinpoint Collection

Shortly after the first version of *AppleWorks* hit the market, Pinpoint Publishing released its collection of mini-programs called *Pinpoint*. These mini-programs are called "Desktop Accessories" because they can be run while you're using *AppleWorks*. That's right, you don't have to quit *AppleWorks* to use *Pinpoint*.

There are eight Desktop Accessories in the original Pinpoint collection: Appointment Calendar, Calculator, Communications, Dialer, GraphMerge, Notepad, QuickLabel, and Typewriter.

Installing *Pinpoint* modifies the *AppleWorks* system file on your *AppleWorks* Startup disk, so be sure to use a copy of the *AppleWorks* disk, not the original. The desk accessories themselves reside on a separate disk, usually in drive 2 (the external drive on a IIc). (*Note: Pinpoint* will work in a one-drive system; two drives are recommended.) The installation process is straightforward. All you have to do is start up the *Pinpoint* disk, select the installation option from the Main Menu, and insert your *AppleWorks* Startup disk when you're prompted.

After you've installed *Pinpoint* on your *AppleWorks* disk, you start *AppleWorks* the way you usually do. The only difference you'll see as the program starts is a *Pinpoint* copyright notice just before the first *AppleWorks* screen. Everything else looks the same, every feature behaves the same way, because nothing in *AppleWorks* has been altered. But something *has* been added. Those eight desktop accessories are available anywhere in *AppleWorks*. All you have to do is hold down the *SOLID*-APPLE key (not the OPEN-APPLE key) and press **P**. (*Note:* Apple IIGS users, don't despair. I know you don't have a SOLID-APPLE key, and so do the folks at Pinpoint Publishing. Use the OPTION key instead.)

Pressing -P displays the *Pinpoint* menu. The menu shows a list of desktop accessories. You select the one you want by highlighting your choice with the up- and down-arrow keys and pressing RETURN. One feature common to all *Pinpoint* desktop accessories is on-screen help. You invoke the Help screen exactly the same way you do in *AppleWorks*, by typing ?. When you quit a *Pinpoint* accessory program, you return to *AppleWorks* just where you left off.

THE APPOINTMENT CALENDAR

The Appointment Calendar lets you keep track of all your appointments on a day-by-day basis. Selecting **Appointments** from the Pinpoint menu displays the current calendar month. (*Note:* If your computer system includes a clock/calendar card, the Calendar desktop accessory will use it to determine the current date. If you don't have a clock/calendar card, the Calendar uses the date you typed in when you started *AppleWorks*.)

You can enter, edit, or look up your appointments for any day through the year 1990. And you can print out daily or weekly schedules at any time. As with all *Pinpoint* desktop accessories, when you quit the Calendar, you return immediately to *AppleWorks*.

THE CALCULATOR

You would think that with the computing power of *AppleWorks*' spreadsheet you'd have little need of a calculator. But suppose you were typing a table of numbers into a word processor document, and you needed to add up a column of numbers. A calculator would sure come in handy.

And that's just why the Calculator accessory is available. The Calculator has four functions: add, subtract, multiply, and divide. It uses scientific notation above 999,999,999. And if your computer system includes a numeric keypad (Apple IIGS's and new Apple IIe's have one), you can use it with the Calculator.

COMMUNICATIONS

This desktop accessory adds data communications to *AppleWorks*. If you've read the description of the *Access //* program above, you'll really appreciate this Communications accessory. With it, you can transmit and receive files from within *AppleWorks*, without having to do any type of file conversion. You can also send text directly from your keyboard. Data received can be read on the screen and/or saved to a file on your data disk.

The Communications accessory lets you select Baud Rate (300 or 1200), Comm. Mode (full or half duplex), Data Bits (7 or 8), Stop Bits (1 or 2), Parity (odd, even, or none), and Line feed after carriage return (yes or no).

There's a phone directory that lets you record the name of the computer service you wish to call (GEnie, CompuServe, etc.), its phone number, and the log-on procedure. Once you've entered this information, a single keystroke tells *Pinpoint* to dial a particular service and automatically transmit the characters necessary to begin a communications session. These characters might include your account number, password, and so forth.

You'll need a modem (a device that lets your computer talk over telephone lines) if you want to use this and the next desktop accessory.

THE DIALER

The Dialer is used to dial phone numbers for you. It uses numbers from the *AppleWorks* document you're using. When you choose this desktop accessory, your document (word processor, data base, or spreadsheet) is scanned for numbers that look like telephone numbers. The first phone number it finds is highlighted. If you want the Dialer to dial this number, you press RETURN. If you want to dial a different number, you press the up- or down-arrow keys to select other phone numbers on the same document.

GRAPHMERGE

GraphMerge lets you combine pictures with your *AppleWorks* word processor documents. You can use pictures from *GraphWorks* (see above) or from other ProDOS graphics programs such as *Dazzle Draw* from Broederbund Software and *MousePaint* from Apple.

The accessory lets you choose a word processor file and then choose a picture file to merge with it. After the picture has been loaded, it's displayed on your screen and you can edit it to the proper shape and size. GraphMerge lets you crop the picture (which means to select any part of it) and stretch or shrink the picture horizontally and/or vertically. The end result is to shape the picture into just the right size for your application.

Once the picture is shaped the way you want it, you can paste it into the word processor document at any spot. GraphMerge automatically makes room for the picture in your document. Then print the document and that's all there is to it.

THE NOTEPAD

The Notepad lets you jot down ideas as they come to you while you're working in *AppleWorks*. Instead of writing your idea on a piece of paper, or going through the trouble of opening a separate word processor document, you can use the Notepad to write up to 32 lines of text. Each note is saved as an *AppleWorks* word processor file, so you can use *AppleWorks* to edit the file later on if you wish. You can add to notes you've already saved, and you can print them anytime.

QUICKLABEL

Have you ever wanted to address a single envelope or type one label? It seems more trouble than it's worth to create a separate data base, then create a Label format, just to print one label. Even setting up a separate word processor document for the three or four lines of an envelope or label is too much trouble.

QuickLabel lets you select the text you want for your label directly from the inside address portion of a business letter. You simply highlight the block of text, call up *Pinpoint*'s QuickLabel, insert the envelope or label in your printer, and print it.

After you've selected the text block, QuickLabel shows you a picture of a standard size envelope. Arrow keys let you position the text block on the envelope. Once you've positioned the text, a single press of the RETURN key prints the envelope.

TYPEWRITER

The last desktop accessory converts your Apple computer and printer into a typewriter. After you select this accessory from *Pinpoint*'s menu, you can type one line of text (up to 70 characters). You can edit the line by pressing the BACKSPACE key. When you press RETURN, the line is immediately printed on your printer. You can type as many lines as you wish.

OTHER *PINPOINT* PROGRAMS

Pinpoint Publishing followed up on its original eight desktop accessories with three other *Pinpoint* packages. *Point-to-Point* is a full-featured data communications program with XMODEM file transfer capability and much more.

InfoMerge is Pinpoint's mail merge utility. It performs the same function as *MegaWorks* or *Spellworks*, or *AppleWorks'* own mail merge feature. And, of course, no desktop would be complete without a *Spelling Checker*.

All three of these new programs install as desktop accessories and are available through the *Pinpoint* menu within *AppleWorks*.

III. USING *APPLEWORKS* WITH OTHER HARDWARE

One of the nicest features of any Apple computer is the ability to expand the computer system with additional hardware. This section discusses three pieces of add-on equipment that can improve the efficiency and/or add extra capabilities to *AppleWorks*.

Large-Capacity Disk Drives

Apple has developed four large-capacity disk drives: the 3.5″ 800-kilobyte (800K) floppy disk drive, the 5-megabyte Profile hard disk drive, and its 10-megabyte big brother, and the new SC20 20 megabyte hard drive. One of the principal reasons for the development of the ProDOS operating system was to allow Apple II computers to access large-capacity disk drives easily. (The older DOS 3.3 operating system could only use standard, 135K disk drives.) Once ProDOS was released, Apple II's could begin using larger capacity disk drives. Since *AppleWorks* was written under ProDOS, it works very well with these larger drives.

The 800K drive lets you place the entire *AppleWorks* program on a single disk, instead of having to use two disks, startup and program. It also provides almost six times the storage space for your data files compared with the original Apple disk drive. This means that you can cut the number of data disks you have lying around your computer by a factor of 6. It makes sense to use 800K drives, especially if you're buying a new Apple system, but it makes even more sense to buy a hard disk drive.

There are two major reasons for wanting to use a hard disk with *AppleWorks*. The first is the ability to store all your data files in one place. This means no more floppy disks that could get lost or damaged. And no more trying to remember *which* disk a particular file was on. The second reason is that you can put the *AppleWorks* program itself on the hard disk. This action speeds up the operation of the program and you no longer have to keep the *AppleWorks* Program disk in drive 1.

There are two ways of using *AppleWorks* with a hard disk. The first is described in Chapter 7 of the *AppleWorks* Reference Manual. The second involves the use of a special program called *Catalyst*. *Catalyst* is kind of a super menu program. It allows you to place virtually any ProDOS based program (*AppleWorks*, *The Sensible Speller*, *HabaMerge*, *Apple Writer*, *Access //*, System Utilities, etc.) on the hard disk, and then select any of them from its menu. When you're through with a program, quitting returns you to *Catalyst's* menu.

One of the major advantages of ProDOS is its ability to create subdirectories within a volume. This feature allows you to group together, under one heading, as many related files as you wish. For example, you might have a data disk that contains copies of business letters you have sent during the year. The volume name of the data disk might be LETTERS and you might set up subdirectories called JANUARY, FEBRUARY, MARCH, etc. (*Note:* There is a command in the

ProDOS System Utilities program that allows you to create subdirectories.) When you want to save a letter you have written in March, you would use the pathname /LETTERS/MARCH/filename.

Subdirectories are convenient when used with floppy disks; they are vital when you use a hard disk. This is because the main (root) directory of *any* ProDOS volume, floppy disk or hard disk, can contain a maximum of only 51 files. If you use a hard disk and you save files indiscriminately to its root directory, you'll soon see an error message (Directory Full) warning you that you can't save any more files on that volume—even though you may have millions of unused bytes of storage space on the hard disk.

There is one caution you should remember if you buy a hard disk drive. Back it up! Sooner or later *everything* breaks. When your hard disk fails and you take it in to be repaired, you will probably lose all of the data you had stored on it. Think about that for a moment. Programs can be easily reloaded on your repaired hard disk. But what about your data files? You will probably have many months, perhaps years, of data files. Does the thought of having to retype all of that data fill you with dread? Good! Then use the backup program that comes with your hard disk to back up your data to floppy disks *regularly*. That way, when you get your repaired hard disk back, all you'll have to do is transfer the data from the floppies back onto your hard disk.

Add-On Memory Cards

AppleWorks is a "memory-based" program. What that means is that the particular file you are working on—word processor, data base, or spreadsheet—is kept in your Apple's memory. That's why *AppleWorks* tells you how much memory remains as you are working. If you have a 128K Apple IIe, IIc, or IIGS, you'll start out with a 56K *AppleWorks* Desktop. This means that you can't create a file of any type larger than 56 thousand bytes. (*Note:* The advantage of a memory-based program is that operations such as searching and sorting can be done in seconds, rather than in half-hours.)

It may seem to you as if a 56K Desktop is more than you'll ever need. And you may be right. But to give you some idea of the limitations of 56K, if you were creating a customer list in the data base, you would have room for about 750 customers before you ran out of memory. Owning a large-capacity disk drive doesn't help. The problem is your Apple's memory, or rather the lack of it.

ADD-ON MEMORY FOR THE APPLE IIe

Three companies, Apple Computer, Applied Engineering, and Checkmate Technology, Inc., currently market memory expansion boards for the Apple IIe. Two of the boards, RamWorks III from Applied Engineering and MultiRam IIe from Checkmate Technology, Inc., are combination memory and 80-column boards. They replace Apple's Extended 80-Column Text Card. Apple's Memory Expansion Card and RamFactor from Applied Engineering plug into one of the other slots (usually slot 4) and add their memory to the memory on the Extended 80-Column Text Card.

All boards come in a variety of memory sizes, ranging from 64K bytes to 1 Meg or more. RamWorks III is available in memory sizes ranging from 64K to 16 Meg—that's 16 million bytes of RAM! RamFactor is also expandable to 16 Meg, in multiples of 256K. MultiRam IIe can be configured in any one of 18 memory amounts, from 64K to 1.5 Meg in multiples of 64K. The Apple memory card comes with 256K and can be expanded to 1 Meg in multiples of 256K.

The RAM on all the cards combines with the 64K of RAM on your IIe's motherboard and Extended 80-column Text Card. But *AppleWorks* can use only part of the total available memory for its Desktop. For example, a 256K Apple memory board plus the 128K of RAM in your Apple IIe would give you a total of 384K. But your *AppleWorks* Desktop would be only 250K, which is still a lot better than 56K.

ADD-ON MEMORY FOR THE APPLE IIc

The same three companies supply add-on memory for the Apple IIc. While the Apple IIe has slots on its motherboard that accept various kinds of add-on boards (memory boards, 80-column cards, printer interface cards, etc.), the IIc was designed without any slots. This fact has hampered the development of third-party accessories (such as memory expansion boards) for the IIc. All three companies (Applied Engineering, Checkmate Technology, and Apple) solved the problem by developing memory expansion boards that mount piggyback fashion on top of the IIc's motherboard.

Applied Engineering makes a memory expansion board called Z-RAM Ultra, and it comes in three models. Z-RAM Ultra 1 provides either 256K or 512K additional RAM to the IIc. Z-RAM Ultra 2 is expandable to 1 Meg of RAM and also has a built-in clock. ProDOS (and, therefore, *AppleWorks*) recognizes this clock and automatically sets the correct date when you start up your computer. Z-RAM Ultra 3 is also expandable to 1 Meg, has a built-in clock, and gives your IIc the ability to run software (such as *WordStar* and *dBASE //*) written under the CP/M operating system. (Ordinarily, your IIc wouldn't be able to run CP/M software. Separate CP/M boards *are* available for the IIe.)

Checkmate Technologies' solution to increasing the IIc's memory is their MultiRam CX board. This board also clips onto the IIc's motherboard and adds 512K of RAM, for a total of 640K. The company also manufacturers an add-on board for their add-on board. The MultiRam CX Plus clips onto their MultiRam CX board and provides an additional 512K of RAM (1152K total).

Apple Computer also sells an add-on memory board for the IIc, but unless you own the newest IIc model, you'll have to replace your IIc's motherboard with a new one. Apple includes the motherboard upgrade at no additional charge when you buy the memory expansion board. Like their memory board for the IIe, the IIc memory board comes with 256K of RAM and can be expanded to 1 Meg.

ADD-ON MEMORY FOR THE APPLE IIGS

Apple Computer's Memory Expansion Board for the IIGS plugs into a special memory expansion slot, and comes in multiples of 256K, up to 1 Meg. (*Note:* At present, Apple strongly suggests that you avoid 768K. It seems that the memory manager has problems with this configuration. 256K, 512K, and 1 Meg work fine. By the time you read this, Apple may have solved the problem.)

RamPak 4GS from Orange Micro, Inc. comes with 512K standard, and can be expanded to 4 Meg.

Applied Engineering offers two memory expansion cards for the IIGS. GSRAM uses the GS's memory expansion slot. It comes with from 256K to 1.5 Meg of memory, and a second version of the card (GSRAM Plus) is expandable to 8 Meg. Their second memory card, RamFactor, doesn't use the IIGS's memory expansion slot. It plugs into any of the other slots, 1–7, and is expandable all the way up to 16 Meg.

APPLEWORKS AND EXPANDED MEMORY

When you use *AppleWorks* with an expanded memory Apple, you get two advantages. One you already know; you can create much larger files because the Desktop is so much larger. Word processor documents can grow from 18 pages (on a 128K Apple) up to a maximum of 511 pages. With a 128K Apple, your data bases can hold about 750 records (assuming an average of 75 characters per record), and no matter how small your records are, you can't have more than 1350 records. If you expand your Apple's memory, the maximum number of records increases to 6350. As for spreadsheets, a 128K Apple can use about 6000 of the 126,873 available cells. Again, the bigger your Apple's memory, the more cells your spreadsheets can use.

Some limits in *AppleWorks* aren't affected by additional memory. The Clipboard can only hold 250 word processor lines, 253 records, or 250 spreadsheet rows. Each entry in a data base category can be no longer than 76 characters, and spreadsheet labels or formulas can't exceed 71 characters.

The other reason to expand your Apple's memory is that version 2.0 of *AppleWorks* automatically looks to see if your Apple has more than the standard 128K of memory. If it does, *AppleWorks* copies itself into some of the additional memory. (You'll see a screen message telling you this is happening.) The advantage of having *AppleWorks* in memory is speed. The program moves more quickly from one section to another because it doesn't have to look to the Program disk for more instructions. The entire program is in memory instead of just part of it.

And speaking of speed, the Applied Engineering folks offer an accelerator board they call TransWarp. This board not only adds 256K of memory to your IIe, it also makes your Apple think about three-and-a-half times faster. This really helps in performing calculations on large spreadsheets and sorting or searching large data bases.

Clock/Calendar Cards

Every time you start up *AppleWorks*, it asks you to type in the current date. The reason for this has to do with ProDOS. When you save a file to disk, ProDOS not only records the file's name, but (if ProDOS knows it) the date and time as well. This "date stamping" of files can be very useful. If you list the directory of your data disk, you can see when a particular file was last updated.

Clock/calendar cards automatically supply the current date and time to ProDOS, as well as to any program designed to look for date and time information (yes, *AppleWorks* will look for this). The cards have batteries that will keep the clock running, even when your Apple is turned off. There are several clock/calendar cards that work properly with ProDOS—ThunderClock from ThunderWare, and Timemaster H.O. from Applied Engineering work with the Apple IIe (Timemaster works with the IIGS as well). And Applied Engineering's IIc System Clock plugs into one of the serial ports at the rear of a IIc.

Final Comments

I thought you might be interested in knowing which computer system and software I used to write this book. (You didn't think I used a typewriter, did you?) The book was entirely written and edited on an Apple IIe with the following peripherals:

Monitor //
2 disk drives
5Meg Profile Hard Disk
256K Apple Memory Expansion Card
ImageWriter II printer w/Super Serial Card
ThunderClock

The software was, what else, *AppleWorks*, running on the Profile, under *Catalyst*. *The Sensible Speller* was used to catch my all-too-frequent spelling errors.

APPENDIX A

MANUFACTURERS' LIST

Company	Product	Description
Advanced Logic System, Inc. 1238 Reamwood Avenue Sunnyvale, CA 94089 408/747-1988	*Spellworks*	Spelling Checker, Mail Merge
Apple Computer, Inc. 20525 Mariani Ave. Cupertino, CA 95014 408/996-1010	Apple IIe, IIc, IIGS Profile ImageWriter Color 100 *AppleWorks* *Apple Writer* *Business Graphics* *Access //* *Quick File* Memory Expansion Card	Computers Hard Disk Drive Printer RGB Color Monitor Integrated Software Word Processing Graph Plotter Data Communications Data Base IIe, IIc, IIGS Memory Card
Applied Engineering P.O. Box 798 Carrollton, TX 75006 214/241-6060	RamWorks, RamFactor GSRAM, GSRAM Plus Z-RAM Ultra TransWarp Viewmaster 80 Pocket Rocket Timemaster H.O.	II+, IIe Memory Card IIGS Memory Card IIc Memory Card II+, IIe Accelerator Card 80-column Card 16K RAM Card Clock Card
Checkmate Technology, Inc. 509 South Rockford Dr. Tempe, AZ 85281 602/966-5802	MultiRam IIe MultiRam CX	IIe Memory Card IIc Memory Card
Discwasher 1407 N. Providence Rd. P.O. 6021 Columbia, MO 65205 314/449-0941	Serial-to-Parallel	IIc Printer I/F
Haba Systems, Inc. 15154 Stagg St. Van Nuys, CA 91405 818/901-8828	*HabaMerge*	Mail Merge, Multi-Label

Company	Product	Description
MegaHaus 5703 Oberlin Dr. San Diego, CA 92121 619/450-1230	*MegaWorks* *ReportWorks*	Mail Merge, Spelling Checker Report Generator
Orange Micro, Inc. 1400 N. Lakeview Ave. Anaheim, CA 92807 714/779-2772	RamPak 4GS	IIGS Memory Card
PBI Software, Inc. 1111 Triton Drive Foster City, CA 94404 415/349-8765	*GraphWorks*	Graph Plotter
Pinpoint Publishing, Inc. Box 13323 Oakland, CA 94661 415/654-3050	*Pinpoint* *InfoMerge* *Point-to-Point* *Spelling Checker*	Desktop Accessories Mail Merge Data Communications Spelling Checker
Sensible Software 210 S. Woodwork, Suite 229 Birmingham, MI 48011 313/258-5566	*The Sensible Speller* *The Graphics Department*	Spelling Checker Graphics Program
Thunderware, Inc. 19G Orinda Way Orinda, CA 94563 415/254-6581	ThunderClock	Clock Card
Video 7, Inc. 12340 Saratoga/Sunnyvale Rd. Sunnyvale, CA 95070 800/238-0101	RGB Adapter	IIc RGB Adapter

APPENDIX B

CONFIGURING APPLEWORKS FOR A CUSTOM PRINTER

The information in this appendix will help you to configure your copy of *AppleWorks* for your custom printer. Please read these instructions first. Then find the Printer Codes Sheet for your printer and enter the codes into *AppleWorks* as described in the following example. (*Note:* If your printer isn't listed here, I apologize. I found as many as I could. If you can't figure out the proper control codes from your printer's manual, try your Apple dealer, who can either figure it out, or call Apple Technical Support for help.)

Let's suppose your printer is the Okidata Microline 92. Find the Printer Codes Sheet for this printer in Appendix B, and refer to it as you go through the example. At this point you should have selected the "Custom printer" from the Add a Printer Menu, named the printer, and selected the slot or port to which it is connected. Your screen should be showing a list of options, the last of which is **Printer codes** (Figure B-1). If you had made any choice other than Custom printer, you wouldn't see the Printer codes option because *AppleWorks* knows the printer codes for all the printers in the list. It's because you have a Custom printer that you have to tell *AppleWorks* how to command your printer to do things like underline and boldface.

Select the Printer Codes option and you'll see four options for printer commands (Figure B-2). (*Note:* If you have an Apple IIc, you will see a fifth option, **Serial Interface settings**, that lets you configure the Apple IIc serial port for your printer. The default settings are 9600 baud, 8 data bits, 1 stop bit, no parity. The configuration switches on your

FIGURE B-1

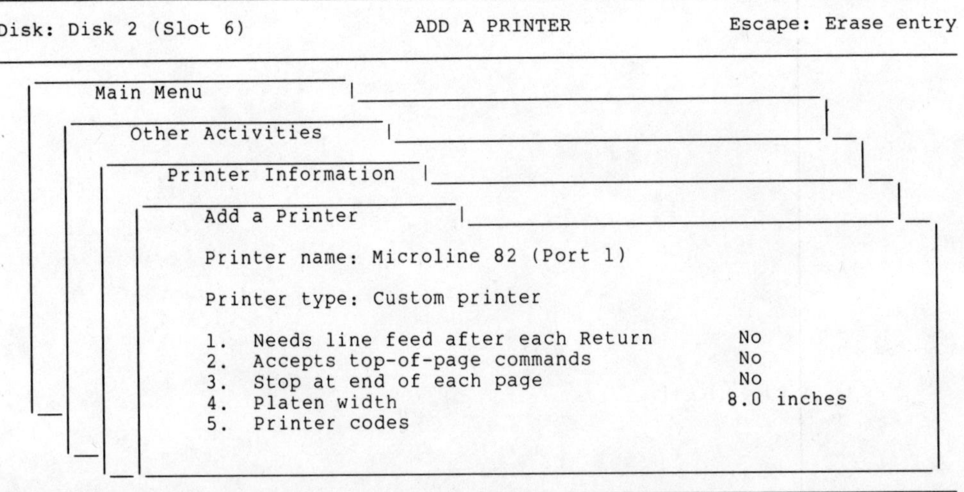

Disk: Disk 2 (Slot 6)
ADD A PRINTER
Escape: Erase entry
Main Menu
Other Activities
Printer Information
Add a Printer
Printer name: Microline 82 (Port 1)
Printer type: Custom printer
1. Needs line feed after each Return No
2. Accepts top-of-page commands No
3. Stop at end of each page No
4. Platen width 8.0 inches
5. Printer codes
Type number, or use arrows, then press Return
56K Avail.

FIGURE B-2

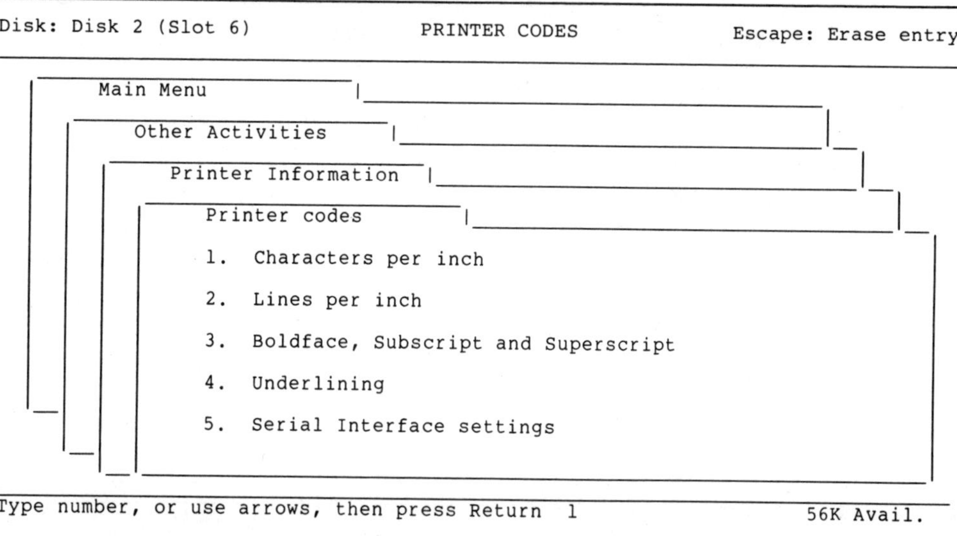

printer should be set to match these values.) You're going to "fill in the blanks" in the first four options with the information from your Printer Code Sheet. For this example, though, I'll use the data from the Microline 92's sheet.

The first type of printer command contains the codes needed to tell your printer how to select the number of characters per inch it prints. Most dot matrix printers offer a variety of print sizes. *AppleWorks* lets you select a print size in the Printer Options section (the CI command) of any of the three applications, word processor, data base, or spreadsheet.

Choose option 1, **Characters per inch**. At the bottom of your screen (Figure B-3), you will be prompted for the number of characters per inch (4–24) you want to define. The Printer Codes Sheet for the Microline 92 lists commands for six different values of characters per inch. Let's enter the first one, 5 characters per inch. Type **5** and press RETURN. The "file folder" on your screen is labeled **5 chars per inch** and says: **Current control characters are None** (Figure B-4). You're going to change that. From the Printer Codes Sheet, you see that the command for 5 characters per inch consists of two characters: CONTROL-^ and CONTROL-_. To get the CONTROL-^ character, hold down the CONTROL key while you type the number 6 (you don't have to hold down the SHIFT key). The word **None** is replaced by CONTROL-^. Type the second character, CONTROL-_, by holding down the CONTROL key while you type a dash, "-" (again, the SHIFT key is

FIGURE B-3

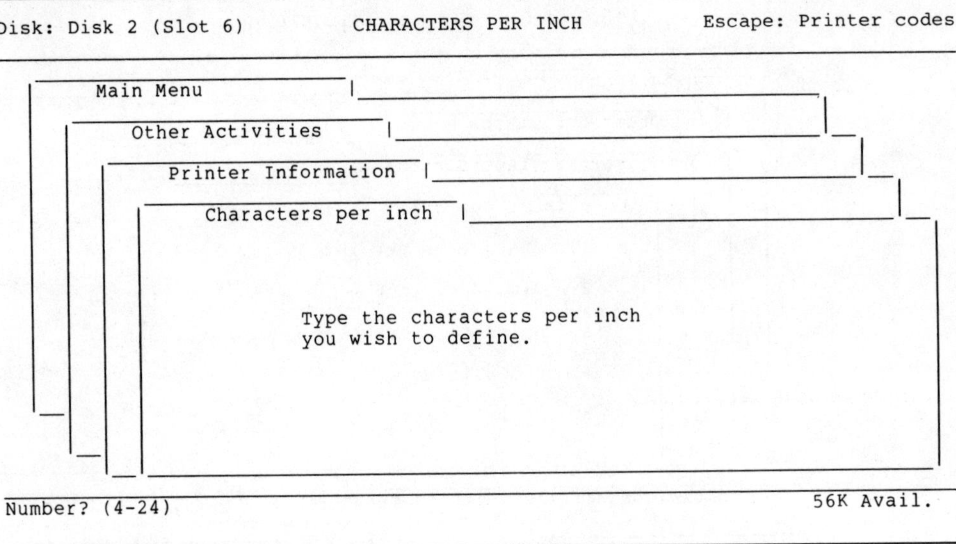

FIGURE B-4

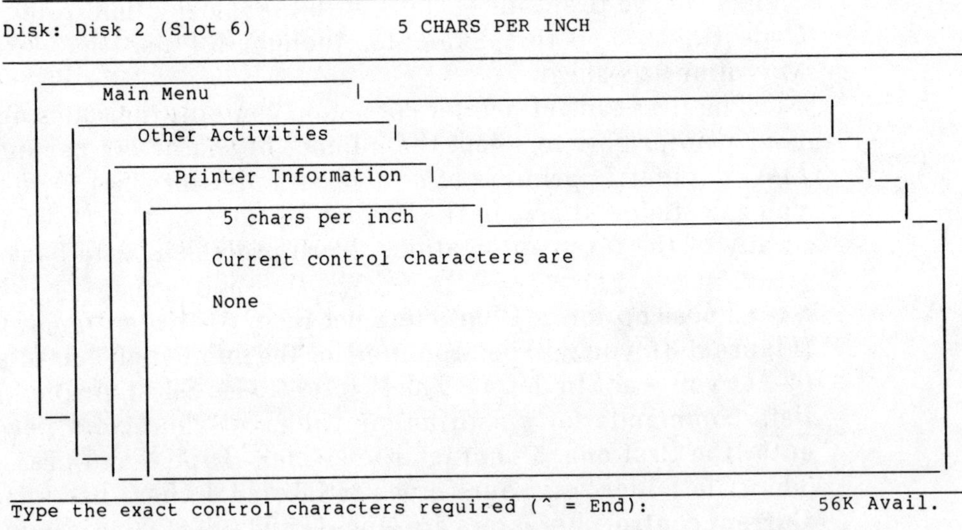

optional). The second control character will appear on your screen (Figure B-5). *Don't press the RETURN key.* You're through entering commands for 5 characters per inch, but pressing RETURN won't get you out of it. Nor will pressing ESC. The only way to terminate entering control characters is to type a "^" (caret) character. (Hold down the SHIFT key while you type a 6.)

FIGURE B-5

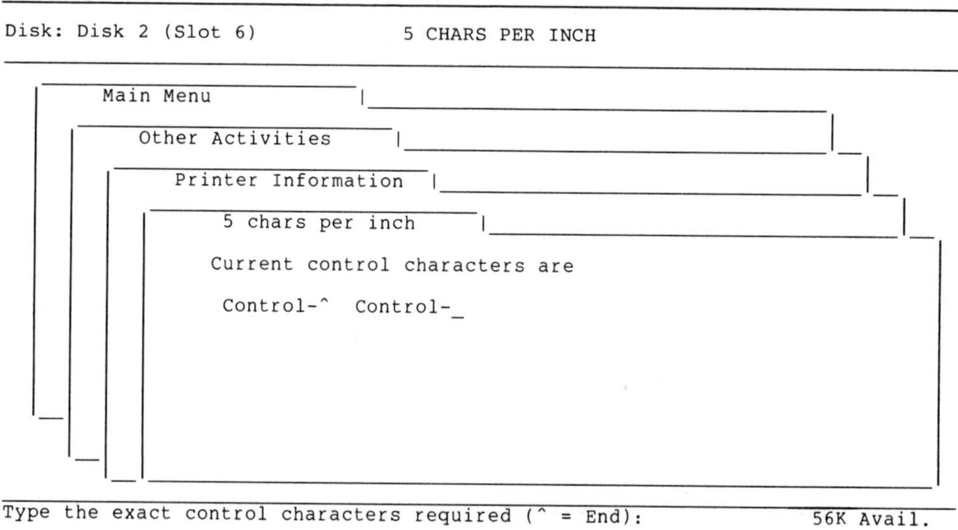

After you type the ^, your screen will again look like Figure B-3. Repeat the above process five more times for 6, 8, 10, 12, and 17 characters per inch. Type in the number of characters per inch (and press RETURN), the control characters from the Printer Codes Sheet, and the ^ character to get out. If you make a mistake, type the ^ character to get out, reenter the same value for Number of characters per inch, type **N** to indicate that the current control characters are wrong, and type in the correct control characters.

When you're finished entering the commands for characters per inch, and you're being asked to type in another value for the Number, press ESC and you'll be back at the Printer Codes screen (Figure B-2).

Take option 2, **Lines per inch** (Figure B-6). Only two values are allowed for vertical spacing, 6 or 8 lines per inch. Choose number 1, **6 lines per inch**. The two characters from the Printer Codes Sheet of the Microline 92 for 6 lines per inch are ESC and 6. ESC represents the Escape character that you enter by pressing the ESC key. The 6 is just a normal 6 (Figure B-7). After you enter the two characters, type a ^ to get out. Then choose 8 lines per inch, enter ESC and 8, and type ^ to get out. ESC back to the Printer Codes screen.

The third Printer Codes option is **Boldface**, **Subscript and Superscript**. Select it (Figure B-8). You'll enter the six commands, one at a time. For Boldface Begin, enter the two characters ESC and T. For Boldface End: ESC and I. For Subscript Begin: ESC and L. For Subscript End: ESC and M. For Superscript Begin: ESC and J. And for Superscript End: ESC and K. These command characters all come from the Printer

FIGURE B-6

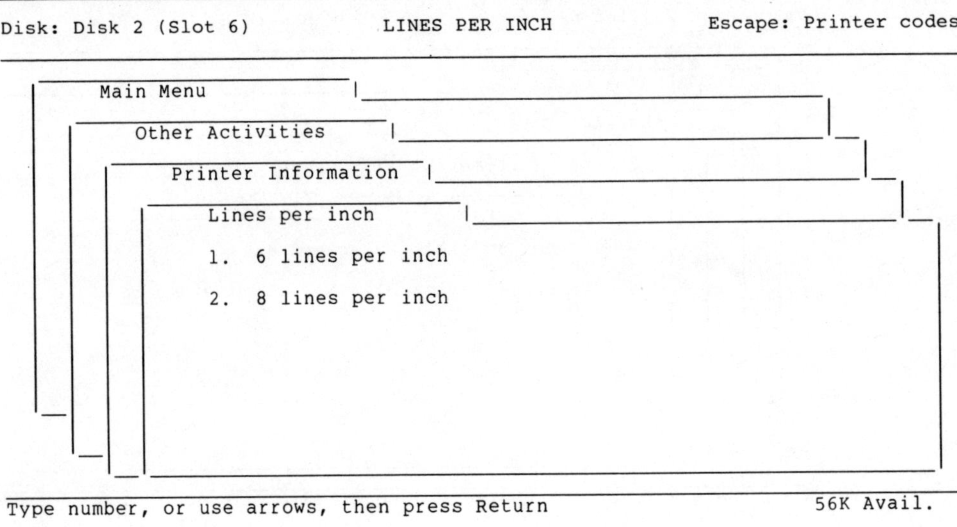

FIGURE B-7

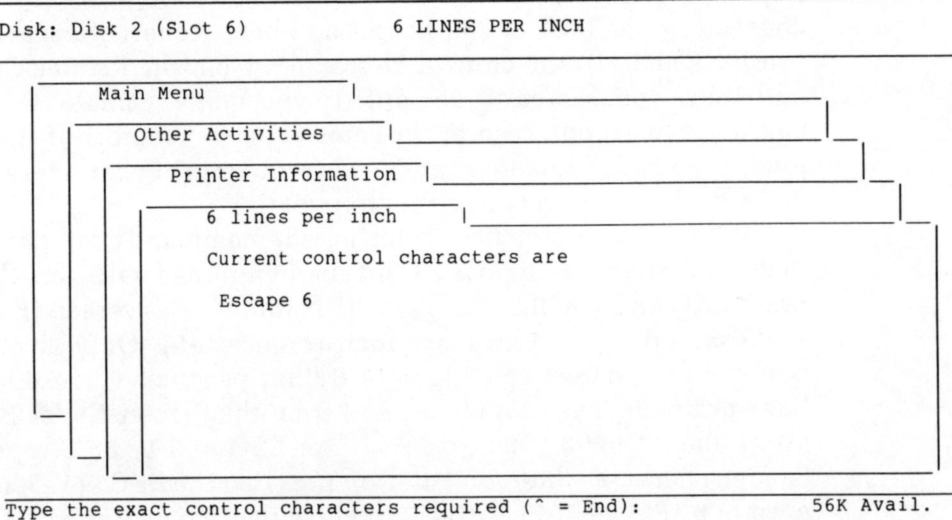

Codes Sheet for the Microline 92. As in previous examples, after the command characters are entered, type a ^ to get out of the option. When you're through with the last one, Superscript End, ESC back to the Printer Codes screen.

The fourth Printer Codes option is for **Underlining**. Select it now (Figure B-9). Some printers can't underline at all. If your printer is one

FIGURE B-8

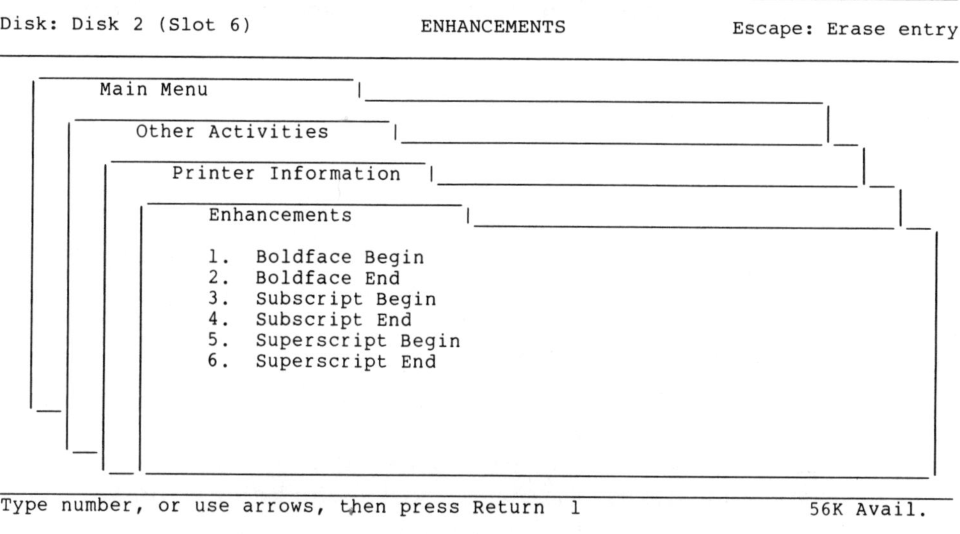

FIGURE B-9

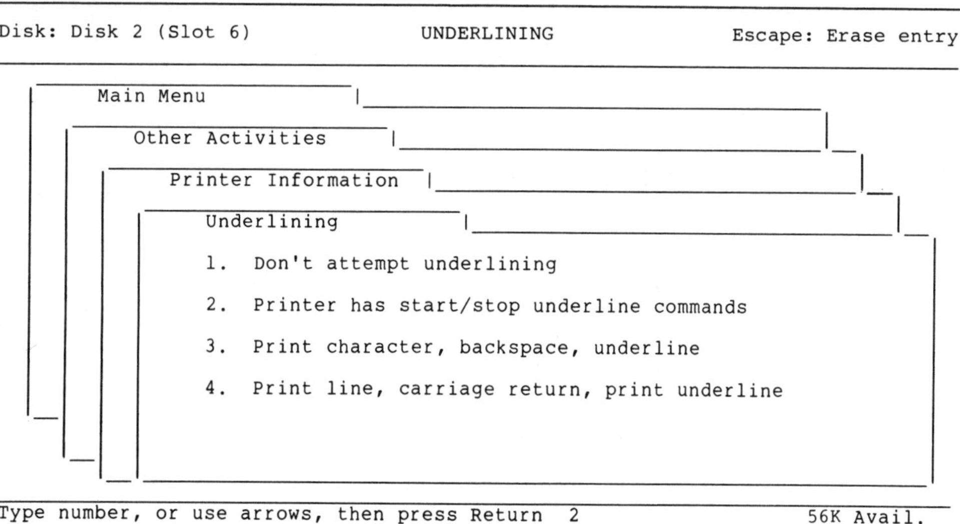

of these, choose option 1, **Don't attempt underlining**. Most printers (such as the Microline 92) have start and stop commands for underlining, so you would choose option 2. You would then select Underline Begin and enter ESC and C; then select Underline End and enter ESC and D.

Some printers underline by typing a character, backing up a space, and typing an underline character. If your printer underlines this way, you should take option 3 from the Underlining Menu. And some printers print the entire line, then go back and underline. Option 4 is for them.

And that completes the custom printer configuration. I know it sounds complicated, but if you take it one step at a time, you should be able to get through it without problems.

Note: Some printers—e.g., C. Itoh 7500 EP and Panasonic KX-P1090—use the CONTROL-@ character in their printer control codes. Earlier versions of *AppleWorks* (1.0, 1.1, 1.2, and 1.3) accepted this character like any other control character. However, *AppleWorks* 2.0 *does not* accept this character. When you try to type it, nothing appears on the screen. Apple has acknowledged the problem, but they haven't said when, or if, they're going to fix it.

The problem may be fixed by the time you read this—look for a change in the *AppleWorks* version number (to 2.01, 2.1, etc.)—but if your printer requires the CONTROL-@ character to access one or more of its features, and *AppleWorks* won't allow you to type the character, here's what to do. Borrow a copy of *AppleWorks* 1.3 (your local Apple dealer will probably have one). Use this version to configure your printer. Then use your System Utilities program to copy the file named SEG.PR from the *AppleWorks* 1.3 program disk to your *AppleWorks* 2.0 program disk.

I. PRINTER CODE SHEETS

Manufacturer: Apple Computer* **Model: LaserWriter**

Characters per Inch
- 5 CPI: ESC CONTROL-_ CONTROL-Y
- 6 CPI: ESC CONTROL-_ CONTROL-U
- 8 CPI: ESC CONTROL-_ CONTROL-P
- 10 CPI: ESC CONTROL-_ CONTROL-M
- 12 CPI: ESC CONTROL-_ CONTROL-K
- 15 CPI: CONTROL-I CONTROL-A ESC CONTROL-_ CONTROL-I CONTROL-A CONTROL-I

Lines per Inch
- 6 LPI: CONTROL-I CONTROL-A ESC CONTROL-^ CONTROL-I CONTROL-A CONTROL-I
- 8 LPI: ESC CONTROL-^ CONTROL-G

Boldface, Subscript and Superscript
    Boldface Begin: ESC 0
    Boldface End: ESC &
    Subscript Begin: ESC U
    Subscript End: ESC D
    Superscript Begin: ESC D
    Superscript End: ESC U

Underlining
    Underline Begin: ESC E
    Underline End: ESC R

*Set printer to "special" (Diablo 630 emulation).

Manufacturer: Brother **Model: HR-15**

Characters per Inch
    10 CPI: ESC S
    12 CPI: ESC CONTROL-_ CONTROL-K
    15 CPI: CONTROL-I CONTROL-A ESC CONTROL-_ CONTROL-I CONTROL-A CONTROL-I

Lines per Inch
    6 LPI: CONTROL-I CONTROL-A ESC CONTROL-^ CONTROL-I CONTROL-A CONTROL-I
    8 LPI: ESC CONTROL-^ CONTROL-G

Boldface, Subscript and Superscript
    Boldface Begin: ESC F
    Boldface End: ESC &
    Subscript Begin: ESC U
    Subscript End: ESC D
    Superscript Begin: ESC D
    Superscript End: ESC U

Underlining
    Underline Begin: ESC E
    Underline End: ESC R

Manufacturer: Brother **Model: HR-25, HR-35**

Characters per Inch
- 10 CPI: ESC S
- 12 CPI: ESC CONTROL-_ CONTROL-K
- 15 CPI: CONTROL-I CONTROL-A ESC CONTROL-_ CONTROL-I CONTROL-A CONTROL-I

Lines per Inch
- 6 LPI: CONTROL-I CONTROL-A ESC CONTROL-^ CONTROL-I CONTROL-A CONTROL-I
- 8 LPI: ESC CONTROL-^ CONTROL-G

Boldface, Subscript and Superscript
- Boldface Begin: ESC O
- Boldface End: ESC &
- Subscript Begin: ESC U
- Subscript End: ESC D
- Superscript Begin: ESC D
- Superscript End: ESC U

Underlining
- Underline Begin: ESC E
- Underline End: ESC R

Manufacturer: Brother **Model: M1409, M1509, M1709**

Characters per Inch
- 5 CPI: CONTROL-R CONTROL-N ESC P
- 6 CPI: CONTROL-R CONTROL-N ESC M
- 10 CPI: CONTROL-R CONTROL-T ESC P
- 12 CPI: CONTROL-R CONTROL-T ESC M
- 17 CPI: CONTROL-T CONTROL-O ESC P

Lines per Inch
- 6 LPI: ESC 2
- 8 LPI: ESC 0

Boldface, Subscript and Superscript
- Boldface Begin: ESC E
- Boldface End: ESC F
- Subscript Begin: ESC S CONTROL-A

Subscript End: ESC T
Superscript Begin: ESC S CONTROL-@
Superscript End: ESC T

Underlining
Underline Begin: ESC- CONTROL-A
Underline End: ESC- CONTROL-@

Manufacturer: C. Itoh **Model: A10 - 20**

Characters per Inch
10 CPI: ESC E 1 2
12 CPI: ESC E 1 0

Lines per Inch
6 LPI: ESC L 0 8
8 LPI: ESC L 0 6

Boldface, Subscript and Superscript
Boldface Begin: ESC O
Boldface End: ESC &
Subscript Begin: ESC U
Subscript End: ESC D
Superscript Begin: ESC D
Superscript End: ESC U

Underlining
Underline Begin: ESC-
Underline End: ESC R

Manufacturer: C. Itoh **Model: 7500 EP**

Characters per Inch
5 CPI: ESC W CONTROL-A CONTROL-R
8 CPI: ESC W CONTROL-A CONTROL-O
10 CPI: ESC W CONTROL-@ CONTROL-R
17 CPI: ESC W CONTROL-@ CONTROL-O

Lines per Inch
6 LPI: ESC 2
8 LPI: ESC 0

Boldface, Subscript and Superscript
- Boldface Begin: ESC E
- Boldface End: ESC F
- Subscript Begin: ESC S CONTROL-A
- Subscript End: ESC T
- Superscript Begin: ESC S CONTROL-@
- Superscript End: ESC T

Underlining
- Underline Begin: ESC- CONTROL-A
- Underline End: ESC- CONTROL-@

Manufacturer: C. Itoh **Model: 8510B**

Characters per Inch
- 5 CPI: CONTROL-N ESC N
- 6 CPI: CONTROL-N ESC E
- 8 CPI: CONTROL-N ESC Q
- 10 CPI: CONTROL-O ESC N
- 12 CPI: CONTROL-O ESC E
- 17 CPI: CONTROL-O ESC Q

Lines per Inch
- 6 LPI: ESC A
- 8 LPI: ESC B

Boldface, Subscript and Superscript
- Boldface Begin: ESC !
- Boldface End: ESC "
- Subscript Begin: Not Available
- Subscript End: Not Available
- Superscript Begin: Not Available
- Superscript End: Not Available

Underlining
- Underline Begin: ESC X
- Underline End: ESC Y

Manufacturer: Canon* **Model: LBP-8 A1/A2**

Characters per Inch
- 5 CPI: ESC CONTROL-_ CONTROL-Y
- 6 CPI: ESC CONTROL-_ CONTROL-U
- 8 CPI: ESC CONTROL-_ CONTROL-P
- 10 CPI: ESC CONTROL-_ CONTROL-M
- 12 CPI: ESC CONTROL-_ CONTROL-K
- 15 CPI: CONTROL-I CONTROL-A ESC CONTROL-_ CONTROL-I CONTROL-A CONTROL-I

Lines per Inch
- 6 LPI: CONTROL-I CONTROL-A ESC CONTROL-^ CONTROL-I CONTROL-A CONTROL-I
- 8 LPI: ESC CONTROL-^ CONTROL-G

Boldface, Subscript and Superscript
- Boldface Begin: ESC O
- Boldface End: ESC &
- Subscript Begin: ESC U
- Subscript End: ESC D
- Superscript Begin: ESC D
- Superscript End: ESC U

Underlining
- Underline Begin: ESC E
- Underline End: ESC R

*Set printer to Diablo 630 emulation.

Manufacturer: Citizen **Model: 120-D**

Characters per Inch
- 5 CPI: CONTROL-R CONTROL-N ESC P
- 6 CPI: CONTROL-R CONTROL-N ESC M
- 10 CPI: CONTROL-R CONTROL-T ESC P
- 12 CPI: CONTROL-R CONTROL-T ESC M
- 17 CPI: CONTROL-T CONTROL-O ESC P

Lines per Inch
- 6 LPI: ESC 2
- 8 LPI: ESC 0

Boldface, Subscript and Superscript
- Boldface Begin: ESC E
- Boldface End: ESC F
- Subscript Begin: ESC S CONTROL-A
- Subscript End: ESC T
- Superscript Begin: ESC S CONTROL-@
- Superscript End: ESC T

Underlining
- Underline Begin: ESC- CONTROL-A
- Underline End: ESC- CONTROL-@

Manufacturer: Computers Intl. **Model: Daisywriter**

Characters per Inch
- 10 CPI: ESC P
- 12 CPI: ESC E
- 15 CPI: ESC M

Lines per Inch
- 6 LPI: Not Available
- 8 LPI: Not Available

Boldface, Subscript and Superscript
- Boldface Begin: ESC O
- Boldface End: ESC &
- Subscript Begin: ESC U
- Subscript End: ESC D
- Superscript Begin: ESC D
- Superscript End: ESC U

Underlining
- Underline Begin: ESC I
- Underline End: ESC J

Manufacturer: Diablo **Model: 630**

Characters per Inch
5 CPI: ESC CONTROL-_ CONTROL-Y
6 CPI: ESC CONTROL-_ CONTROL-U
8 CPI: ESC CONTROL-_ CONTROL-P
10 CPI: ESC CONTROL-_ CONTROL-M
12 CPI: ESC CONTROL-_ CONTROL-K
15 CPI: CONTROL-I CONTROL-A ESC CONTROL-_ CONTROL-I CONTROL-A CONTROL-I

Lines per Inch
6 LPI: CONTROL-I CONTROL-A ESC CONTROL-^ CONTROL-I CONTROL-A CONTROL-I
8 LPI: ESC CONTROL-^ CONTROL-G

Boldface, Subscript and Superscript
Boldface Begin: ESC O
Boldface End: ESC &
Subscript Begin: ESC U
Subscript End: ESC D
Superscript Begin: ESC D
Superscript End: ESC U

Underlining
Underline Begin: ESC E
Underline End: ESC R

Manufacturer: Integral Data Sys. **Model: 440 & 445**

Characters per Inch
5 CPI: CONTROL-A CONTROL-]
6 CPI: CONTROL-A CONTROL-^
8 CPI: CONTROL-B CONTROL-\
10 CPI: CONTROL-B CONTROL-]
12 CPI: CONTROL-B CONTROL-^
15 CPI: CONTROL-B CONTROL-_

Lines per Inch
6 LPI: Not Available
8 LPI: Not Available

Boldface, Subscript and Superscript
Boldface Begin: Not Available
Boldface End: Not Available
Subscript Begin: Not Available
Subscript End: Not Available
Superscript Begin: Not Available
Superscript End: Not Available

Underlining
Choose option 1: **Don't attempt underlining**

Manufacturer: Integral Data Sys. Model: 460 & 560

Characters per Inch
5 CPI: CONTROL-A CONTROL-]
6 CPI: CONTROL-A CONTROL-^
8 CPI: CONTROL-A CONTROL-_
10 CPI: CONTROL-B CONTROL-]
12 CPI: CONTROL-B CONTROL-^
17 CPI: CONTROL-B CONTROL-_

Lines per Inch
6 LPI: ESC B 8
8 LPI: ESC B 6

Boldface, Subscript and Superscript
Boldface Begin: Not Available
Boldface End: Not Available
Subscript Begin: CONTROL-T
Subscript End: CONTROL-Y
Superscript Begin: CONTROL-Y
Superscript End: CONTROL-T

Underlining
Choose option 1: **Don't attempt underlining**

Manufacturer: Integral Data Sys. Model: Prism 80 & 132

Characters per Inch
5 CPI: CONTROL-A CONTROL-]
6 CPI: CONTROL-A CONTROL-^

8 CPI: CONTROL-A CONTROL-_
10 CPI: CONTROL-B CONTROL-]
12 CPI: CONTROL-B CONTROL-^
17 CPI: CONTROL-B CONTROL-_

Lines per Inch
6 LPI: ESC B 8 $
8 LPI: ESC B 6 $

Boldface, Subscript and Superscript
Boldface Begin: Not Available
Boldface End: Not Available
Subscript Begin: CONTROL-T
Subscript End: CONTROL-Y CONTROL-Y CONTROL-T
Superscript Begin: CONTROL-Y CONTROL-Y CONTROL-T
Superscript End: CONTROL-T

Underlining
Choose option 3: **Print character, backspace, underline**

Manufacturer: Juki **Model: 6000, 6100, 6300**

Characters per Inch
10 CPI: ESC S
12 CPI: ESC CONTROL-_ CONTROL-K
15 CPI: CONTROL-I CONTROL-A ESC CONTROL-_ CONTROL-I CONTROL-A CONTROL-I

Lines per Inch
6 LPI: CONTROL-I CONTROL-A ESC CONTROL-^ CONTROL-I CONTROL-A CONTROL-I
8 LPI: ESC CONTROL-^ CONTROL-G

Boldface, Subscript and Superscript
Boldface Begin: ESC W
Boldface End: ESC &
Subscript Begin: ESC U
Subscript End: ESC D
Superscript Begin: ESC D
Superscript End: ESC U

Underlining
Underline Begin: ESC E
Underline End: ESC R

Manufacturer: Leading Edge **Model: Prowriter**

Characters per Inch
5 CPI: CONTROL-N ESC N
6 CPI: CONTROL-N ESC E
8 CPI: CONTROL-N ESC Q
10 CPI: CONTROL-O ESC N
12 CPI: CONTROL-O ESC E
17 CPI: CONTROL-O ESC Q

Lines per Inch
6 LPI: ESC A
8 LPI: ESC B

Boldface, Subscript and Superscript
Boldface Begin: ESC !
Boldface End: ESC "
Subscript Begin: Not Available
Subscript End: Not Available
Superscript Begin: Not Available
Superscript End: Not Available

Underlining
Underline Begin: ESC X
Underline End: ESC Y

Manufacturer: NEC **Model: E.L.F. 360**

Characters per Inch
8 CPI: ESC] O
10 CPI: ESC] L
12 CPI: ESC] J
15 CPI: ESC] H
17 CPI: ESC] G

Lines per Inch
6 LPI: ESC] W
8 LPI: ESC] U

Boldface, Subscript and Superscript
Boldface Begin: ESC *
Boldface End: ESC ,
Subscript Begin: ESC :
Subscript End: ESC ;
Superscript Begin: ESC ;
Superscript End: ESC :

Underlining
Underline Begin: ESC-
Underline End: ESC '

Manufacturer: NEC **Model: PC 8023A-C**

Characters per Inch
5 CPI: CONTROL-N ESC N
6 CPI: CONTROL-N ESC E
8 CPI: CONTROL-N ESC Q
10 CPI: CONTROL-O ESC N
12 CPI: CONTROL-O ESC E
17 CPI: CONTROL-O ESC Q

Lines per Inch
6 LPI: ESC A
8 LPI: ESC B

Boldface, Subscript and Superscript
Boldface Begin: ESC !
Boldface End: ESC "
Subscript Begin: Not Available
Subscript End: Not Available
Superscript Begin: Not Available
Superscript End: Not Available

Underlining
Underline Begin: ESC X
Underline End: ESC Y

Manufacturer: NEC **Model: Spinwriter 3350**

Characters per Inch
- 5 CPI: ESC CONTROL-N
- 10 CPI: ESC S
- 12 CPI: ESC I
- 15 CPI: ESC CONTROL-O

Lines per Inch
- 6 LPI: ESC 2
- 8 LPI: ESC 0

Boldface, Subscript and Superscript
- Boldface Begin: ESC E
- Boldface End: ESC F
- Subscript Begin: ESC :
- Subscript End: ESC ;
- Superscript Begin: ESC ;
- Superscript End: ESC :

Underlining
- Underline Begin: ESC -
- Underline End: ESC '

Manufacturer: Okidata **Model: Microline 92**

Characters per Inch
- 5 CPI: CONTROL-^ CONTROL-_
- 6 CPI: CONTROL-\ CONTROL-_
- 8 CPI: CONTROL-] CONTROL-_
- 10 CPI: CONTROL-^
- 12 CPI: CONTROL-\
- 17 CPI: CONTROL-]

Lines per Inch
- 6 LPI: ESC 6
- 8 LPI: ESC 8

Boldface, Subscript and Superscript
- Boldface Begin: ESC T
- Boldface End: ESC I
- Subscript Begin: ESC L
- Subscript End: ESC M

Superscript Begin: ESC J
Superscript End: ESC K

Underlining
Underline Begin: ESC C
Underline End: ESC D

Manufacturer: Panasonic **Model: KX-P1090**

Characters per Inch
5 CPI: CONTROL-R CONTROL-N ESC P CONTROL-A
6 CPI: CONTROL-R CONTROL-N ESC P CONTROL-@
10 CPI: CONTROL-R CONTROL-T ESC P CONTROL-A
12 CPI: CONTROL-R CONTROL-T ESC P CONTROL-@
17 CPI: CONTROL-O CONTROL-T

Lines per Inch
6 LPI: ESC 2
8 LPI: ESC 0

Boldface, Subscript and Superscript
Boldface Begin: ESC E
Boldface End: ESC F
Subscript Begin: ESC S CONTROL-A
Subscript End: ESC T
Superscript Begin: ESC S CONTROL-@
Superscript End: ESC T

Underlining
Underline Begin: ESC- CONTROL-A
Underline End: ESC- CONTROL-@

Manufacturer: Panasonic* **Model: 1080i**

*Use Epson RX series

Manufacturer: Panasonic* **Model: 1092i**

*Use Epson FX series

Manufacturer: Panasonic* **Model: 1592**

*Use Epson FX series

Manufacturer: Silver-Reed **Model: EXP-400**

Characters per Inch
10 CPI: ESC S
12 CPI: ESC CONTROL-_ CONTROL-K
15 CPI: CONTROL-I CONTROL-A ESC CONTROL-_ CONTROL-I CONTROL-A CONTROL-I

Lines per Inch
6 LPI: CONTROL-I CONTROL-A ESC CONTROL-^ CONTROL-I CONTROL-A CONTROL-I
8 LPI: ESC CONTROL-^ CONTROL-G

Boldface, Subscript and Superscript
Boldface Begin: ESC O
Boldface End: ESC &
Subscript Begin: ESC U
Subscript End: ESC D
Superscript Begin: ESC D
Superscript End: ESC U

Underlining
Underline Begin: ESC E
Underline End: ESC R

Manufacturer: Silver-Reed **Model: EXP-500 & EXP-550**

Characters per Inch
10 CPI: ESC S
12 CPI: ESC CONTROL-_ CONTROL-K
15 CPI: CONTROL-I CONTROL-A ESC CONTROL-_ CONTROL-I CONTROL-A CONTROL-I

Lines per Inch
6 LPI: CONTROL-I CONTROL-A ESC CONTROL-^ CONTROL-I CONTROL-A CONTROL-I
8 LPI: ESC CONTROL-^ CONTROL-G

Boldface, Subscript and Superscript
- Boldface Begin: Not Available
- Boldface End: Not Available
- Subscript Begin: ESC U
- Subscript End: ESC D
- Superscript Begin: ESC D
- Superscript End: ESC U

Underlining
- Choose option 3: **Print Character, backspace, underline**

Manufacturer: Teletex Comm. **Model: TTX-1014**

Characters per Inch
- 10 CPI: ESC P
- 12 CPI: ESC F
- 15 CPI: ESC M

Lines per Inch
- 6 LPI: ESC 6
- 8 LPI: Not Available

Boldface, Subscript and Superscript
- Boldface Begin: ESC O
- Boldface End: ESC &
- Subscript Begin: ESC U
- Subscript End: ESC D
- Superscript Begin: ESC D
- Superscript End: ESC U

Underlining
- Underline Begin: ESC E
- Underline End: ESC R

Manufacturer: Toshiba **Model: P1340**

Characters per Inch
- 5 CPI: ESC E 2 4
- 6 CPI: ESC E 2 0
- 10 CPI: ESC E 1 2

12 CPI: ESC E 1 0
15 CPI: ESC E 0 8
17 CPI: ESC E 0 7

Lines per Inch
6 LPI: ESC L 0 8
8 LPI: ESC L 0 6

Boldface, Subscript and Superscript
Boldface Begin: Not Available
Boldface End: Not Available
Subscript Begin: ESC U
Subscript End: ESC D
Superscript Begin: ESC D
Superscript End: ESC U

Underlining
Underline Begin: ESC I
Underline End: ESC J

APPENDIX C

APPLEWORKS AND THE APPLE II+

AppleWorks was originally written for the Apple IIe and Apple IIc models, and it works great on the IIGS. But what about the million or so Apple II and II+ owners? Well take heart, Apple II people, you can use *AppleWorks* 2.0, too.

There are four factors that have to be dealt with before an Apple II/II+ can run *AppleWorks*. First, the number of characters your Apple II/II+ displays per line on its screen has to be changed from 40 to 80. You will need to get an 80-column card, which plugs into one of the slots, usually slot 3, on your Apple's motherboard (main circuit board). In addition to 80-column text, it will display letters in both upper and lower case. This upper/lower case feature requires a special "shift key modification" so that the card recognizes when you depress either SHIFT key on your keyboard. The 80-column card manual describes this modification, and you can either do it yourself or have your dealer do it for you.

Second, the standard 48K of memory on the Apple's motherboard has to be increased to at least 128K. This is usually accomplished with two cards. One is called a 16K RAM card, and plugs into slot 0 on the motherboard. The other is a memory expansion card that will plug into one of the other 7 slots.

The third step is to modify *AppleWorks* so that it will run on your Apple II/II+. This is done by rewriting part of the *AppleWorks* program. Don't worry, you don't have to become a programmer to do this. Several companies supply "patch" disks that modify *AppleWorks* to run on your computer with their 80-column or 16K RAM cards. These patch disks permanently modify the *AppleWorks* program, so you only have to use them once. (*Note:* Be sure when you do this that you use a *copy* of your *AppleWorks* disk, and *not* the original.)

Finally, because the Apple II/II+ does not have OPEN-APPLE, up- or down-arrow, TAB, DELETE, or CAPS LOCK keys, these functions must be generated some other way. Different companies use different schemes to simulate these function keys.

Up until now, I have intentionally refrained from discussing specific manufacturers or products. If you check any of the national Apple II computer magazines, you'll find several companies offering various computer boards that will let your Apple II/II+ run *AppleWorks*. Many of these companies sell only one type of card (e.g., only 80-column cards, or only memory cards). And some of these "solutions" only work with older versions of *AppleWorks* (1.3 or older).

One company seems to have put it all together. Applied Engineering (AE) supplies a total package for upgrading your Apple II/II+ to use *AppleWorks* 2.0. Their 80-column card is the Viewmaster 80 ($149 as I write this). The patch disk that modifies *AppleWorks* to work with your Apple II/II+ is included with Viewmaster 80, at no additional charge.

AE provides two ways to increase your Apple's memory to 128K and beyond. Their 16K RAM card (called "Pocket Rocket") gives your Apple a total of 64K ($79). Their TransWarp card ($279) increases the Apple II/II+'s memory to 128K, *and* more than triples its speed of operation. If you want to increase your *AppleWorks* desktop beyond the standard size, you can add AE's RamFactor memory board. For example, the 256K RamFactor board ($239) not only increases *AppleWorks'* desktop to 250K, but also allows the entire *AppleWorks* program to be loaded and run in memory. This significantly improves *AppleWorks'* efficiency.

AE handles the missing OPEN-APPLE key by using the ESC key. For example, if you want to print a document, instead of typing ⌘P, you'd press ESC, then the letter "P." To go from Review/Add/Change to *AppleWorks'* Main Menu, you'd press ESC twice. The up- and down-arrow keys are simulated with CONTROL-K and CONTROL-J, respectively. The TAB key function is achieved with CONTROL-I, and so forth.

Whichever solution you decide to use, the bottom line is that *AppleWorks* and your Apple II/II+ *will* work together.

GLOSSARY

Abort to terminate a procedure or operation prematurely.

Alignment describes the way text is printed, relative to fixed margins. In *AppleWorks,* text can be aligned in four ways: Left, Right, Centered, and Justified.

Arranging sorting a list of entries. The arrange option is available in the data base and the spreadsheet applications.

ASCII a generally accepted method of representing characters by number values. Stands for: the American Standard Code for Information Interchange.

Backslash a character (\) used in the *MegaWorks* program from Megahaus. It is located just under the DELETE key on your keyboard.

Blanking erasing the contents of a cell in a spreadsheet.

Block in the spreadsheet, a group of cells in adjacent rows and/or columns.

Boldface a printing feature offered by most printers. Characters printed in boldface appear darker than normal text.

Boot computerese term that means to start a program from the beginning. It also can mean to start up your computer.

Byte a unit of computer memory or disk storage. One byte of memory can store one character (letter, number, or symbol) of information.

Calculated Category in the data base Tables report, a category that is created at the time the report is printed. It is the result of a mathematical operation (sum, product, etc.) involving one or more other categories.

Caret sometimes called the circumflex symbol (ˆ), it is used by the word processor to indicate the beginning and ending of special printer features such as boldfacing and underlining. It is also used as the termination character when entering printer control codes.

Category in the data base, a topic or heading under which data can be entered. Other data base programs refer to categories as "fields."

Cell in the spreadsheet, the area indicated by the intersection of a row and a column. Individual cells may hold nothing (blank), words (labels), or numbers or formulas (values).

Circumflex see *Caret.*

Clipboard part of *AppleWorks'* desktop metaphor. It is a section of computer memory that can be used to store part of a document. Later, the contents of the Clipboard can be pasted into another document.

Configure customizing a computer program for your particular equipment.

Control Codes sequences of characters that instruct your printer to perform certain features, such as boldfacing and underlining.

Copy an *AppleWorks* command that duplicates a section of a document into a separate area of computer memory (the Clipboard) so that it can be pasted into a different document (or the same document in a different place).

Cursor a blinking character on your screen that tells you where the next typed character will appear.

Cut with the Copy or Move command, places the indicated section of a document on *AppleWorks*' Clipboard.

Default values for options that are selected for you by the program. For example, in the word processor, *AppleWorks* selects a value of 1″ for the left (and right) margin. You are always free to change the default values to something different.

Desktop an *AppleWorks* term. All documents you are currently working with are said to be "on the Desktop," meaning that they are being held in your computer's memory and can be examined without accessing your data disk.

DIF stands for Data Interchange Format. A popular format for recording data from data base and spreadsheet programs. Files recorded in DIF from one program can be read by other programs that also use DIF files.

Disk Drive the component of your computer system that records or plays back your documents from disks.

Disk or Diskette the medium upon which your computer records (saves) your documents.

DOS 3.3 an operating system for Apple II computers, in use for many years.

Elite on a printer, a printing width of 12 characters per inch.

ESC represents the ESCAPE key on the keyboard. This key is used to move from one part of *AppleWorks* to another.

Exponentiation the raising of a number to a power. For example, 3 raised to the fourth power is 81.

Filename the name associated with a document you wish to store on (or retrieve from) disk. In ProDOS, a filename can be up to 15 characters (letters, numbers, or periods) long. The first character must be a letter. The filename is the last component of the pathname.

Folder part of *AppleWorks*' desktop metaphor. Every section of *AppleWorks* exists in its own file folder. You generally move from one folder to another through menu selection or the ESC key.

Footer in the word processor, a single line that is printed at the bottom of each page of a document.

Formats set ways of printing out data. In the data base section, there are two report formats: Labels and Tables.

Formatting a process that prepares a blank disk to receive data. All newly purchased disks must be formatted before they can be used.

From Scratch to create a document by yourself, rather than using a previously created file.

Global referring to the entire document. For example, a global search would be a search through the document from beginning to end.

Header in the word processor, a single line that is printed at the top of each page of a document.

Heading in the data base or spreadsheet, one or more lines printed at the top of each page of a report. Headings contain information such as the name of the document, the date, category names (in a data base Tables report), report name, page number, etc.

Highlight on the screen, to show a word (or group of words) with black letters against a light background.

Initialization Code required by all printer interface cards used on the Apple II+, IIe, and IIGS. It consists of a string of characters, usually beginning with CONTROL-I. The code sequence is generally different for each brand of interface card.

Insert Cursor indicated by a blinking underline. This cursor causes typed characters to be inserted into the existing text at the cursor position.

Integrated a term used to describe two or more applications that can share data.

Justified to print out text even with the left and right margins.

Kilobyte one-thousand bytes of computer memory or disk storage.

Labels Report one of two report formats in the data base. It features multiple line output with one or more categories per line and is used primarily to produce mailing labels.

Layout in the data base, describes the placement of categories on the screen. In the spreadsheet, describes the way labels and values will be displayed.

Marker in the word processor, an invisible indicator that can be inserted into the text of a document so that you can find this point at some later time with the Find: Marker command.

Megabyte one-million bytes of computer memory or disk storage space.

Merge combining two or more documents. The usual merge is with a word processing letter and a data base file to create personalized form letters.

Modem stands for MOdulator/DEModulator. It is a computer peripheral that allows your Apple to send and receive data over telephone lines.

Motherboard your Apple's main logic circuit board.

Move an *AppleWorks* command that copies a section of a document into a separate area of computer memory (the Clipboard), and then erases the section from the document. The Clipboard's contents can then be pasted into another document, or into in a different spot in the same document.

Multiple Record Format one of two display formats in the data base. It displays up to 80 characters of data from up to 15 records on a single screen.

 represents the OPEN-APPLE key on your keyboard.

Operating System a set of instructions telling your computer how to save and load programs and data from disks. DOS 3.3 and ProDOS are operating systems.

Overstrike Cursor indicated by a blinking box. This cursor causes typed characters to replace existing ones at the cursor position.

Pagination automatic page numbering. In the word processor, you must set up pagination. In the data base and the spreadsheet, *AppleWorks* will number the pages for you.

Parallel one of two methods of transmitting data to printers; the other is Serial.

Paste inserts text from *AppleWorks*' Clipboard into a document at the location of the cursor.

Pathname a combination of the volume name, subdirectory name (optional), and filename. The pathname begins with a slash (/) and uses a slash to separate each component.

Peripherals devices for getting data into and out of your computer. Keyboards and printers are examples of peripherals.

Pica on a printer, a printing width of 10 characters per inch.

Platen Width the actual distance your printer's print head moves from full left to full right positions.

Port on an Apple IIc, one of two serial outputs used to communicate between the IIc and a printer or modem.

Prefix the volume name (and, optionally, the subdirectory name) part of a file's pathname. *AppleWorks* allows you to set a particular

ProDOS prefix instead of specifying disk drives.

Processor sometimes referred to as the CPU (Central Processing Unit), it is the brain of your computer. Modern Apple II's use the 65C02 as their CPU; older models use the 6502.

ProDOS a new operating system for Apple II computers. *AppleWorks* is written under ProDOS.

Profile a hard disk drive mass storage device. It comes in 5 and 10 Megabyte sizes. The 5 Megabyte version can store the equivalent of 35 5.25″ disks of data.

Program Disk the second of two *AppleWorks* 5.25″ disks.

Proportional Printing on a printer, advancing the print head by different widths, depending on the width of the character being printed. In nonproportional printing, the print head always advances by the same amount for each character, regardless of the character's width.

RAM acronym for Random Access Memory. It refers to your computer's internal memory (128K or more). This is the maximum memory your computer starts with when you turn it on. Both the *AppleWorks* program and the documents you're working on are kept in RAM.

Serial one of two methods of transmitting data to printers; the other is Parallel.

Single Record Format one of two display formats in the data base. It displays all of the data from all of the categories in a single record.

Slot on the Apple IIe and IIGS, slots are connectors inside the computer that allow you to attach peripherals such as disk drives, printers, etc.

Spreadsheet one of three *AppleWorks* applications. It allows you to create mathematical models of situations such as mortgage payment schedules, expense reports, etc.

Startup Disk the first of the two *AppleWorks* 5.25″ disks.

String a group of characters (letters, numbers, and symbols).

Subdirectory a portion of a disk volume. In ProDOS, a disk may be subdivided into one or more sections, called subdirectories. Subdirectories can, themselves, be further divided into separate subdirectories.

Subscripting the printing of characters half a line below the normal printed line.

Superscripting the printing of characters half a line above the normal printed line.

Synchronize in the spreadsheet, when the split screen option is used, the Synchronize option causes the two views of the spreadsheet to scroll together.

Tables Report one of two report formats in the data base. It features single line output, category totals, group totals, and calculated categories.

Tractor on a printer, the mechanism that holds and moves pin-feed paper through the printer.

Truncate with the INT function in the spreadsheet, to throw away the part of the number that follows the decimal point.

Unsynchronize in the spreadsheet, when the split screen option is used, allows each of the two views of the spreadsheet to scroll independently of the other.

Volume Name in ProDOS, the name given to each disk when it is initialized. The volume name is always the first component of the pathname.

Word Wraparound in the word processor, this feature assures that a word at the end of a line on your screen will not be split, with some of it at the end of one line and the rest at the beginning of the next line. Instead, the entire word is brought to the beginning of the next line.

Zoom in the word processor, allows you to see print formatting commands. In the data base, switches between single and multiple record formats. In the spreadsheet, switches between formulas and results in value cells.

INDEX